T0100066

SYSTEMS ENGINEERING METHODS, DEVELOPMENTS
AND TECHNOLOGY

NETWORKED CONTROL SYSTEMS WITH THEIR APPLICATION IN INDUSTRY

SYSTEMS ENGINEERING METHODS, DEVELOPMENTS AND TECHNOLOGY

Additional books in this series can be found on Nova's website under the Series tab.

Additional e-books in this series can be found on Nova's website under the eBooks tab.

SYSTEMS ENGINEERING METHODS, DEVELOPMENTS
AND TECHNOLOGY

NETWORKED CONTROL SYSTEMS WITH THEIR APPLICATION IN INDUSTRY

GENG LIANG
WEN LI
AND
GUOPING LIU

nova
science publishers
New York

Copyright © 2018 by Nova Science Publishers, Inc.

All rights reserved. No part of this book may be reproduced, stored in a retrieval system or transmitted in any form or by any means: electronic, electrostatic, magnetic, tape, mechanical photocopying, recording or otherwise without the written permission of the Publisher.

We have partnered with Copyright Clearance Center to make it easy for you to obtain permissions to reuse content from this publication. Simply navigate to this publication's page on Nova's website and locate the "Get Permission" button below the title description. This button is linked directly to the title's permission page on copyright.com. Alternatively, you can visit copyright.com and search by title, ISBN, or ISSN.

For further questions about using the service on copyright.com, please contact:
Copyright Clearance Center
Phone: +1-(978) 750-8400   Fax: +1-(978) 750-4470   E-mail: info@copyright.com.

NOTICE TO THE READER

The Publisher has taken reasonable care in the preparation of this book, but makes no expressed or implied warranty of any kind and assumes no responsibility for any errors or omissions. No liability is assumed for incidental or consequential damages in connection with or arising out of information contained in this book. The Publisher shall not be liable for any special, consequential, or exemplary damages resulting, in whole or in part, from the readers' use of, or reliance upon, this material. Any parts of this book based on government reports are so indicated and copyright is claimed for those parts to the extent applicable to compilations of such works.

Independent verification should be sought for any data, advice or recommendations contained in this book. In addition, no responsibility is assumed by the publisher for any injury and/or damage to persons or property arising from any methods, products, instructions, ideas or otherwise contained in this publication.

This publication is designed to provide accurate and authoritative information with regard to the subject matter covered herein. It is sold with the clear understanding that the Publisher is not engaged in rendering legal or any other professional services. If legal or any other expert assistance is required, the services of a competent person should be sought. FROM A DECLARATION OF PARTICIPANTS JOINTLY ADOPTED BY A COMMITTEE OF THE AMERICAN BAR ASSOCIATION AND A COMMITTEE OF PUBLISHERS.

Additional color graphics may be available in the e-book version of this book.

Library of Congress Cataloging-in-Publication Data

ISBN: 978-1-53613-528-2

Published by Nova Science Publishers, Inc. † *New York*

CONTENTS

Preface   **xi**

Acknowledgment   **xiii**

Chapter 1   General Introduction   **1**
                   1.1. Introduction   1
                   1.2. History of Industrial Field-Bus   8
                   1.3. Development of Industrial Field-Bus   11
                   1.4. Communication Protocol of Industrial
                        Field-Bus   14
                   1.5. Field-Bus Types   29
                   1.6. Scheduling and Managements for Industrial
                        Field-Bus   35

Chapter 2   Timed-Token Networked Control System
                   with Its Application in Industry   **41**
                   2.1. Introduction   41
                   2.2. Timed Token Mechanism   43
                   2.3. FDDI Technology   54
                        2.3.1. Description   *54*
                        2.3.2. Topology   *55*
                        2.3.3. Frame Format   *55*
                        2.3.4. Deployment   *56*

Chapter 3   Networked Control System Based on PROFIBUS
with Its Application in Industry   **57**

3.1. Introduction to PROFIBUS   57

3.2. History and Developments of PROFIBUS   92

    3.2.1. Origin of PROFIBUS   *92*

    3.2.2. Technology   *93*

    3.2.3. Profiles   *97*

    3.2.4. Standardization   *98*

    3.2.5. Organization   *98*

3.3. PROFINET Technology   99

    3.3.1. Related Technology   *99*

    3.3.2. Peripherals   *100*

    3.3.3. IO Addressing   *101*

    3.3.4. Real-Time Characteristics   *101*

    3.3.5. Isochronous Communication   *102*

    3.3.6. Profiles   *102*

    3.3.7. Organization   *103*

3.4. PROFIBUS Protocol   103

    3.4.1. General Description   *103*

    *3.4.2. Medium Access Control Mechanism
in PROFIBUS*   *104*

    *3.4.3. Real-Time Characteristics of
the PROFIBUS*   *107*

    3.4.4. PROFIBUS Timing Analysis   *110*

Chapter 4   Networked Control System Based on FF
Field-Bus with Its Application in Industry   **115**

4.1. Introduction of Foundation Field-Bus   115

    4.1.1. History and Development   *116*

    4.1.2. Performance Features   *117*

4.2. Protocol Model   119

    4.2.1. Physical Layer   *120*

    4.2.2. Protocol Stack   *126*

4.3. Performance Analysis for FF   142

    4.3.1. Introduction   *142*

    4.3.2. Analytical Model   *143*

    *4.3.3. Cyclic Communication and Scheduling
of FF*   *152*

4.4. Analysis and Practice on Performance
Improvement in FF-Based Control System   154

4.4.1. Nomenclature   *154*
4.4.2. Introduction   *155*
4.4.3. Principles for Control System
Implementation   *158*
4.4.4. Experimental Control Systems   *161*
4.4.5. Analysis and Improvements   *169*
4.4.6. Conclusion   *184*

Chapter 5   Networked Control System Based on WorldFIP
with Its Application in Industry   **187**

5.1. Introduction to WorldFIP Field-Bus   187

5.1.1. History of FIP   *187*
5.1.2. Use of WorldFIP   *188*
5.1.3. Configuration of the WorldFIP   *188*
5.1.4. Physical Laver in WorldFIP   *189*
5.1.5. Data Link Laver (DLL) in WorldFIP   *191*
5.1.6. Application Laver in WorldFIP   *207*

5.2. Performance Analysis of WorldFIP Field-Bus 212

5.2.1. PDC Communication Model   *212*
5.2.2. Bus Scheduling Mechanism   *213*
5.2.3. Non-Periodic Communication
Mechanism   *215*
5.2.4. Construction of Bus Scheduling Table   *217*

5.3. Communication Performance Analysis
for WorldFIP   223

5.3.1. Introduction   *223*
5.3.2. Communication Patterns for WorldFIP   *224*
5.3.3. Communication Performance Analysis
for WorldFIP by Variable Exchange   *226*
5.3.4. Communication Performance Analysis
for WorldFIP by Periodic Message   *234*
5.3.5. Comparison of Communication
Performance   *240*
5.3.6. Conclusion   *243*

Chapter 6   Networked Control System Based on CAN Its
                  Application in Industry   **245**
                  6.1. Introduction to CAN   245
                  6.2. CAN Messages   246
                      6.2.1. The CAN Messages   *246*
                      6.2.2. Message Types   *246*
                  6.3. Physical Layers in CAN   253
                      6.3.1. Minimum Bus Speed   *255*
                      6.3.2. Bus Termination   *255*
                  6.4. CAN Error Handling   257
                      6.4.1. Errors Handling Mechanisms   *257*
                      6.4.2. Error Detection Mechanisms   *257*
                      6.4.3. Error Confinement Mechanisms   *259*
                  6.5. Higher Layers in CAN Protocol   261
                  6.6. Simulation and Performance Analysis for
                      CAN Communication   262

Chapter 7   IEC61499 for Networked Control System   **267**
                  7.1. Introduction to IEC61499   267
                  7.2. Key Points in IEC61499   268
                  7.3. Improvement in the IEC61499 2nd Edition   272
                      7.3.1. Execution Control   *272*
                      7.3.2. Temporary Variables   *275*
                      7.3.3. Network and Segments   *275*
                      7.3.4. Integration with PLCs   *275*
                      7.3.5. Simplified Data Access   *276*
                      7.3.6. Additional Changes and Corrections   *276*
                  7.4. Developments in the Future   277
                  7.5. Benefits of IEC61499   277
                  7.6. Integration   280
                  7.7. Examples   281
                      7.7.1. Example 1: Processing a Message   *281*
                      7.7.2. Example 2: Processing an Input Event *282*
                  7.8. Configuration   282
                  7.9. Software Tools   283
                  7.10. Conclusion   283

References **285**

About the Authors **295**

Index **297**

PREFACE

A recent trend in networked control systems is to interconnect the distributed elements by means of a multipoint broadcast network, instead of using the traditional point-to-point links. Within industrial communication systems, industrial networks are specially intended for the interconnection of process controllers, sensors, and actuators at the lower levels of the factory automation hierarchy. It is known that time constraints are more stringent as we go down in the automation hierarchy. In this book, we consider the application of networked control systems in their industrial environments. Some factors such as message cycle delay, the access and queuing delays, the transmission time (frame length/ transmission rate), and the protocol processing time all have effects on control performance.

ACKNOWLEDGMENT

This book was supported by "the Fundamental Research Funds for the Central Universities" of China (2017MS073).

Chapter 1

GENERAL INTRODUCTION

1.1. INTRODUCTION

A complex automated industrial system — such as manufacturing assembly line — usually needs a distributed control system—an organized hierarchy of controller systems—to function. In this hierarchy, there is usually a Human Machine Interface (HMI) at the top, where an operator can monitor or operate the system. This is typically linked to a middle layer of programmable logic controllers (PLC) via a non-time-critical communications system (e.g., Ethernet). At the bottom of the control chain is the field-bus that links the PLCs to the components that actually do the work, such as sensors, actuators, electric motors, console lights, switches, valves and contactors.

Field-bus is an industrial network system for real-time distributed control. It is a way to connect instruments in a manufacturing plant. Field-bus works on a network structure which typically allows daisy-chain, star, ring, branch, and tree network topologies. Previously, computers were connected using RS-232 (serial connections) by which only two devices could communicate. This would be the equivalent of the currently used 4-20 mA communication scheme which requires that each device have its own communication point at the controller level, while the field-bus is the equivalent of the current LAN-type connections, which require only one communication point at the controller level and allow multiple (hundreds) of analog and digital points to be connected at the same time. This reduces both the length of the cable required and the number of cables required. Furthermore, since devices that communicate through field-bus require a microprocessor, multiple points are typically provided by the same device. Some field-bus devices now support control schemes such as PID control on the device side instead of forcing the controller to do the processing.

One of the main disadvantages of the previously presented situations is that wiring costs are one of the most important part of the distributed system cost. They require a lot of manual work and they are difficult to reconfigure. The total wiring length easily attains several miles and the cost to install or reconfigure them becomes important regarding the overall system cost. This was the main motivation for the emergence of networks to directly interconnect sensors, actuators and controllers in a bus topology which is much more cost effective than point-to-point connections. These networks are called field-buses, as they are very close to the physical process.

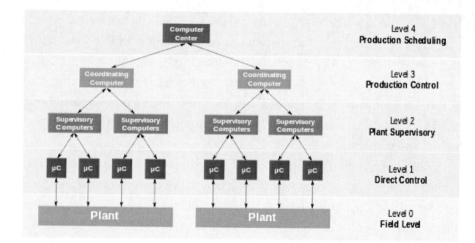

Figure 1.1. Framework of DCS.

In the industrial automatic control system area, people always need a high speed and low cost network for dispersive field equipments controlling. In the past, distributed control system (DCS) were widely used as a mature technology, but in the DCS, machine or plant automation was based on a centralized system with individual connections to each field device (e.g., sensor and actuators), the framework of the DCS shown as Figure 1.1.

Assembly mistakes were easily made but not so easily solved. Further, it wasn't possible to set-up and maintain a field device centrally. Users had to go to each device in turn to change its operating parameters. For solving above problems, people devised field-bus control systems (FCS), FCS is a kind of industrial networking system developed to replace centralized parallel wiring and prevailing analog signal transmission, the aim is to create a single-cable solution that could provide substantial cost reductions, the framework of the FCS shown as Figure 1.2.

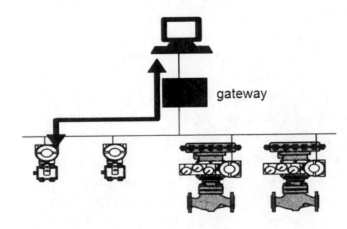

Figure 1.2. The framework of the FCS.

Nowadays, FCS technology has various standards belongs to different corporation alliance, such FIELD-BUS FOUNDATION, PROFIBUS, CANBUS, MODBUS, HART and so on. Every kinds of field-bus has their own protocol and protocols are incompatible, harmonize different devices will pay out abnormal cost, and that will limit user to choose devices in a wider range. Ownership always needs a faster, cheaper and easier to be integrated network in the process control and automation industry field-bus has some more advantages:

- *Increased noise immunity.* The information transmitted over a field-bus is digital, not analog, and hence it has an increased immunity to the inevitable noise. Long point-to-point analog connections are always subject to undesirable interferences which affect the values read from sensors or sent to actuators. After A/D conversion an analog value may be transmitted over the bus covering the necessary distances without any degradation of the digital information. If distances to be covered are so large that even digital information would be plenty of noise, it is always possible to use repeaters which actually regenerate the digital information.

- *Easier reconfiguration.* As the equipment (sensors, actuators or controllers) is connected to the network by a single interface, it becomes easier to reconfigure the connections. If the central controller has to be moved, we just need to reconnect it on any point of the field-bus. This is a strong advantage compared to a situation, where the controller is connected to all the sensors by point-to- point connections. In the former only one connection is to be moved, whereas in the later one has to reconfigure all the existing connections related to the moved controller.

- *Accessibility to the information.* All the information sent over a field-bus is broadcast over the bus and may be read by any node connected to the field-bus, independently of the node on which they produced. Moreover, the protocol may guarantee that all nodes compute with the same values.

- *Decreasing hardware costs.* The connection of a sensor/actuator to a field-bus has a certain cost. Besides the sensing element one has to introduce at least a processor to perform the acquisition of the signal, some indispensable memory and the field-bus interface circuits. This has a certain cost and this is the main reason why we still have to wait till the emergence of common-market cheap standard sensors/actuators. However, it is known that hardware costs are always reducing and if a standard field-bus would emerge, these additional costs would be hardly reduced in a near future.

- *Transducers become smart!* Smart is maybe a badly chosen word but it is true that a sensor/actuator with some processing capabilities and a standard interface network may provide much more services than a classical one. These standard interfaced sensors/actuators are called "smart transducers/transmitters." The main idea to make them "smart" was to take advantage of the processing capabilities of the probably under-loaded processors of smart transducers/transmitters to process some tasks that usually were done by the controlling PLCs. Examples of these tasks are variable pre-processing tasks like linearization of the produced value, filtering and so on. If these tasks are distributed among the processors of smart transmitters/transducers instead of being all allocated to the central controlling device, this will actually free a non negligible part of the central controller load.

- *Distribution of the system's intelligence.* This advantage is a consequence of the generalization of the previous one. If the central controller is free of all pre-processing tasks, why not do the same to the rest of the tasks? These tasks may be distributed among all the processors of the smart transducers/transmitters and there would be no more need of a centralized controller! All the tasks become distributed among the several transducers, as an actual distributed system. In such a system, tasks co-operate with each others (by means of message exchange) to achieve the overall goal, without any centralized hierarchical controller. Moreover, tasks may be allocated dynamically, allowing the possibility of migration, which strongly enhances the system's fault tolerance. In spite of the above advantages, the introduction of field-buses brings up some disadvantages too. Let us mention some of them:

- The field-bus is a communication bottleneck/Classical sensors are connected to the controllers by dedicated connections. The physical medium of a field-bus is no longer dedicated to each sensor but must be shared by all the connected devices. The controllers may no longer read/send the information whenever they want. On the contrary, they must wait for access to the medium (this depends on the type of MAC protocol) to perform the desired input/output operations. The network traffic must hence be carefully scheduled, to guarantee that information will arrive to the consumers within a given time window to meet the timing constraints. Thus, we should not use MAC protocols in which all possible traffic generators may transmit messages at random times, provoking collisions or other sorts of delay, if there is no guarantee that the time window to pass a message is bounded. In other words, protocols like CSMA/CD should not be used for field-buses.

- *Lack of consistency.* A field-bus has the usual problems of distributed systems. As it has no central memory, protocols to guarantee that the copies of each variable have the same value must be provided [6]. As it has no single clock, clock synchronization must be provided to ensure a consistent time stamping of variables and events occurrences. Nowadays a lot of algorithms exist ensuring a more or less accurate synchronization of the clocks, depending mostly on the drift of each clock and the period between resynchronization operations.

- *Fault tolerance.* A real-time system must be intrinsically fault tolerant (i.e., the system must continue to work correctly even in the presence of local faults). Concentrating all the information on a single support may be a strong disadvantage when the medium becomes faulty. For instance, if the bus is accidentally cut, no more messages may be transmitted, resulting in a global fault of the system. This problem is solved by duplicating the physical supports.

From the above discussion, it seems that even if a field-bus may pose new problems, the presented advantages do largely compensate the disadvantages.

Field-bus technology represents a wide domain of problems which are similar, but not exactly identical in nature. Field-bus technology involves a variety of solutions and techniques which, although frequently seen as closely related, are different from each other. Field-bus technology is a kind of technical, political, and human adventure, which for more than 30 years has led to a lot of papers in journals, a lot of announcements, a lot of so-called scoops, a lot of conferences and workshops, and a lot of products and standards.

The following reasons justified the coexistence of multiple standards in field-bus area nowadays.

- The need for a field-bus technology identified by a number of different end-user companies in a number of different sectors.
- The variety of possible hosts to be connected (the variety of sensors, of actuators, of controllers).

Initially, there was no existing standard so each information technology (IT) provider developed their own solutions in a given sector. These companies realized the strategic importance of the field-bus in the industrial automation systems. Once their products were developed, they pushed to have them standardized, and hence we have the current vast range of standards.

The section of the book established the origins and current status of several typical field-bus technology, including technical and scientific analysis, and standardization. Taking into account the number of systems and the number of contenders, the history of the field-bus is long and the different episodes are numerous. Because of this, a lot of details will not be included, and we shall simply focus on the essential steps in its evolution. The section of the book also focuses on the origin of the concept of the field-bus and on the requirements which led to the beginning of field-buses, ending with the current state of standardization. The second part is dedicated to the technical aspects, the services, the protocols, and then the QoS, ending with some communication architecture considerations.

1.2. HISTORY OF INDUSTRIAL FIELD-BUS

The field-bus concept has several origins, but they can be classified into two main groups: the end-user needs and the technological capabilities.

It is appropriate to start with the history of field-buses, in order to understand the differences in approaches. As with most histories, this one has a prehistory. The field-bus ancestors which stood out the most in industrial automation were Modbus from Modicon (Modicon Bus) and the Westinghouse Distributed Processing Family (WDPF) from Westinghouse because of their seniority, their functionalities, and their worldwide acceptance.

Other networks were already in existence, but did not go beyond a few specific applications or domains. For example, the Alliance Research Centre Network (ARCNET) started in 1977 and primarily covered office communication needs, before being used in data acquisition [19]. Another network which was highly used in avionics and aerospace applications was the Military Standard 1553. In the nuclear instrumentation domain, the CAMAC [28] network, created in the 1960s, is considered as the first instrumentation network. Several proprietary networks were in use at the end of the 1970s to connect programmable logic controllers (PLCs) (Allen Bradley Data HighWay and Tiway-Texas Instrument Way), as well as in the process industry.

The integration of heterogeneous systems was difficult due to the lack of standards and was expensive on account of necessary gateways, adaptors, and protocol converters. It was at this moment that two U.S. companies started two projects, the aim of which was "the definition of a standard communication profile." Boeing Company launched the TOP project [26, 36], and General Motors the MAP project [41, 48, 79, 145]. The main objective of the MAP project was the definition of a standard communication profile suited for communication between the design offices and factories and, inside the factory, between workshops and machine tools or robots. General Motors wanted a communication profile for manufacturing applications that could allow all devices to communicate without having to develop specific hardware and/or software. Boeing's idea with the TOP project was similar but concerned another issue, namely, communication between business and technical offices.

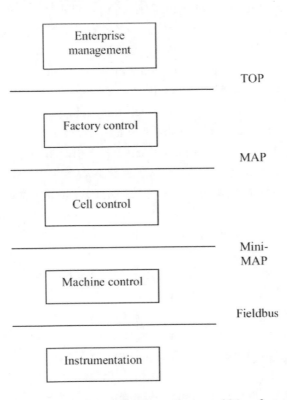

Figure 1.3. Implementation models of Computer Integrated Manufacturing.

Computer Integrated Manufacturing refers to automated manufacturing, automated transport of pieces and materials, using computer technologies at all the stages of a product from its design to the manufacture and the quality control. The idea of structuring applications in a hierarchical way by abstracting levels has been used for decades to simplify their design. Figure 1.3 shows the five levels model of application architecture defined by the National Bureau of Standards (NBS) in the United States [13, 79]. These models were initially functional, meaning that the main interest lay in the function organization, but not in how it was implemented. They were based on the structure of discrete part manufacturing factories. It was later that they were also used as implementation models (or operational models) (as in Figure 1.3).

Each network governs the functions of the layer below and serves as an interface for the layer above. This is how a MAP network in a factory works. All the controllers of cells or of a workshop are connected to the MAP backbone. But each of these controllers is connected to a mini-MAP network which interconnects the machines in the cell. And each machine can use one or several field-bus which interconnects the instrumentation to the machine controllers. Notice that the field-bus and the mini-MAP locations and roles are more or less similar.

In Figure 1.3, a TOP network is situated between the enterprise and the factory control levels, a MAP network is between the latter and the cell control level, mini-MAP or sometimes process data highway, just below that, and then finally the field-bus network between the machine control and the sensor–actuator levels, leading to the operational architecture. Mini-MAP [58] or MAP/enhanced performances architecture (MAP/EPA) was added, based on the factory automation interconnect system (FAIS) specification developed in Japan.

This notion of hierarchical architecture was also developed in process industries, [11, 159] but with a difference in functions. Indeed, the following layers were most often considered: a first layer for reflex automation, a second for the supervision, and a third for optimization.

At the lowest level of communication, before the field-bus era, a lot of standards reigned, for example, the 4–20 mA standard for analog sensors or the 0–24 V for digital inputs, etc. These standards led to a cabling of two wires for each analog point and for each Boolean point (true, false), or each binary digit in a number. The result was the need for a great number of cables in the factories. The design and installation of the wiring were expensive operations, and maintenance or evolution was difficult. This was one of the reasons why end users requested a solution for simplifying these operations: the field-bus was an answer to this request. This need had already been stated in 1971.

1.3. DEVELOPMENT OF INDUSTRIAL FIELD-BUS

In the beginning of the 1980s, several projects started in Europe after the MAP project had began in the United States. In France, the FIP field-bus project saw light in 1982 under the aegis of the French Ministry for Research and Industry. It is a similar process which led to the Process Field-Bus (PROFIBUS [9, 37]) field-bus project in Germany in 1984, and to the P-Net [40] project in Denmark in 1983. At the same time, in 1983, the Bosch Company developed the specifications of the Controller Area Network (CAN) for cars manufactured in Germany. FIP stands for Factory Instrumentation Protocol and is now known as WorldFIP.

The standardization process began at this time in these different countries and at an international level, with IEC TC 65/SC65C/WG6 [51], simultaneously with the Instrumentation Society of America (ISA) in the United States (in the ISA SP50 (ISA-Standard Practice).

The contenders for the IEC international standard at the early beginning were classified into two subgroups: the first group included solutions based on existing protocols; the second group included only new paper proposals without experiments. Some details on these proposals can be found in several publications. Two field-bus types were to be considered, the H1 field-bus at a low data rate for the connection of some sensors essentially in process control, and the H2 field-bus at high data rate for manufacturing or for interconnection of several H1 networks.

The U.K. ERA Technology proposed a field-bus based on the existing Mil Std 1553B. The proposal extended the current standard for physical performances:

- 1900 m at a data rate of 62.5 kb/s, 750 m at the data rate of 250 kb/s, and 350 m at the data rate of 500 kb/s;
- changes to specifications for spur isolation resistors;
- optional addition of power;
- 32 nodes possible with power and active repeaters.

A U.S. group proposed a field-bus based on the P1118 project (based on Bit bus [10] from Intel) dedicated to exchanges between microcontrollers for all types of applications. The specifications covered the physical, the data link, and the application layers.

- *Physical layer:* The covered distance was from 2000 to 5000 m with data rates between 50 and 500K bit/s. The proposed medium was a twisted pair with possible redundancy.
- *Data link layer:* A master/slave protocol with an optional backup master was required. In case of failure with initial master, the backup master assured availability.
- *Application layer:* Different types of messages and services were specified (broadcast and multicast, datagram, acknowledged datagram, connection oriented) with a response time between 10 and 50 ms, and a minimum of 1 millisecond, to ensure the physical procedures. The field-bus had to be optimized for small frames (128 b), with downloading and task control, management tools for device status. The P1118 proposal scope was underlined for distributed intelligent devices in all industries.

The Foxboro company presented two complementary solutions for the H1 applications, using enhanced high-level data link control (HDLC) with Manchester encoding and baseband communication and HDLC with non-return to zero inverted (NRZI) encoding, and RS 485 for H2 networks. The enhancements of HDLC were related to the error detection mechanism.

The number of undetected errors is to be less than one such error in 40 years [6] at a data rate of 1 Mb/s.

Rosemount Inc. presented two solutions, one for the H1 bus using IEEE 802.4 with frequency shift keying (FSK) phase coherent, and one for H2 using IEEE 802.4 with FSK phase continuous. Rosemount started the development of the Hart system in 1985.

Two European proposals, FIP and PROFIBUS, were only paper proposals at this time.

The FIP requirements, published in 1984, were developed by a group of end users and labs. The requirements focused on the application needs, periodic updates of data, independence of addresses and locations, coherence and consistency of data. The FIP Club was created in 1986 for the promotion of these specifications.

The PROFIBUS Field-bus Message Specification (FMS) field-bus was already a technical solution: a character-based transmission, according to the RS 485 standard, with a token passing method distinguishing master and slave stations. Only the master stations were included in the virtual ring. FMS was a subset of the Manufacturing Message Specification (MMS) [89].

The technical committee IEC TC65C/WG6, after having defined Proway (IEC 955) [52] "Inter subsystem communications for industrial process," was in charge of the field-bus standardization after a meeting in Montreal, QC, Canada, in May 1985.

The American position was given by ISA SP50. ANSI entrusted ISA for the definition of the American field-bus standard. The position was that it was not necessary to develop a specific American standard, as they had to cooperate directly with the IEC committee for a unique international standard. After a "call for proposals," the diversity of the protocols proposed made any convergence difficult, if not impossible. The group SP50 of ISA then defined their requirements, which were not very different from those of IEC, and tried to find a common solution among the proposals (Rosemount, PROFIBUS, FIP, ERA, Foxboro).

In the United States, the National Electrical Manufacturers Association (NEMA) created a task force (SC21) which worked with ISA SP50 and IEC to determine a single American and international standard.

The proposals were very different in terms of requirements and solutions. Many concerned the physical layer, and related aspects such as connectivity, topology, and distances, without any deep investigation into the functional application aspects. All this was something new. For the first time ISA and IEC had to consider:

- on the one hand, existing products;

- on the other, paper proposals, largely based on different views of what a field-bus should be.

The decision was to write requirements in order to define a field-bus. The contenders tried to push for the requirement(s) corresponding to their solutions. These requirements are presented in the following section.

1.4. COMMUNICATION PROTOCOL OF INDUSTRIAL FIELD-BUS

In 1978, work on the communication reference architecture model started in the International Organization for Standardization (ISO), and was to become the Open System Interconnection model (OSI) that we all know today. This model, originally conceived for computer interconnection, brought the right concepts for the understanding of data communication, for the design and standardization of new communication protocols. The 1980s were to be a very rich period in creativity and innovation in the field of services as well as in protocols. The OSI/ISO model was shown in Figure 1.4.

The OSI reference model was introduced to clearly identify and isolate the communication problems that may exist between two stations. A complete equivalence between messages and tasks should hence be sought for taking into account all the seven layers of the OSI model. However, in practice, real-time communication systems do not need the services proposed by all the seven layers. Let us summarize the services of each layer and analyse their importance from the scheduling viewpoint. The first layer, the physical layer, is responsible for bit transmission over the physical medium. It defines the features of the physical support and specifies electrical and mechanical specifications of the physical interface plugs and sockets. In other words, this layer is irrelevant from the scheduling viewpoint.

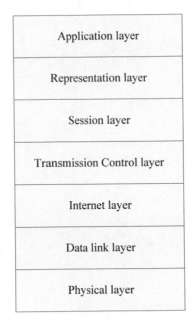

Figure 1.4. OSI/ISO model.

The Medium Access Control (MAC) sub-layer defines the policy how nodes access the physical medium. As the medium is a resource shared by a set of tasks, this layer is of extreme importance from the scheduling viewpoint.

The Logical Link Control (LLC) sub-layer defines the procedure for opening and closing connections, flow control and error management. From the scheduling viewpoint this is equivalent to a fault-tolerance technique similar to the "watch dog" technique used for tasks. The main difference is that in message communication the fault tolerance technique is almost inevitable (most network protocols support some sort of acknowledgement to prevent the inevitable noise over the medium), whilst for processors fault-tolerance techniques are not inevitable, they are used only for applications where dependability is a must. The network layer is responsible for routing messages among different networks. Its protocols are used mainly in highly interconnected networks (like telecommunication networks). Field-bus protocols do not include this layer because they are usually composed by a single segment. The transport layer is responsible for end-to-end flow control. It is more or less equivalent to the LLC sub-layer, in that the LLC sub-layer ensures reliable communication among directly connected stations whilst the transport layer performs the same function but between end-to-end stations which may be connected passing through a huge number of intermediate stations and networks. Another function of the transport layer is to segment messages to keep them at a reasonable size. From the scheduling point of view this is equivalent to limit each task execution time in order to allow other tasks to execute in the mean time. This is a common practice for real-time operating systems called time sharing.

The session layer is responsible for maintaining associations between two or more application entities. In the case of loss of a communication connection, the session layer may provide check points to allow recovery from a known state. This is equivalent to some task error recovery procedures used in fault-tolerant systems.

The presentation layer is responsible for solving differences in information representation between application entities and provides services like data transformation, formatting, structuring, encryption and compression. For instance, this layer is necessary to provide a standard representation for integers, real numbers and characters codes among heterogeneous computers [10]. From the scheduling viewpoint this layer is irrelevant. The application layer is responsible for protocols corresponding to end to end applications like electronic mail, file transfer protocols, etc. This layer is relevant for task scheduling, since user tasks are located at this layer. In LANs, the stations shared the same transmission support. Logically, without some kind of intervention, all stations would transmit simultaneously. For one station to send at a time, it was necessary to develop medium access control (MAC) protocols. Some of these protocols were called deterministic, i.e., a transmission could occur within a bounded delay. The other protocols, which did not have this property, were called nondeterministic. A deterministic MAC protocol based on the token mechanism [88] was chosen by the MAP project. The TOP project chose a nondeterministic protocol called Ethernet [Carrier Sense Multiple Access-Collision Detection (CSMA-CD)].

Because Ethernet lacked the ability to guarantee latency delay, research for making Ethernet deterministic led to the protocols known as CSMA-Bitwise Arbitration (CSMA-BA), CSMA-Collision Avoidance (CSMA-CA), and CSMA-DCR (CSMA-Deterministic Collision Resolution).

With all these varieties of MAC protocols, LANs exploded. It was attractive to specify one's own protocol, well suited to one's need. The trend was facilitated by the progress made in microelectronics, and design automation.

From another point of view, the LAN technology gave an opportunity to a lot of users to experiment with the distribution of applications. It was a great temptation to experiment with distributing functions on microcomputers, and testing their cooperation through a network. It was the moment in the evolution of industrial applications that the digital control system (DCS) or the direct digital control (DDC) migrated to the distributed control system (DCS), ultimately leading to the systems used today.

The 1970s and the 1980s saw the development of microelectronics, of semicustom and full-custom integrated circuits, the development of microcontrollers, and of digital signal processing (DSP). These were the state-of-the-art technologies that made it possible to design new communication controllers. The first Inter Integrated Circuits (I2C) network was created in 1982 by Philips for the interconnection of ICs in television sets [124]. However, the perspective was not only the integration of protocols into silicon, but also the capability to put "intelligence" inside the smallest device, inside any sensor, or actuator. This digital treatment capability found in each sensor and actuator necessitated new communication means. This was another reason for the development of the field-bus, and was stated in a report from Prof. Soutif of Grenoble University, Grenoble, France and during a dedicated colloquium in the UK.

All the elements were in place for entering into the field-bus saga. The discussion at that time centered on sensor and actuator networks or instrumentation networks.

The needs were many and the provider companies recognized great potential in this emerging market. Perhaps the most important reason for field-bus development was the awareness that it could become the backbone of the future distributed and real-time systems for automation (and then the bone of contention for the competition between automation companies). Thus, the specification and the design of numerous field-buses began. An initial experiment of a digital field-bus (1981) was carried out by Brown Bovery Company and Electricité de France with the KSU network at the Thémis solar power plant in the south of France.

In parallel with this innovative design work was the real start of protocol engineering activity, formalization of protocols in terms of automata, Petri nets, etc., and proofs of property, development of languages for specification (ESTELLE, LOTOS, SDL), conformance testing methods, conformance testing procedures and institutions, and arrangements and recognition between national organizations.

The establishment of field-bus requirements started the standardization by both the IEC and ISA committees. Before examining the different proposals, it was decided to first express the requirements before choosing or defining a standard solution. ISA SP50 gave a questionnaire to all the members to try to state the real needs of the user. ISA and IEC committees started writing the requirements in 1986.

Without going into details, a very deductive approach was advocated and described in an ISA document entitled "Field Instrument Bus Standard Specification." But it was difficult to follow the stages described in this document strictly because of the various levels of progress. Some were working on the needs analysis, others on the protocol specifications, and still others on the first implementations. However, it was only in February 1987 that the first version of the final requirements was drafted. For one year, new needs or requirements were proposed at each meeting. But work on the definition of a solution started in Spring 1987. Therefore, we can see an evolution in the requirements from end users' needs at the beginning moving to more and more technical aspects in the later versions.

This next section presents, first, the questionnaire by ISA SP50, then a table summarizing the requirements issued from IEC and ISA. Some requirements from the FIP proposal are included [50] because of their specificity in this arena; an example of operational architecture issued from [166] is also given.

ISA published a 15-page "Discussion draft and questionnaire for functional requirements" [82]. This document discussed the requirements for a "low level" industrial field-bus that connected field devices to higher level monitoring and control systems. Some of the following features were used to distinguish a "low level" field-bus from a "high level" bus system such as Proway or MAP. It was structured in four chapters: "Benefits of field-buses," "Describing field devices," "Information flows," and "Application environment."

Seven benefits were identified, and each was to be qualified according to its importance from greatest to least. The benefits were:

- lowering the installation costs;
- ease of adding field devices;
- providing two-way communication with field devices;
- improving the accuracy of information delivered at control room;
- enhancing the maintainability of field devices;
- providing remote access to measurement data through handheld interface;
- more advanced control strategies can be implemented because of improved field data.

The description of the devices consisted essentially of (for each type of sensor):

- the maximum message response time (time between request and delivery of information);
- the message frequency (in average).

The "information flows" part dealt with

- the design philosophies (grouping of devices on a bus based on functional analysis, on geography, etc.);
- the bus control and the exchanges (master/slave; peer-to-peer, etc.);
- the address allocation;
- the field-bus topology (with distinction of lengths between master and junction box and between junction box and slaves);
- the field-bus size in number of stations;
- the redundancy possibility.

The application environment analyzed the power requirements, the type of wires, the insulation requirements, and the capability to support flammable atmospheres.

As can be seen, the questions were very end user oriented at this early stage; the environment and management were the two key points of the questionnaire. Technical communication aspects were not dealt with, except on a few points such as the notion of masters and slaves and bidirectional communications. It was implicit that the field-bus had to provide two services READ and WRITE. Other services were not considered.

The committees were very optimistic. At the end of 1986, it was expected that the functional guidelines would be available in January 1987 and a standard set in June 1989 [84, 85]. The tables of contents of two future documents (Architecture and Overview; Messaging Service) were published in the working groups on 11 December 1986.

The field-bus will be a serial digital communication standards which can replace present signaling techniques such as 20 mA and 24 VDC, so that more information can flow in both directions between intelligent field devices and the higher level control system over shared communication medium.

Just one field-bus is needed to allow multipoint attachments for a number of addressable devices. The most common justifications for this design are:

- better quality and quantity of information flow;
- save cable and installation cost;
- ease of adding or deleting field devices in a system;
- fewer connections to devices mounted on moving equipment;
- fewer penetrations through process containment walls;
- save cable and installation weight;
- reduce installation errors;
- reduce terminal and junction boxes.

The official requirements stated that two field-buses were needed, H1 and H2. Even if they presented some similar functionalities, they differed in speed, distances between stations, number of stations, and services to the user. We can see the needs expressed on the one hand for the low-speed process control applications (H1), and on the other hand for high-speed process applications (H2) (in discrete part manufacturing or in certain process control). The former required a robust physical layer, with a powered bus, with intrinsic safety, and possible reuse of the existing wiring, but in terms of services, it needed READ and WRITE services, without particular synchronization needs. The latter expressed more requirements in terms of synchronization and distributed control.

Field-bus traffic was either periodic or non-periodic, that it was composed of data and of messages. The data was coming from or going to the final elements in the devices; it was transmitted with status. The messages contained other information.

Regarding the services provided to the user, the requirements cited the services for the exchange of values (READ, WRITE, Information Report, or Notification) and for synchronization. Time stamping was required, but the concepts of consistency or of coherence were not really recognized as necessary. The concept of response time, even if cited and quantified, was not really studied. A rapid classification distinguished process control and manufacturing.

Regarding the mechanisms relevant to MAC and LLC, the question seemed to be eluded; they were to become the major point of discussion and the stumbling block throughout the following years.

The field-bus was not yet considered as a real-time network but as relative to MAP and Mini-MAP [6]. This was reinforced by the position of PROFIBUS FMS, which appeared at this moment more as a mini-MAP network than a field-bus.

It was after the appearance of the field-bus in other applications that the concept of a real-time network would be considered at the international level for standardization. It was after the publication of real-time communication needs by the European MAPs users' group [45, 127] that the work group ISO TC 184, SC5, WG6 TCCA was created to study real-time communication independently of the network's position in the system's architecture.

At the beginning of the field-bus era, only two main domains of application (process control and discrete manufacturing) were considered by the standardization bodies (IEC and national organizations). We have seen that the requirements were quite similar in both cases. And now, as field-bus technology has penetrated all application domains, it is interesting to observe their similar needs, even a posteriori. This section analyzes the different application domains in order to show that the variety of field-bus existing today is also a result of these different requirements.

The applications can be seen as a set of criteria for classification of industrial LANs and, more especially, field-buses. The criteria are related to:

- The types of traffic, which influence the services and the required QoS (real-time constraints, synchronization needs, etc.);
- The environment characteristics (electromagnetic compatibility (EMC), intrinsic safety, power);
- The dependability constraints (availability, reliability, safety, security, etc.).

We shall not analyze the environment and dependability characteristics because they are too dependent upon the application itself, and dependent even on the location of the application.

The question of real time is common to all domains as well. It is not expressed in the same "units," but the constraints are potentially the same.

Now, as traffic is always periodic or non-periodic, we shall briefly analyze its characteristics for the following types of applications: discrete manufacturing applications, process control industry including energy production, building automation, control of utilities networks, transportation systems, and embedded systems.

A discrete manufacturing application is characterized by the fact that, between two operations, a product is in a stable state, i.e., it is not damaged if stocked between these operations. This criterion allows for decomposing the application into sub-applications relatively independent from a time point of view, with each sub-application being attached to an operation or to a machine.

In such applications, it is then natural to distinguish the communications within a machine from those between machines. In the former, the stations are the sensors, the actuators, the axis controllers, the regulators, and other PLCs. Traffic is essentially periodic and is relevant to the field-bus. There are needs for broadcasting, for distribution of control algorithms, and for synchronization between application processes.

In the latter, the exchanges are more asynchronous [production orders, report of activity, downloading of programs (or of "domains" in MMS terminology)]. The synchronization between the sub-applications is more relevant to production management and productivity criteria than to real-time constraints and process dependability or of product quality criteria. Indeed, such a synchronization failure does not affect the process nor the product. Even if this traffic may be supported by some field-buses, it is more the role of cell networks or factory networks.

The environment depends essentially on the factory domain and may lead to the use of special media adapted to the EMC.

The reliability criterion applies to the field-bus inside a machine, for the quality of the products and for human (operators) safety. Other criteria, such as availability, are not usually critical but are important for productivity.

The continuous processes are characterized by the fact that the products are continuously produced through a sequence of operations (assumed by different machines) with no stable state between two successive operations. Iron–steel industry processes, many chemical and biological processes, the paper mill industry, and energy production are considered in this category.

Inside a given machine, the traffic is very similar to that described in the previous section. The field-bus must assume real-time traffic between sensors, controllers, and actuators. But considering the need for synchronization between successive machines, some real-time traffic introduced by the distributed control between the concerned controllers is also supported by the field-bus.

The characteristics of these processes differ essentially in their time constants, e.g., the speed control in a steel mill and the temperature control in a blast furnace. The lack of a stable state leads to very strict time constraints for the synchronization of operations, e.g., the controller coordination of the sequential elements of a rolling mill. The real-time QoS depends on the criticality of the application.

In terms of environment, continuous processes, especially in the chemical industry, are the domain of intrinsic safety for devices powered by the network. It is also the domain for protection against electromagnetic perturbations (industries with electrical motors). Redundancy is often desired, sometimes necessary, for dependability and safety (people, environment, production tools).

This type of application concerns the surveillance of houses or buildings, access control, heating and air conditioning, and management of utilities and electric domestic appliances. The applications are more relevant to data acquisition and supervision than to control. The control functions are often very simple.

The range of sensors is very broad. A lot of sensors are On/Off (open/close, enable/disable). Others measure the usual physical input variables (temperatures, levels, speeds, etc.). Finally, some are camera based and need image analysis for remote monitoring. The real-time constraints are not numerous. Only some cases, such as burglar alarms or control of elevators and access, are constrained.

As far as the wiring is concerned, it usually represents a significant part of the cost. Therefore, wireless or power line communications are being used more and more in this kind of application. The environmental conditions are not really too demanding, but the great number of devices and controllers lead to very complex systems. All possible topologies must be available for adapting the architecture of the system to any type of building or group of buildings. The dependability is not specified as in industry but it is also very important:

- reliability—an elevator or a heating system cannot fail on Christmas evening;
- availability of communication resources in case of an emergency in a remote health care monitoring;
- safety and security for protection against vandalism or unauthorized people.

These applications consist of the remote monitoring and the control of very large networks for the distribution of water, gas, hot steam, or electricity. They are no longer located in a small area such as a factory or a building, and the networks are no longer really LANs, and yet these applications really are of the same nature as the previous. The functions are the remote monitoring and control of stations (pumping, stocking, transformer stations), pipes, and lines. Operators are only in central control rooms for exploitation and maintenance organization.

Traffic consists of status variables and events as well as the transfer of information between the intermediate stations of fluid/current transport.

The synchronization of data acquisition is often important for establishing the order of events. The data rate depends on the complexity of the system considered.

The networks that convey the data for monitoring and control have the same dependability roles as a field-bus in a factory. The only difference is in the distances covered; the medium and the physical layer protocol must be adapted to the distance. Power line protocols are used in electrical networks. Optic networks are used in transformer stations. Radio waves are often used to connect very remote stations. It is also now a preferred domain for Internet use.

A transport system is an infrastructure for the transport of people and/or freight. The applications in these systems cover the management of a railway network, the remote control of urban traffic, the monitoring of highways, etc.

Traffic is composed of status variables, events, and device command and control. The topology of the field-bus depends on the geography of the system considered. The safety constraints are often very important. Dependability is also very crucial, especially availability, even during maintenance or updating operations.

It is possible to include in this category of applications the control and management of telecommunications networks (telephone networks, mobile networks, etc.)

These systems are now in many products, from cars to buses to trains, but also in major electrical domestic appliances (refrigerators, etc.). In vehicles, the application consists of various functions:

- control of the motor(s), of the braking system, of the stability, of the gearbox;
- assistance to the driver, or to automatically pilot the vehicle (as in some trains);
- other functions are related to the energy consumption, such as optimization;
- management of lights, glass-cleaner;
- management of passenger access in trains, ticketing;
- maintenance;

The distances are short; the environment possibly very demanding (in cars, for example); safety is a major constraint.

These applications present time constraints depending on the functions considered. The motor is controlled every 10 ms; the response time of a braking request must be as short as possible.

The term "embedded system" is also used for different equipment such as refrigerators, coffee machines, and washing machines. Each time a piece of equipment is built with "intelligence" and communication capabilities, it can be considered as an embedded system. We also speak of "ambient intelligence" [1] with the expectation of a fully communicating environment and many autonomous intelligent devices in the near future. New problems will occur such as connectivity, safety, confidentiality, integrity, etc.

This brief study of the application domains shows that the basic field-bus specifications in terms of functions and of services are very similar in each of the applications.

The exchange of data (values, status, and events) is the main function of the field-buses for automatic control, but also for maintenance and management. We shall see that if the requirement is relatively simple, the solutions are numerous (in terms of protocols). Other functions are required but as options. Synchronization is one of these functions. It is, nevertheless, necessary for the management of distributed systems. The fact that this function was not considered 20 years ago shows that a lot of people did not think that the field-bus would change the application architecture and design. They thought it would only be a simplification of the wiring. Consequently, the only cited time constraints were the response time and the frequency of the exchanges, which allow for a very simple calculation of the load on a field-bus and then its proportioning.

The maximum values given for each field-bus (maximum length, maximum number of stations, maximum data rate, maximum frequency of data update, etc.) are limitations for each application design. Because of these limitations it is sometimes necessary to use several field-buses (and other networks) on which the architecture of the application will then depend.

This notion of architecture is not as simple as is usually understood. The word "architecture" is sometimes used for topology; it may be used with the same sense as in the title of the OSI model, and in this case, it then represents an organization of services and protocols. Here, the word "architecture" represents the organization of the automatic control application implemented around a field-bus and other industrial networks. Architecture is typically defined by diagrams as seen in Figure 1.4. The question of architecture is inherent in the requirements for setting up a field-bus. This was not the question before.

Figure 1.4 shows an operational architecture, because it indicates the devices and the field-buses actually in operation. But this kind of diagram leaves much to be desired. Indeed, nothing is said about the functions implemented in each station represented by a box, and nothing is said about the cooperation between functions and the exchanges supported by the field-buses and other networks. Before designing such architecture, it is necessary to carry out a functional analysis which must specify the application, the functions and sub-functions, their interactions, and their communications. The result is a functional architecture which ideally may relegate the components and the networks to second place, focusing on the functions. A functional architecture being specified, the designer has to choose the networks, the components, the devices, and the distribution of the functions in the devices. This is the real design stage of the solution, taking into account the constraints, defining which station is connected to which field-bus, and distributing the functions in the devices.

It is only after this stage that the choice of the architecture takes place, along with the choice of the field-bus. Now it is the choice of the field-bus which has an impact on, and sometimes imposes, the choice of the architecture, depending on the services provided by the communications system. It is clear that the existence of certain services determines the distribution facilities.

These architectures will be applied to all domains of application, with a hierarchy from the first-level field-bus, up to the highest level. Let us take some examples.

In a train, the usual architecture has two levels; each wagon has its own field-bus, and another field-bus interconnects them all and has a gateway to the external world.

In a building, architecture with three levels can be considered; here, each apartment has its own field-bus; they, in turn, are interconnected by a floor field-bus, themselves interconnected by a building field-bus. Other field-buses may be associated with the control of the elevators.

In the control of a pipe (be it for gas or water, or some other medium), we could have a field-bus along the pipe, structured in "segments" of the maximum length for the chosen field-bus. Each field-bus of a segment connects all the devices of the segment, and a special site serves as concentrator. The concentrators may be interconnected by another upper level field-bus or network.

1.5. FIELD-BUS TYPES

Recently, efforts by standardization bodies as IEC and technical societies as ISA have led to the IEC61158 norm [2], which defines eight distinct field-buses as an international standard.

Field-bus standardization is a subject which has led to a great number of publications for the past twenty years. Regularly, during the 1990s journals published the progress of the standardization process (control and instrumentation, control engineering, measurement and control). Words such as "war," "battle," "winner," "peace" appear in the titles. Optimistic opinions ("a standard will be obtained at the end of the 1980s") expressed in 1987 all the way up to 1996 decrease after this period. Skepticism and interrogations start to appear.

Several updates on the situation have been regularly published; some are listed here in chronological order.

The international standardization concerned essentially the IEC, but also the ISO (TC 184 SC5 WG6), which was in charge of the Time Critical Communication Architecture (TCCA) specification. In Europe, in the middle of the 1990s, the CENELEC decided to define European norms while waiting for an international solution from IEC. Indeed, at the beginning of the 1990s, different lobbying groups appeared only to disappear: the Open Field-bus Consortium (OFC), the International Field-bus Group (IFG), the Interoperable System Project (ISP), etc. There was no compromise and no possible consensus between any two opposing blocks. Even though a group of experts wrote a complete specification for the data link layer [70, 71], including the different concepts and mechanisms, the opposition continued. Because this specification was refused by the minimum minority in 1998, and caused a great problem at the highest IEC level, the Committee of Action of the IEC issued some kind of ultimatum for the working group. The result today is the current content of the IEC 61 158 with eight completely heterogeneous and incompatible field-bus families.

After a lot of episodes and developments, the IEC 61 158 standard, including a large set of services and protocols, is defined as follows. It is structured by layer, according to the OSI model architecture reduced as mini-MAP, or MAP-EPA, to the physical layer, the data link layer including the MAC and the application layer (cf. Section III-A).

The main standard is IEC 61 158. The first standard (IEC 61 158-2), published in 1993 [67], defined the physical layer.

The other parts are:

- 61 158-3: data link layer service specification;
- 61 158-4: data link layer protocol specification
- 61 158-5: application layer service specification
- 61 158-6: application layer protocol specification.

These specifications are a collection of different national standards or specifications.

The data link pars (IEC 61 158-3 and 61 158-4) cover eight types listed below:

- Type 1 is the TR1158, the compromise standard proposal refused by a minority of members in 1999, which led to a publication of indignation by Patricio Leviti [104].

- Type 2 is the ControlNet specification.
- Type 3 is the PROFIBUS specification.
- Type 4 is the P-Net specification.
- Type 5 is the FOUNDATION Field-bus specification.
- Type 6 is the SwiftNet specification.
- Type 7 is the WorldFIP specification.
- Type 8 is the INTERBUS specification.

The application layer specifications (IEC 61 158-5 and 61 158-6) covered ten different types. The first eight are associated with the data link layer. The two others, Type 9 and Type 10, define the FOUNDATION Field-bus H1 network and PROFINET, respectively.

Two other parts were planned, 61 158-7 for network management and 61 158-8 for conformance testing procedures. They were canceled, because of the existence of proprietary tools for configuration and network management, and for conformance tests of the different types. The maintenance of this standard is now entrusted to SC65C/MT1 (MT stands for Maintenance Team).

A project for a new standard has also been started for the definition of the Communication Profile Families (CPFs) inside the IEC 61 784 standard. Its objective is to clarify the situation created by the number of variants and options in the IEC 61 158 standard. While it defines services and protocols by layer, according to the OSI model reference architecture, the 61 784 standard proposes a specification for a complete stack of protocols based on the previous options. These communication stacks are called profiles.

This standard is composed of two parts; the first, the IEC 61 784-1 standard, is composed of 18 profiles; and the second part, 61 784-2 on Real-Time Ethernet, in progress (work started mid–2003), is composed of nine proposals, all based on Ethernet.

This new project has been entrusted to the new working group IEC SC65C WG11. It is structured as follows.

Structure of IEC 61 784-1:

- The current CPFs are defined in the first part.
- CPF 1 FOUNDATION field-bus CPF 1/1 H1, CPF 1/2 High-Speed Ethernet (HSE).
- CPF 2 ControlNet CPF 2/1 ControlNet, CPF 2/2 EtherNet/IP.
- CPF 3 PROFIBUS, CPF 3/1 PROFIBUS-DP, CPF 3/2 PROFIBUS-PA, CPF 3/3 PROFINET.
- CPF 4 P-Net, CPF 4/1 P-Net RS 485, CPF 4/2 P-Net RS 232.
- CPF 5 WorldFIP, CPF 5/1 WorldFIP, CPF 5/2 WorldFIP Device WFIP.
- CPF 6 INTERBUS, CPF 6/1 INTERBUS, CPF 6/2 INTERBUS TCP/IP, CPF 6/3 subset.
- CPF 7 SwiftNet, CPF 7/1 SwiftNet transport (without application layer), CPF 7/2 Full stack.

Structure of 61 784-2, under current specification:

- CPF 2 ControlNet;
- CPF 3 PROFIBUS, PROFINET;
- CPF 6 INTERBUS;
- CPF 10 VNET/IP (Virtual Network Protocol);
- CPF 11 TCnet;
- CPF 12 EtherCAT (Ethernet for control automation technology);
- CPF 13 EPL (Ethernet PowerLink)
- CPF 14 EPA (Ethernet for plant automation);
- CPF 15 MODBUS-RTPS (real-time publish–subscribe).

In 1990, a new work item for the ISO TC184 SC5 WG6 Time-Critical Communication Architecture (TCCA) group was started, following the analysis of the MAP experiments to define real-time communication requirements and recommendations [127]. The European MAP user group published a list of requirements for real-time communication. At the same time, the field-bus appeared as a real-time network [130]. The study of a communication architecture was published as a technical report [57, 90]. Following this work, the network management of time-critical communication systems (TCCS) was also studied [93].

Four European standards have been published and updated several times in order to provide international standards where the IEC lacked.

The EN 50170 was published in 1996 with three national standards: P-Net from Denmark, PROFIBUS-FMS from Germany, and WorldFIP from France. FOUNDATION Field-bus was added to EN 50170 as an addendum in 2000, jointly with ControlNet [27] and PROFIBUS-PA [39].

The EN 50254 was also published to include field-buses with higher performances for the transmission of short frames: INTERBUS, PROFIBUS DP, and Device WorldFIP [3, 22].

The EN 50325 standard covers the profiles derived from the CAN protocol (and of the ISO 11 898 standard), as DeviceNet, SDS, and CANopen, which are also parts of the IEC 62 026.

The EN 50295 standard is a standard defining the actuator and sensor interface (AS-i) protocol [7].

Different communication protocols have distinct temporal behavior characteristics, which depends on factors such as transmission rate, bus length, and medium access control strategies. To take into account all these different parameters during distributed automation systems development becomes a very complex task and therefore the availability of tool support is very important.

Over the last decades some interesting approaches for assessing timing behavior characteristics, such as temporal determinism and guarantees of messages latencies, of field-bus-based automation applications have been proposed.

Control loops that are closed over a communication network get more and more common as the hardware devices for network and network nodes become cheaper. A control system communicating with sensors and actuators over a communication network will be called a *distributed real-time control system*. In distributed real-time control systems, see Figure 1.1, data are sent and received by network nodes of different kind and manufacturers. Network nodes that are of specific interest for distributed control are sensor nodes, actuator nodes, and controller nodes. Sensor nodes measure process values and transmit these over the communication network. Actuator nodes receive new values for the process inputs over the communication network and apply these on the process input. Controller nodes read process values from sensor nodes. Using a control algorithm control signals are calculated and sent to the actuator nodes. The system setup with a common communication network reduces cost of cabling and offers modularity and flexibility in system design. The distributed control setup is powerful, but some caution must be taken. Communication networks inevitably introduce delays, both due to limited bandwidth, but also due to overhead in the communicating nodes and in the network. The delays will in many systems be varying in a random fashion. From a control perspective the control system with varying delays will no longer be time-invariant. As an effect of this the standard computer control theory cannot be used in analysis and design of distributed real-time control systems. The thesis addresses the problem of analysis and design of control systems when the communication delays are varying in a random fashion. Models for communication network delays are developed. The most advanced model has an underlying Markov chain that generates the probability distributions of the time delays. Measurements of transfer delays are presented for two commercially used networks, a CAN-network and an Ethernet network.

Nowadays, FCS technology has various standards belongs to different corporation alliance, such FIELD-BUS FOUNDATION, PROFIBUS, CANBUS, MODBUS, HART and so on. Every kinds of field-bus has their own protocol and protocols are incompatible, harmonize different devices will pay out abnormal cost, and that will limit user to choose devices in a wider range. Ownership always needs a faster, cheaper and easier to be integrated network in the process control and automation industry. Ethernet gives a good solution. In the past several years, the standard of Ethernet had been improved much especially on determination, speed and information priority, Because of the rapid development of the exchanging technology the impediment of adopting Ethernet in control area is eliminated greatly. Now many organizations and companies are engaged in mixing Ethernet and existing field-bus protocol together and spreading it in plant level.

1.6. SCHEDULING AND MANAGEMENTS FOR INDUSTRIAL FIELD-BUS

Modern industrial automation solutions employ distributed networks which use industrial communication protocols, such as PROFIBUS, Foundation Field-bus, and CAN. These technologies allow a real distribution of processing over the network having positive influence on aspects such as system's reliability, expansibility, and maintenance.

It is widely accepted that the performance of an industrial automation system does not only depend on the function of the individual components, (sensors, actuators, PLCs, workstations), but also and mainly on its communication system because of its distributed structure. Local Area Networks (LAN) are used for such applications, especially the industrial LANs (field-busses), in order to provide in a reliable way the necessary communication paths. The protocols that are used for the implementation of the MAC sub-layer strongly affect the performance of the industrial networks.

In the industrial and some security key systems, usually a node transmits categories data frame with different requirements for time performance [1, 2], so safety critical systems communication network realization and information scheduling theory needs to be solved urgently [3]. In the existing references [4-10] the field-bus application layer real-time information scheduling mostly reference single processor task scheduling, but whether static scheduling or dynamic scheduling, many defects existed, and the MAC (Media Access Control) mechanism has not been considered in these application layer scheduling algorithms either. In fact, it is MAC mechanism determines the rules of node access bus. Therefore, the real-time information scheduling method based on centralized MAC mechanism has been presented in this paper to solve the real-time information scheduling problem of field-bus system which a node with a variety of information that have different requirements for real-time characteristics. In real-time systems the deadlines of each task must be met. A pre-run-time schedule ability analysis becomes necessary to prove that the existing software and target hardware will meet the real-time application constraints. In a real-time distributed system, the messages transmitted through the network are also time constrained. However, some new problems arise when one applies existing task scheduling algorithms to schedule the network traffic. A real time system must produce correct responses in a specified time, because a result produced out of time is useless even if it was correctly computed [1, 2]. A result produced after its deadline is a wrong result and may lead to severe consequences. A current practice to build a centralized real-time system is to choose a robust and last generation not cumbersome PLC from the huge variety available on the market. (PLCs have benefited from the evolution of microprocessors and have become much less voluminous, more robust and with increasing performance.) All PLC centralized real-time system is to choose a robust and last generation not cumbersome PLC from the huge variety available on the market. (PLCs have benefited from the evolution of microprocessors and have become much less voluminous, more robust and with increasing performance.) All PLC manufacturers propose a large variety of modular I/O cards which offer a sufficiently large number of I/O ports per card. The user "just" needs to connect each sensor/actuator to the corresponding I/O port and the software installed on the PLC will control the process as wished. Another advantage is that connections are more or less standard like the 4-20 mA current loop which is, in practice, the standard connection for the transmission of analog signals.

The research in real-time communications can be grouped into two categories: soft real-time and hard real-time communication. The primary performance objective of the first category is to maximize the percentage of data packets successfully transmitted within a predetermined time constraint. Applications of this category include packaged voice/video communication, in which a certain amount of packet loss is usually tolerable and a packet which is not successfully delivered within a certain time limit is considered lost [14]. Classical applications of hard real-time networks are the industrial networks in which several packets, such as alarm and control signals, must reach their destination before a certain time (time deadline). The hard real-time MAC protocols aim at improving the throughput while ensuring all time constrained packets to meet their time deadlines (bounded packet delay).

Most of the CSMA/CD-based networks (IEEE 802.3 Standard) [15] have been mainly aimed at commercial rather than real-time applications, due to their non-deterministic nature. However, in the literature, several studies examined the feasibility of using CSMA/CD (or Ethernet) for real-time applications, either without any kind of modification [15-171, or by introducing (implicit or explicit) priorities for the high-priority packets [18, 19]. A general conclusion of these studies is that, under certain assumptions, the requirements of several soft real-time applications are met by the CSMA/CD protocol. Various schemes which are based on deterministic retransmission delays for the collided packets of a CSMA/CD protocol [20] result in an upper-bounded delay for all the transmitted packets. However, this is achieved at the expense of inferior performance to CSMA/CD at low to moderate channel utilization in terms of delay-throughput.

On the other hand, token passing protocols (like the IEEE 802.4 Standard) [22] have been widely used as MAC protocols for many of the existing popular industrial LANs, like the MAP network [23]. This is done because token passing is both efficient and deterministic at high loads. However at low channel traffic, its performance is not as good as that of contention protocols (e.g., CSMA/CD). This lack of efficiency becomes more serious as the number of nodes, the (bandwidth) X (distance) product and the token size are increased. The complementary behavior of the token passing and CSMA/CD access protocols has led to the suggestion that they could combined in order to form more complex reservation or hybrid protocols with high performance [20, 21, 24-301. Two high-performance protocols of this category are the CSMA/CD-DP [20] and the Virtual Token [24] protocols. The CSMA/CD-DP is a CSMA/CD-like protocol with dynamic priorities and low collision probability. It "switches" between two operational modes, the contention mode when the channel is idle and the reservation mode when the channel is busy. This protocol uses an algorithm which assigns priorities to the network stations by using larger delays for the retransmission of the low-priority packets. The CSMA/CD-DP protocol combines the advantages of the CSMA/CD and token passing access mechanisms, uses priorities and guarantees none or only one collision per frame transmission. However, this protocol does not offer good performance for the middle range of the throughput values. The Virtual Token protocol is another MAC-level hybrid protocol for bus-type networks which offers high performance and bounded packet delay. A number of back-off algorithms (VT,, VT,, VIP, VT01 which guarantee bounded packet delay were tested and the result was that the Virtual Token protocol performs better than the standard Token Bus in terms of mean delay-throughput; its performance is also comparable to CSMA/CD for low and moderate loads, being much better for heavy traffic conditions.

To guarantee that the application timing constraints will always be met, one must do a pre-run time schedule ability analysis of the system. From the scheduling point of view, distributed real-time systems impose much more problems and constraints than centralized systems. Whereas in centralized mono processor-based systems the main problem is to schedule tasks on a single processor, in distributed systems the problem is not only to decide "when" to execute a task, but also to decide "where" the task should be executed. It is up to the global scheduler to decide which is the most suitable node (or nodes) to execute a given task and to give a warranty that it will be able to schedule all the tasks and network traffic, meeting all the application timing constraints. There are some fundamental differences concerning message scheduling and task scheduling. Although messages are somewhat different from tasks, a lot of analogies do exist between task scheduling and message scheduling.

In order to be executed tasks may require a set of resources (processors, memory, I/O ports, etc.). Similarly, to be transmitted, messages require a set of resources (physical medium, memory, etc.). Resource constraints complicate the scheduling problem, leading to undesirable situations like deadlocks. In the case of tasks, a deadlock arises, for instance, when a task uses a resource R 1 and requires a resource R2 which is being used by another task requiring the resource RI: the two tasks are blocking each other. In a multiple-connection network, the same situation may arise. For instance, if one message has to be broadcast over two channels at the same time, the sender may fall in a deadlock if another sender tries to do the same operation, but reserving the channels in an opposite order. A special class of resource constraints is known as allocation constraints; tasks may not be placed on any processor of the network because of several reasons, like micro-code compatibility. Similarly, sending messages may require the use of a specific network.

In this book, analysis and evaluation of communication performance in real time industrial field-bus, including timed-token MAC, Foundation Field-bus (FF), PROFIBUS, WorldFIP and CAN, were presented. It is very helpful for university students and researchers in their research in the related field. FF is based on token mechanism and the relationship between periodic and non-periodic traffic is relatively loose. In non-periodic traffic, the time resource is limited and has close relationship with data priority and token priority. The priority of token can be adjusted automatically in FF when a token rotation is finished. Target Token Rotation Time (TTRT) is a critical parameter in the non-periodic traffic for FF field-bus. TTRT can be viewed as time resource to be allocated. Actual Token Rotation Time (ATRT) can be viewed as the time resources consumed. Time resource is surplus and more data can be allowed to consume the time resource in the next round if TTRT > ATRT. Time resource is not enough and less data can be allowed to consume the time resource in the next round if TTRT < ATRT. PROFIBUS is also TTRT based protocol but the value of TTRT is not adjusted when a token rotation is finished. Once the value of TTRT (representing time resource) is set, it is fixed and the time resource can only be contended by nodes. Therefore the setting of TTRT is quite important. Essential element of the communication performance analysis lies in the node data to be served. All performance analysis can be carried out based on the analysis for the relationship between those data with different priority. Assignment of different priority to different node data was also quite important in the analysis. This is also called node-data oriented analysis. WorldFIP field-bus is Link Activity Scheduler (LAS) based and the relationship between periodic and non-periodic traffic is relatively tight. Non-periodic traffic is dependent on periodic traffic and initialized with registration to LAS in periodic traffic. That means the time resource is only available to some variables that has been listed in scheduling table (named class 1 variables, C1V for short) and those variables connected to C1V. Those variables that have nothing to do with C1V cannot obtain time resource to send data. Therefore, the equity of allocation of time resource needs to be discussed further if we regard data-sending as a right of a variable. It is possible that the designer of the WorldFIP protocol thought that WorldFIP field-bus is a demand-oriented system. Variables acquiring data is not active to providing data. Only the variables need remote data are active in "pulling" remote data.

Chapter 2

TIMED-TOKEN NETWORKED CONTROL SYSTEM WITH ITS APPLICATION IN INDUSTRY

2.1. INTRODUCTION

It has become a common practice to use digital computers for embedded real-time distributed applications such as space vehicle systems, image processing and transmission, and the integration of expert systems into avionics and industrial process control. A salient feature of these computations is that they have stringent timing requirements. A failure to meet the computational deadlines could lead to a catastrophe. Further, these systems are often distributed. This is not only because the applications themselves are often physically distributed, but also due to the potential that distributed systems have for providing good reliability, good resource sharing, and good extensibility. The key to success in using a distributed system for these applications is the timely execution of computation tasks that usually reside on different nodes and communicate with one another to accomplish a common goal. Distributed realtime systems may be categorized as soft real-time systems or hard real-time systems. In soft real-time systems tasks are performed by the system as fast as possible but are not constrained to finish by a specific time. In hard real-time systems tasks must satisfy explicit time constraints; otherwise, grave consequences may result. Consequently, the messages transmitted in the network by the hard real-time tasks are also time constrained. End-to-end deadline guarantees are possible only if a communication network supports the timely delivery of inter-task messages. The main focus of this study is to address important issues related to guarantees of synchronous message deadlines. A guaranteed message will always be transmitted before its deadline (unless a network fault occurs).

GUARANTEEING message deadlines is a key issue in distributed real-time applications. The timed token medium access control (MAC) protocol is suitable for real-time applications due to its special timing property of bounded token rotation time. Timed token means a limited time resource shared among different nodes over network.

In a distributed system for hard real-time applications, communication through message exchange between tasks residing on different nodes must happen in bounded time, in order to guarantee that end-to-end deadline requirements are met. This motivates the use of medium access control (MAC) communication protocols proposed for hard real-time communications, which provide the guaranteed connection and guaranteed amount of channel bandwidth to sup- port timely delivery of inter-task messages. With the special timing property of bounded time between any v (v is an integer no less than two) consecutive visits of the token to a node, which is necessary for real-time communication, the timed token protocol becomes one of the most suitable and attractive candidates for (hard) real-time applications. The timed token protocol has been incorporated into many network standards including the Fibre Distributed Data Inter- face (FDDI), IEEE 802.4, the High-Speed Data Bus (HSDB), the High-Speed Ring Bus (HSRB) and the Survivable Adaptable Fibre Optic Enbedded Networks (SAFENET), which are used as backbone networks in many embedded real-time applications. The important concept of "timed token" protocol was first proposed in 1982 by Grow [Gro82] where the framework (the basic idea) of the timed token protocol, adaptable to either a physical or a logical ring, was described in detail. Ulm[Ulm82] then studied the proto- col proposed by Grow and its performance characteristics. The timing properties of the timed token protocol were formally analyzed by Johnson and Sevcik in [Joh87, Sev87] where it is shown that the average token rotation time is bounded by TTRT (the Target Token Rotation Time) and the maximum token rotation time cannot exceed twice the TTRT. Chen et al[Che92a] made a detailed study on the timing behavior of the timed token protocol and generalized the upper bound derived by Johnson and Sevcik on the maximum token rotation time.

With the timed token protocol, messages are grouped into two separate classes: the synchronous class and the asynchronous class. Synchronous messages arrive in the system at regular intervals and may be associated with deadline constraints. The idea behind the timed token protocol is to control the token rotation time. At network initialization time, a protocol parameter called Target Token Rotation Time (TTRT) is determined, which indicates the expected token rotation time. Each station is assigned a fraction of the TTRT, known as synchronous bandwidth,' which is the maximum time for which a station is permitted to transmit its synchronous messages every time it receives the token. Once a node receives the token, it transmits its synchronous messages, if any, for a time no more than its allocated synchronous bandwidth. It can then transmit its asynchronous messages only if the time elapsed since the previous token departure from the same node is less than the value of TTRT, i.e., only if the token arrived earlier than expected.

2.2. TIMED TOKEN MECHANISM

It is well known that token protocols can be classified into non-timed-token protocols and timed-token protocols (TTPs). The non-TTP including its queuing models and mathematical analyses have been studied for a long time, and significant results have been obtained [1]. The TTP is studied recently with the development of the technology of fiber distributed data interface (FDDI) in MAN. Pang, Jain discussed the throughput of the TTP under different conditions [2] and [3]. In 1992, Rubin developed an approximate M/G/1/S vacation model for FDDI asynchronous TTP systems [4]. In 1997, Rubin presented an exact analysis of an asymmetric multiple-priority token ring network supporting stations with single packet buffers under a TTP, and illustrated the application of the analytic approach through numerical examples representing FDDI network systems under various traffic loading conditions [5].

With the timed token protocol, messages are distinguished into two types: synchronous and asynchronous. Synchronous messages are periodic with delivery time constraints. Asynchronous messages are non-periodic with no delivery time constraints. During network initialization time, all nodes negotiate a common value for the Target Token Rotation Time (TTRT) which should be small enough to meet responsiveness requirements of all nodes. However, the value of TTRT cannot be too small for TTRT represents the time resource shared by all network nodes. The network nodes cannot get enough time to send their data if TTRT is too small. Each node i is assigned a fraction of the TTRT, denoted as Hi, as its synchronous bandwidth, which is the maximum time the node is allowed to transmit its synchronous messages every time it receives the token [3, 4]. Whenever a node receives the token, it transmits its synchronous messages (if any) firstly for a time up to Hi. If the time elapsed between the previous and the current token arrivals at the same node i is less than TTRT (i.e., the token arrived earlier than expected), node i can then send asynchronous messages to make up the difference. It is to be noted that time elapse begin to count after the token has been used by node i for this node, as shown in Figure 2.1.

Chord ABCA represents the Actual Token Rotation Time (ATRT). If the token rotation time (chord ABC) was less than TTRT, then the time used by node i is $T_{AC}=(TTRT- T_{ABC})$. ATRT is reset to 0 in node I after the token is used by this node, which is indicated as point A in Figure 2.1. Johnson [5] first proved that the token rotation time cannot exceed 2 _ TTRT. Chen et al. [3, 4] generalized the bound derived by Johnson on the maximum token rotation time, extending it from between any two to between any v (integer v>= 2) successive token's arrivals at a node. This result was widely used in studying various synchronous bandwidth allocation (SBA) schemes.

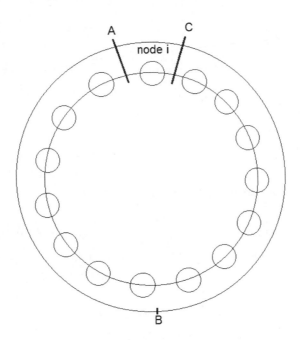

Figure 2.1. Illustrations of timed token mechanism.

In the timed token network, it is assumed to consist of n nodes forming a logical ring. All token protocols below operate on a ring consisting of a number of stations (repeaters), each connected to two others by a unidirectional medium that forms a single closed path. A small frame, called *token,* circulates when all stations are idle. A station desiring to transmit waits to grasp the token before transmitting. After transmitting, the station releases the token.

The message transmission is controlled by the timed token MAC protocol [2]. Let T_i be the maximum amount of overhead incurred from the token's arrival at node i till its immediately subsequent arrival at node (i+ 1), then the maximum time unavailable for message transmission during one complete token rotation, denoted as T, can be expressed by $T = \sum_{i=1}^{n} T_i$. Since T forms part of the token rotation time and synchronous transmission with guaranteed bandwidth precedes synchronous transmission, clearly, as a protocol constraint on the allocation of synchronous bandwidth $\sum_{j=1}^{n} H_j \leq TTRT - T$ must be met.

The following points hold for timed token protocol.

1. The total time resource, represented by TTRT, is a constant. That means that if the data transmission time is consumed a lot in a node then the data transmission times consumed by its successive nodes are greatly reduced.

2. The first node in the token passing ring is the node that preempt in the occupation of the limited time resource. That means the first node can use up all the TTRT time resource once regardless of other nodes.

3. If the time resource is released by a precedent node then the node next to it become the most immediate beneficiary. That means that the next node can occupy the time resource to its greatest extent.

Guaranteeing a message deadline implies transmitting the message before its deadline. With a token passing protocol, a node can transmit its message only when it captures the token. This implies that if a message deadline is to be guaranteed, the token should visit the node where the message is waiting before the expiration of the message's deadline. That is, in order to guarantee message deadlines in a token ring network, it is necessary to bound the time between two consecutive visits of the token to a node (called the token rotation time or access time). The timed token protocol possesses this property. In [21, 41], Johnson and Sevcik formally proved that when the network operates normally (i.e., there is no failure), the upper bound on the token rotation time (or the time elapsed between two consecutive visits to a node) is twice the expected token rotation time (TTRT). Although the prerequisite of "bounded token rotation time" is indispensable, it is insufficient for guaranteeing message deadlines. A node with inadequate synchronous bandwidth may be unable to complete the transmission of a synchronous message before its deadline. On the other hand, allocating excess amounts of synchronous bandwidth to the nodes could increase the token rotation time, which may also cause message deadlines to be missed. Thus, guaranteeing message deadlines is also dependent on the appropriate allocation of synchronous bandwidth to the nodes. As pointed out in [21], the allocation of synchronous bandwidth is an open problem. The main objective of this study is to analyze and evaluate the synchronous bandwidth allocation schemes used with the timed token protocol in a hard real-time communication system. Before discussing details of our work, we will first present an analogy between real-time communication and scheduling to motivate the readers towards the use of our methodology. For real-time systems, the basic design requirements for a communication protocol and for a centralized scheduling algorithm are similar: both are constrained by time to allocate a serially used resource to a set of processes. Liu and Layland [25] addressed the issue of guaranteeing the deadlines of synchronous (i.e., periodic) computation tasks in a single CPU environment. They analyzed a fixed priority preemptive algorithm, called the rate monotonic algorithm, which assigns priorities to tasks in a reverse order of the task's periods. They showed that the worst case achievable utilization of the algorithm is 69%. AS long as the utilization of the task set is no more than 69%, task deadlines are guaranteed to be satisfied. The algorithm was also proven to be optimal among all the fixed priority scheduling algorithms in terms of achieving the highest worst case utilization. The rate monotonic scheduling algorithm has been subsequently extended by many researchers [9, 42] and is used in many hard real-time applications [IO]. Intuitively, one would believe that a protocol which implements the rate monotonic transmission policy is the most desirable for a real-time environment. However, implementation of the rate monotonic policy requires global priority arbitration every time a node in the network is ready to transmit a new frame. In a high-speed network, such as the FDDI network, where the bandwidth can be as high as 100 Mbps, the overheads involved in global priority arbitration would be too prohibitive in comparison to the transmission times of the messages themselves. Consequently, it is difficult, if not impossible, to implement the rate monotonic transmission policy in such environments. However, the methodology for analyzing this algorithm has a more profound significance than merely its relevance to the rate monotonic scheduling. The methodology stresses the fundamental requirement of predictability and stability in hard real-time environments and is therefore also befitting to other hard real-time scheduling problems. In this methodology, the worst case achievable utilization is used as a metric for evaluating the predictability of a scheduling algorithm. That is, if the CPU utilization of all tasks is within the bounds specified by the metric, all the tasks will meet their deadlines. This metric also gives a measure of the stability of the scheduling algorithm in the sense that the tasks can be freely modified as long as their total utilization is held within the limit. These advantages (of predictability and stability) have led us to adopt the same methodology in our study of guaranteeing message deadlines with the timed token protocol. We aim to analyze synchronous bandwidth allocation schemes based on the worst case achievable utilization.

The problem of guaranteeing synchronous message deadlines in token ring networks where the timed token medium access control protocol is employed was studied already by some researchers. Synchronous bandwidth, defined as the maximum time for which a node can transmit its synchronous messages every time it receives the token, is a key parameter in the control of synchronous message transmission. To ensure the transmission of synchronous messages before their deadlines, synchronous capacities must be properly allocated to individual nodes. The issue of appropriate allocation of the synchronous capacities was also studied by some researchers. Several synchronous bandwidth allocation schemes are analyzed in terms of their ability to satisfy deadline constraints of synchronous messages. We show that an inappropriate allocation of the synchronous capacities could cause message deadlines to be missed, even if the synchronous traffic is extremely low.

The basic ideas of the timed token protocol on which the FDDI protocol is based were originally presented by Grow. With the protocol, messages are distinguished into two types. Synchronous messages, such as voice or video traffic, are periodic messages which come to the system at regular intervals and have delivery time constraints. Asynchronous messages are nonperiodic messages which have no time constraints or have the time constraints measured at least in units that are large relative to the token rotation time. Synchronous traffic is assigned a guaranteed bandwidth while the leftover bandwidth (unallocated, unused or both) is dynamically shared among all the nodes for asynchronous traffic. In network initialization time, all nodes negotiate a common value for the target token rotation time (TTRT), an important protocol parameter which gives the expected token rotation time, since each node has different synchronous transmission requirements to be met. The TTRT should be chosen small enough to meet responsiveness requirements of all nodes, i.e., the negotiated value for TTRT should be fast enough to satisfy the most stringent response-time requirements of all nodes. Each node is assigned a fraction of the TTRT, known as its synchronous capacity (denoted as H i for node i), which is the maximum time for which the node is allowed to transmit its synchronous messages every time it receives the token [Mal93b, Che92b, Agr92a]. Whenever a node receives the token, it is permitted to transmit its synchronous mes- sages, if any, for a time period no more than its allocated synchronous bandwidth. The asyn- chronous messages can then be initiated (if any), but only if the token has rotated sufficiently fast that it is earlier than expected since the token's last arrival at the node.

Each node has the following counters:

1. Token Rotation Timer of node i (TRT i): This counter is initialized to TTRT and is always enabled. TRT i counts down until it either expires (i.e., TRT i = 0) or the token is received early (i.e., earlier than expected since the token's last arrival at the node). In either situation, the TRT i is reinitialized to TTRT and enabled again (starting the counting down process).

2. Late Counter of node i (LC i): This counter is initialized to zero and used to record the number of times that TRT i has expired since the token last arrived at node i. LC i is incremented each time TRT i expires and is reset to zero whenever node i receives the token. During the normal ring operation, LC i should not exceed one. However, if LC i exceeds one by any reasons of faults, the ring recovery process will be initialized. The token is said to arrive

early at node i if LC i is zero when the token arrives at node i. Otherwise, if LC i is one, the token is considered to be late.

3. Token Holding Timer of node i (THT i): This counter also counts down, but is enabled only during asynchronous transmission in order to control the amount of time for which the node i can transmit asynchronous messages. THT i is set to zero at ring initialization.

When the token arrives early at node i, the current value of TRT i is placed in THT i and TRT i is then reset to TTRT. Synchronous frames, if any, can be transmitted for a time not to exceed its allocated synchronous bandwidth (H i). The node may then transmit its asynchronous frames (if any) until THT i or TRT i expires (i.e., as long as both THT i and TRT i are greater than zero). On the other hand, when the token is late on its arrival at node i (i.e., LC i = 1), the LC i is reset to 0 and TRT i continues to count down. Node i can transmit synchronous frames for a time no more than its allocated synchronous bandwidth (H i) and no asynchronous frames are allowed. Note that TRT i is not reset to TTRT as in the case when node i receives the token early. Refer to [Jai94, Gro82, Ros86, Ros89] for a more detailed description of the timed token protocol and/or of FDDI. Due to inevitable overheads involved, such as ring latency and other protocol/network dependent overheads, the total bandwidth available for message transmission during one complete traversal of the token around the ring is less than TTRT. Let τ be the portion of TTRT unavailable for transmitting messages. The ratio of τ to TTRT is denoted by α. So the usable ring utilization available for message transmission, synchronous and asynchronous, would be $(1 - \alpha)$. Because synchronous transmission with the guaranteed bandwidth allocated precedes asynchronous transmission, it is clear that as a protocol constraint on the allocation of synchronous bandwidth, the sum total of the synchronous bandwidths allocated to all nodes in the ring should not exceed the available portion of the Target Token Rotation Time (TTRT).

We consider a token ring network under a TTP similar to that employed by the FDDI Media Access Control. There are N stations (labeled as 0,1,..., N−1) in the network, each has a buffer to accommodate customers. A token rotates around the ring and visits station-0, station-1,...,station-N−1 cyclically, as shown in Figure 2.2.

The network supports synchronous and asynchronous service. Multiple priority levels of asynchronous service are distinguished by the use of distinct timing thresholds: T_{pr-i}, for asynchronous priority-i service, $i \geqslant 1$, and $T_{pr-i} < T_{pr-j}$, $i > j \geqslant 1$, priority-i customers assume lower priority than priority-j customer. TTRT, the target token rotation time selected during ring initialization, is the timing threshold for the highest priority of asynchronous customer i.e., T_{pr-1}. The TRT at a station is equal to the time between successive token arrivals at the station. When the server (token) arrives at station-i with customers queued, the station is allowed to transmit the synchronous customer during SAi, (the timing threshold for synchronous customers), then transmit the asynchronous customers with priority-k if the TRT$\leqslant T_{pr-k}$ $(k \geqslant 1)$.

The operation described by the model presented above is similar to that exhibited by an FDDI network under the corresponding setups of the timing threshold for synchronous and asynchronous services.

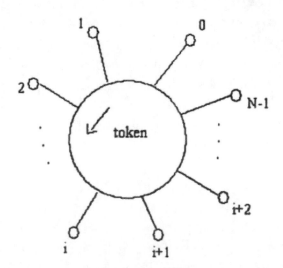

Figure 2.2. A token ring network under a TTP.

The arrival of synchronous customer and asynchronous customer constitute the above two kinds of customers' arrival. The customers' arrival can be divided into independent arrival and correlated arrival. For independent arrival, each station has two queues, which are synchronous and asynchronous customer queues. Typically, the two kinds of customers in independent arrival abide by Poisson arrival. For correlated arrival, each station has only one queue. A station generates a batch of synchronous customers or a batch of asynchronous customers each time. Typically, a station generates one customer each time, either a synchronous customer or a asynchronous one, no new customer will be generated before the current one leaves, so the customers' arrival abides by binomial distribution.

When the token arrives at station-i, the virtual server of station-i begin its service (transmits packets). A batch of packets will be transmitted during limited time i.e., time-limited batch service. After the transmitting, the token runs to the downstream stations, providing possible service for stations that have customers (this is the basic difference between timed-token and non-timed-token protocols). The virtual server ends its service when the packets from station-i return and begins its next service when the token arrives at station-i again after the packets from other stations passing by station-i. The virtual service is intermittent because the server does not work from the end of current service to the next arrival of token. The normalized length of intermittent period is defined as Mi, which equals to the number of transmitted packets during a token rotation cycle from all of stations except station-i.

The use of priority makes the analysis difficult, it is necessary to handle the priority in different cases:

a. *Station priority:* The priority of a asynchronous customer is decided by a station. In this case, there is only one kind of asynchronous customers in each station besides synchronous customers. There exist N kinds of asynchronous customer priorities in a LAN with N stations.

b. *Customer priority:* The priority of an asynchronous customer is defined by the class of the customer. If there are L kinds of customers, for example, there exist L kinds of priorities. The service for one station in the custom priority system is similar to the others, and therefore, the stations are symmetric in the sense of statistics.

According to the above discussion, FDDI can be considered as a multiple-queuing system with two kinds of customers' arrival, batch process of time-limited service and intermittent service with multiple virtual servers. As one station is concerned, FDDI can be described as a queuing system with two kinds of customers' arrival, batch process of time-limited service and intermittent service with a virtual server. The queuing models for FDDI can be divided into four kinds:

1)
$M^2/G/1$ [K, Ba, Customer Priority, Time-limited service]/∞/FCFS,

2)
$M^2/G/1$ [K, Ba, Customer Non-Priority, Time-limited service]/∞/FCFS,

3)
L/G/1 [K, Station Priority, Time-limited service]

4)
L/G/1 [K, Station Non-Priority, Time-limited service]

where M^2: two ways Poisson arrival, G: general distribution of service time, 1: one virtual server, K: intermittent service, Ba: batch service, Customer priority: synchronous customer has the highest priority, asynchronous customer has its priority, Time-limited service: the number of customers (synchronous and asynchronous) being served is confined by TTRT, TRT, and T_{pr}-i, ∞: the capacity of buffer is infinite, FCFS: first come, first served, Customer non-priority: Asynchronous customer has no priority, synchronous customer has higher priority than asynchronous customer, L: binomial arrival, Station priority: each station has its own priority.

2.3. FDDI TECHNOLOGY

Fiber Distributed Data Interface (FDDI) is a standard for data transmission in a local area network. It uses optical fiber as its standard underlying physical medium, although it was also later specified to use copper cable, in which case it may be called CDDI (Copper Distributed Data Interface), standardized as TP-PMD (Twisted-Pair Physical Medium-Dependent), referred to as TP-DDI (Twisted-Pair Distributed Data Interface).

2.3.1. Description

FDDI provides a 100 M bit/s optical standard for data transmission in local area network that can extend in range up to 200 kilometers (120 mi). Although FDDI logical topology is a ring-based token network, it did not use the IEEE 802.5 token ring protocol as its basis; instead, its protocol was derived from the IEEE 802.4 token bus timed token protocol. In addition to covering large geographical areas, FDDI local area networks can support thousands of users. FDDI offers both a Dual-Attached Station (DAS), counter-rotating token ring topology and a Single-Attached Station (SAS), token bus passing ring topology [1].

FDDI, as a product of American National Standards Institute X3T9.5 (now X3T12), conforms to the Open Systems Interconnection (OSI) model of functional layering using other protocols. The standards process started in the mid 1980s [2]. FDDI-II, a version of FDDI described in 1989, added circuit-switched service capability to the network so that it could also handle voice and video signals [3]. Work started to connect FDDI networks to synchronous optical networking (SONET) technology.

A FDDI network contains two rings, one as a secondary backup in case the primary ring fails. The primary ring offers up to 100 M bit/s. When a network has no requirement for the secondary ring to do backup, it can also carry data, extending capacity to 200 M bit/s. The single ring can extend the maximum distance; a dual ring can extend 100 km (62 mi). FDDI had a larger maximum-frame size (4,352 bytes) than the standard Ethernet family, which only supports a maximum-frame size of 1,500 bytes [a] allowing better effective data rates in some cases.

2.3.2. Topology

Designers normally constructed FDDI rings in a network topology such as a "dual ring of trees". A small number of devices, typically infrastructure devices such as routers and concentrators rather than host computers, were "dual-attached" to both rings. Host computers then connect as single-attached devices to the routers or concentrators. The dual ring in its most degenerate form simply collapses into a single device. Typically, a computer-room contained the whole dual ring, although some implementations deployed FDDI as a metropolitan area network.

FDDI requires this network topology because the dual ring actually passes through each connected device and requires each such device to remain continuously operational. The standard actually allows for optical bypasses, but network engineers consider these unreliable and error-prone. Devices such as workstations and minicomputers that might not come under the control of the network managers are not suitable for connection to the dual ring.

As an alternative to using a dual-attached connection, a workstation can obtain the same degree of resilience through a dual-homed connection made simultaneously to two separate devices in the same FDDI ring. One of the connections becomes active while the other one is automatically blocked. If the first connection fails, the backup link takes over with no perceptible delay.

2.3.3. Frame Format

The FDDI data frame format is:

PA	SD	FC	DA	SA	PDU	FCS	ED/FS
16 bits	8 bits	8 bits	48 bits	48 bits	up to 4478x8 bits	32 bits	16 bits

where PA is the preamble, SD is a start delimiter, FC is frame control, DA is the destination address, SA is the source address, PDU is the protocol data unit (or packet data unit), FCS is the frame check Sequence (or checksum), and ED/FS are the end delimiter and frame status. The Internet Engineering Task Force defined a standard for transmission of the Internet Protocol (which would be the protocol data unit in this case) over FDDI. It was first proposed in June 1989 [5] and revised in 1990. Some aspects of the protocol were compatible with the IEEE 802.2 standard for logical link control. For example, the 48-bit MAC addresses that became popular with the Ethernet family. Thus other protocols such as the Address Resolution Protocol (ARP) could be common as well.

2.3.4. Deployment

FDDI was considered an attractive campus backbone network technology in the early to mid 1990s since existing Ethernet networks only offered 10 M bit/s data rates and token ring networks only offered 4 M bit/s or 16 M bit/s rates. Thus it was a relatively high-speed choice of that era. By 1994, vendors included Cisco Systems, National Semiconductor, Network Peripherals, SysKonnect (acquired by Marvell Technology Group), and 3Com.

FDDI was effectively made obsolete in local networks by Fast Ethernet which offered the same 100 M bit/s speeds, but at a much lower cost and, since 1998, by Gigabit Ethernet due to its speed, and even lower cost, and ubiquity.

Chapter 3

NETWORKED CONTROL SYSTEM BASED ON PROFIBUS WITH ITS APPLICATION IN INDUSTRY

3.1. INTRODUCTION TO PROFIBUS

PROFIBUS is an open field, supplier-independent network standard, whose interface permits a vast application in processes, manufacture and building automation. This standard complies with EN 50170 e EN 50254 standards. Since January, 2000, PROFIBUS is firmly established with IEC 61158, alongside seven other field-bus systems. IEC 61158 is divided in seven parts, named 61158-1 a 61158-6, which contain the OSI model specifications. This version was expanded to include the DPV-2.

Worldwide, users can now use as a reference an international standard protocol, whose development aims at reducing costs, gaining flexibility, trust, orientation to the future, suit the most varied applications, interoperability and multiple suppliers.

Today, more than 23 million of PROFIBUS nodes are installed and more than 1000 plants with PROFIBUS PA technology are running. They are 24 regional organizations (RPAs) and 33 PROFIBUS Competence Centers (PCCs) located strategically worldwide, as to offer support to their users, including Brazil. The São Carlos Engineering School (University of São Paulo) has the only PCC in Latin America.

- Over 1300 members al over the world;
- More than 23 million nodes installed successfully;
- Over 2800 products and more than 2000 suppliers serve the widest possible application needs;

PROFIBUS is based on master/slave topology, on which masters can initiate a communication in the bus, being responsible for network monitoring, configuration and cyclical data exchange with slaves (intelligent sensors/actuators). A slave station monitors the medium waiting for a message addressed to it, when it will process the transmited information, and, if necessary, send a reply.

For medium access control between masters, PROFIBUS adopts the token passing concept. Each master station knows the addresses of its previous master station (PS), of the next master station (NS) and its own address, TS (This Station). When a master receives the token, it can transfer or receive information to/from its slave stations. The time that a master holds the token is given by a pre-determined interval, called token holding time (Tht). The Tht interval should include necessary time for the master to perform a complete data exchange cycle with all its slaves plus the time for acyclical message transmissions. The sum of the Tht for all masters defines the so called token rotation time, Trt, which is an important timing characteristic of a PROFIBUS network and defines the application macro-cycle.

PROFIBUS data link layer defines three acyclic services: SDA (Send Data with Acknowledge), SRD (Send and Request Data with reply) and SDN (Send Data with No acknowledge), as well as one cyclic service: CSRD (Cyclic Send and Request Data with reply). The PROFIBUS-DP protocol uses only two of these services: SRD and SDN. The former is used for information exchange, allowing a master station to send and request data to/from a slave in a single message sequence. SDN service allows transmission of information without receiving confirmation for a group of stations (multicast) or for all stations (broadcast).

The frame typically used to provide cyclical data exchange by PROFIBUS-DP protocol is the variable length frame. As depicted in Figure 3.1 it is composed by a message start delimiter, message's length byte, target and source address fields. Frame control byte, data field, frame check conference byte and message end delimiter. A PROFIBUS station can transfer or receive up to 246 bytes when using variable length frames. Each station in the bus has an unique identification with values from 0 to 126 (address 127 is used for global broadcast messages).

PROFIBUS provides 127 different Service Access Points (SAPs) for communication between stations. PROFIBUS SAPs implement some special services for bus programming/configuration. PROFIBUS-DP SAPs include SAP values from 54 to 62 plus the value 0 (default), allowing services as slaves configuration, diagnosis request, global input sampling (FREEZE mode), and synchronization of output updates (SYNC mode).

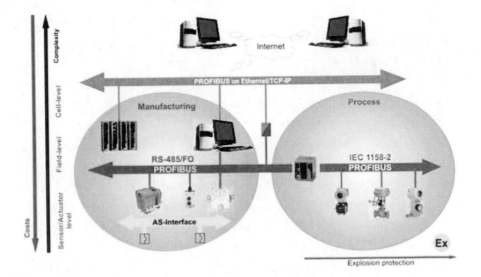

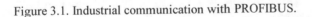

Figure 3.1. Industrial communication with PROFIBUS.

The information technology played a decisive role in the development of the automation technology and changed the hierarchies and structures of offices. It now arrives to the industrial environment and its several sectors, from process and manufacture industries to buildings and logistic systems. The possibility of communication between devices and the use of standardized, open and transparent mechanisms are essential components of today's automation concept.

The communication expands rapidly in the horizontal direction at the field level, as well as in the vertical direction integrating all of the hierarchy levels of a system. According to the characteristics of the application and the maximum cost to reach, a gradual combination of different communication systems like Ethernet, PROFIBUS and AS-Interface are the ideal open networks conditions for industrial processes.

With respect to actuators/sensors the AS-Interface is the perfect data communication system, as the binary data signals are transmitted through an extremely simple and low-cost data bus, together with the 24Vdc power supply required to feed those sensors and actuators. Another important feature is that the data are transmitted in cycles, in a very efficient and fast way.

At field level, the peripherals distributed, like I/O modules, transducers, drives, valves and operation panels' work in automation systems, through an efficient, real-time communication system, the PROFIBUS DP or PA. The process data transmission is made in cycles, while alarms, parameters and diagnostics are transmitted only when necessary, in a non-cyclic way.

As to cells, the programmable controllers like the PLCs and the PCs communicate between themselves and so require that large data package be transferred in several and powerful communication functions. Furthermore, the efficient integration to the existing corporate communication systems, such as Intranet, Internet and Ethernet is absolutely mandatory. This need is met by PROFINET protocol.

The industrial communication revolution in the technology plays a vital role in the optimization of the process systems and has made a valuable contribution toward improving the use of resources. The information below will summarize the importance of PROFIBUS as a central connecting link on the automation of data flow.

The PROFIBUS, in its architecture, is divided in three main variants:

3.1.1. PROFIBUS DP

It is the high-speed solution for PROFIBUS. It was developed specifically for communication between automation systems and decentralized equipments. It is applicable on control systems where the access to I/O-distributed devices is emphasized and substitutes the conventional 4 to 20 mA, HART systems or in 24 Volts transmissions. It uses the RS-485 physical medium or fiber optics. It requires less than two minutes to transmit 1 I/O Kbyte and is largely used in critical time controls.

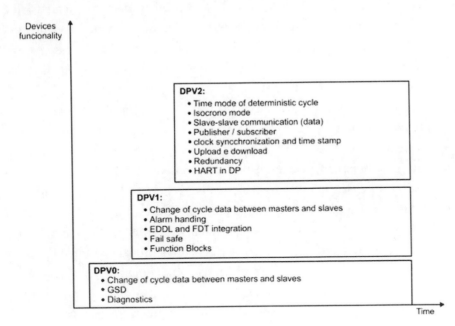

Figure 3.2. PROFIBUS Versions.

Currently, 90 percent of the applications involving slaves PROFIBUS utilize the PROFIBUS DP. This variant is available in three versions: DP-V0 (1993), DP-V1 (1997) e DP-V2 (2002). The origin of each version occurred alongside the technological advancement and the long-time growing demand for the applications.

3.1.2. PROFIBUS FMS

The PROFIBUS FMS provides the user with a wide selection of functions when compared to other variants. It is the solution in universal communication standard that may be used to solve complex communication tasks between PLCs and DCSs. This variant supports the communication between automation systems besides the exchange of data between intelligent equipments, generally used in control level. Recently, since its primary function is the peer-to-peer communication, it is being replaced by application in Ethernet.

3.1.3. PROFIBUS PA

The PROFIBUS PA is the solution PROFIBUS that attend to the requisites of process automation, where automation systems and process control systems connect with field equipments, like pressure and temperature transmitters, converters, positioning devices, etc. It may also replace the 4 to 20 mA standard.

There are potential advantages for using this technology, which carry functional advantages such as the transmission of reliable information, variable status dealing, failure safety systems, and the feature of auto-diagnosis equipment, equipment rangeability, measuring with high resolution, Integration with high speed discreet control, etc. In addition to the economical benefits pertinent to the installations (cost reduction up to 40% comparable to the conventional systems in some cases), maintenance costs reduction (up to 25%. against the conventional systems), smaller startup time, it offers a significant increase in functionality and safety.

PROFIBUS PA permits measurement and control through one line and two single cables. It also powers the field equipment in intrinsically safe areas. PROFIBUS PA allows maintenance and connecting/disconnecting equipment even during operation without interfering in other stations in areas potentially explosive. PROFIBUS PA was developed in cooperation with the Control and Process Industry (NAMUR), in compliance with the special requirements on this application area:

- The original application profile for the process automation and interoperability of field equipments from different manufacturers;
- Addition and removal of bus stations even in intrinsically areas without affecting other stations;
- A transparent communication through the couplers of the segment between the PROFIBUS PA automation bus and the PROFIBUS-DP industrial automation bus.
- Power and data transmission on the same pair of cables based on the IEC 61158-2 technology;
- Use in potentially hazardous areas with "intrinsically safe" or "intrinsically unsafe" explosive-proof protection shield.

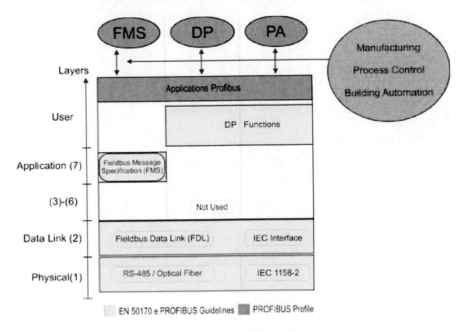

Figure 3.3. PROFIBUS Protocol Communication Architecture.

The connection of the transmitters, converters in a PROFIBUS DP network is made by a DP/PA coupler. The twisted pair cable is used as power supply and data communication for each equipment, which makes the installation easier and lower the cost of hardware, thus resulting in less initiation time, problem-free maintenance, low engineering software cost and highly reliable operation.

All of the PROFIBUS variants are based in the OSI (Open System Interconnection) network communication model, in compliance with the ISO 7498 international standard. Due to the field requirements, only levels 1 and 2 and also level 7 on the FMS have been implemented, for efficiency reasons.

On the three variants the two lower levels are very similar, their biggest difference being the interface with the application programs. Level 1 defines the physical medium.

Level 2 (data transportation level) defines the access protocol to the bus. Level 7 (application level) defines the application functions.

This architecture ensures fast and efficient data transmission. The applications available to the user, as well as the behavior of the several types of PROFIBUS-SP devices, are specified on the user interface.

The PROFIBUS-FMS has levels 1, 2 and 7 defined, where the application level is made up of FMS (Field-bus Message Specification) messages and the lower layer interface (LLI). The FMS defines a large number of powerful communication services between the masters themselves and master and slaves. The LLI defines the representation of FMS services on the level 2 transmission protocol.

The PROFIBUS PA communication protocol uses the same communication protocol as the PROFIBUS DP. This is because the communication and the messages services are identical. In fact, the PROFIBUS PA = PROFIBUS DP – communication protocol + Extended Acyclic Services + IEC61158 that is the Physical Layer, also know as H1. It allows a uniform and complete integration between all the automation levels and the plants of the process control area. This means that the integration of all the plants areas can be accomplished with a communication protocol that uses different variations.

3.1.3.1. RS485: The Most Used PROFIBUS Physical Medium

The RS 485 transmission is the transmission technology most used on PROFIBUS, although the fiber optics may be applied on long distances (over 80 Km). Its main characteristics are:

- NRZ Asynchronous Transmission;
- 9.6 K bit/s to 12 M bit/s configurable baud rates;
- Twisted pair shielded cable;
- 32 stations per segment, 127 stations max;
- Distance dependent on the transmission rate (Table 3.1);
- 12 M bit/s = 100 m; 1.5 M bit/s = 400m; < 187.5 K bit/s = 1000 m;
- Expansible distance up to 10 Km with the use of repeaters;
- 9 PIN, D-Sub connector.

Normally it is applied in areas involving high transmission rate, simple installation and low cost. The bus structure allows the addition and removal of stations without affecting others stations with further expansions, without affecting stations in operation.

When the system is configured, only one transmission rate is selected for all the devices in the bus.

There is the need for an active termination on the bus, at the beginning and the end of each segment, according to Figure 3.4, while both terminators must be energized in order to keep the transmission signal integrity.

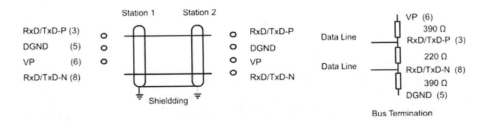

Figure 3.4. Cabling and Termination for RS-485 Transmission in the PROFIBUS.

Table 3.1. Length according to the Transmission rate with Type A Cable

Baud rate (K bit/s)	9.6	19.2	93.75	187.5	500	1500	2000
Segment Length (m)	1200	1200	1200	1000	400	200	100

For cases with more than 32 stations or for dense networks, repeaters should be used. The maximum length of cabling depends on the transmission rate, according to Table 3.1.

3.1.3.2. PROFIBUS PA Transmission Technology

The transmission technology is synchronous with Manchester codification in 31.25 Kbits/s (voltage mode); it is defined according to the IEC 61158-2 and was elaborated aiming to satisfy the requisites by chemical and petrochemical industries: intrinsic safety and the possibility of power the field equipment through the bus. The work options and limits in potentially explosive areas were defined as per the FISCO (Field-bus Intrinsically Safe Concept) model.

Table 3.2 shows some of the IEC 61158-2 features.

Table 3.2. Feature as of IEC 61158-2 Transmission Technology

CHARACTERISTICS	PHYSICAL MEDIUM COMPLYING WITH IEC61158-2, H1 VARIANT
Cable	31.25 kbits/s
Topology	Bus, tree, point to point.
Power Supply	Via bus or external medium
Intrinsic Safety	Possible
Number of equipments (depends on current devices consumption)	Maximum 32(*non-Ex*) *Explosion Group* IIC: 9 *Explosion Group* IIB: 23
Maximum Cabling	1900 m, expansible to 10 Km with 4 repeaters.
Spur Maximum	120m/spur
Communication Signal	Codification, with voltage modulation

3.1.3.3. Fiber Optics Transmission

The fiber optics solution meets the needs for eliminating noises, potential differences, long distances, ring architecture and physical redundancy and high speed transmission.

Table 3.3. Types of Fiber and their Characteristics

FIBER TYPE	CHARACTERISTICS
Monomode Glass Fiber	2 – 3 Km mean distance
Multimode Glass Fiber	Long Distance > 15 Km
Synthetic Fiber	Short Distance > 80 km
PCS/HCS fiber	Short Distance > 500 m

3.1.3.4. The Communication System and Its Safety and Access Layer

The efficiency of communication is determined by the level-2 functions, which specify the tasks of access to the bus, data frame structures, communication basic services and many other functions.

Level-2 tasks are executed by FDL (Field-bus Data Link) and FMA (Field-bus Management), the first one performing the following tasks:

- Control of access to the bus (*MAC-Medium Access Control*);
- Telegrams structure;
- Data safety;
- Availability of data transmission services:
  - SDN (*Send Data with no acknowledge*)
  - SRD (*Send and Request Data with reply*)

The FMA provides several management functions, such as:

- Configuration of operation parameters;
- Events report;
- Activation of services of access points (SAPs).

Multi-master Communication

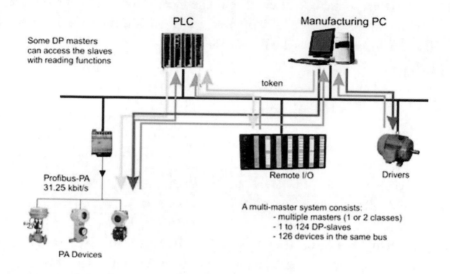

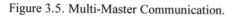

Figure 3.5. Multi-Master Communication.

Master and Slave Communication

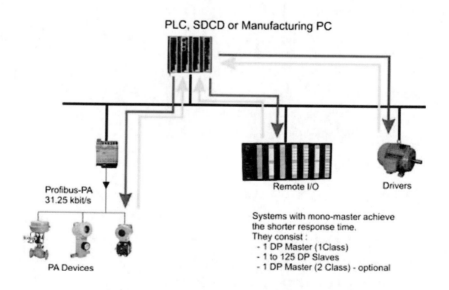

Figure 3.6. Master-Slave Communication.

Table 3.4. PROFIBUS Level-2 Services

SERVICE	FUNCTION	DP	FMS	PA
SDA	*Send Data with Acknowledgment*	no	yes	no
SRD	*Send and Request Data with Reply*	yes	yes	yes
SDN	*Send Data with No Acknowledgment*	yes	yes	yes
CSRD	*Cyclic Send and Request Data with Reply*	no	yes	no

The PROFIBUS protocol architecture and philosophy ensure to every station involved in the exchange of cyclic data the time sufficient to execute their communication task within a defined time period. For this, they use the "token" passage procedure from the bus master stations when communicating between themselves, and the master-slave procedure to communicate with the slave stations. The token message (a special frame to enable the right of passage from one master to another) must circulate one time for each master within the maximum rotation time defined (which is configurable). On PROFIBUS the token passage procedure is used only for masters to communicate with each other.

The master-slave communication enables the active master (with the token) to access its slaves through the reading and writing services.

PROFIBUS uses different subsets of level-2 services in each of its profiles (DP, FMS, PA). See Table 3.4.

Addressing services with 7 bits identify the network participants, and on 0 to 127 range the following addresses are reserved:

- 126: standard address attributed via master;
- 127: used to send frames in broadcast.

3.1.3.5. PROFIBUS DP and High Speed Communication Rate

The PROFIBUS DP profile was developed to answer in cyclic communication in a quick way among the distributed devices. In addition, PROFIBUS DP provides functions for acyclic access services, like configuration, monitoring, diagnostics and field equipment alarm management.

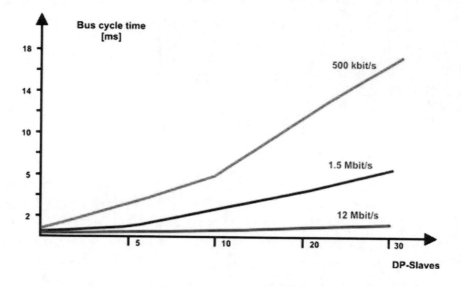

Figure 3.7. Bus Cycle Time for a DP Mono-master System.

In 12M bit/s, the PROFIBUS-DP needs only 1 ms to transmit 512 input bits and 512 output bits distributed by 32 stations. This profile is recommended for discreet control, which requires high speed processing. Figure 3.7 shows the PROFIBUS-DP typical transmission time, according to the number of stations and the transmission speed, where each slave has 2 input bytes and 2 output bytes and the minimal slave interval time is 200 µs.

3.1.3.6. PROFIBUS: Telegram

The telegrams are defined by the FDL, as follows:

- Telegrams without data field (6 bytes control);
- Telegrams with one fixed length data field (8 bytes data and 6 bytes control);
- Telegrams with variable field data (from 0 to 244 bytes data and 9 to 11 bytes control);
- Fast recognition (1 byte);
- Token telegram for access to bys (3 bytes).

Principle of User Data Transfer

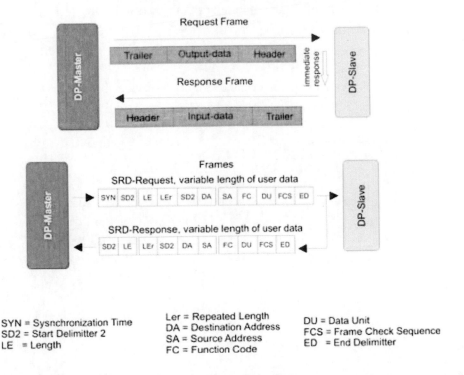

SYN = Sysnchronization Time
SD2 = Start Delimitter 2
LE = Length

Ler = Repeated Length
DA = Destination Address
SA = Source Address
FC = Function Code

DU = Data Unit
FCS = Frame Check Sequence
ED = End Delimitter

Figure 3.8. Principle of Users Data Transfer Used by FDL.

The integrity and the safety of the information are kept in all of the transactions, as the frame parity and checking to reach the HD = 4 hamming distance.

Figure 3.8 illustrates the user data transference principle, while recalling that on the DP side, the data are transmitted in asynchronous way under 485 and on the PA side, in bit-asynchronous way on H1.

In order to exchange data with a slave, it is totally essential that the master follows the sequence below during the startup:

- Station address;
- Request for diagnostics;
- Slave parameterization;

- Diagnostics request check before cyclic data exchange, as confirmation that the initial parameterization is OK;
- Cyclic data exchange;
- Global control.

Figure 3.9 shows mandatory and optional services between a DP slave and class 1 and 2 masters that masters and slaves should have.

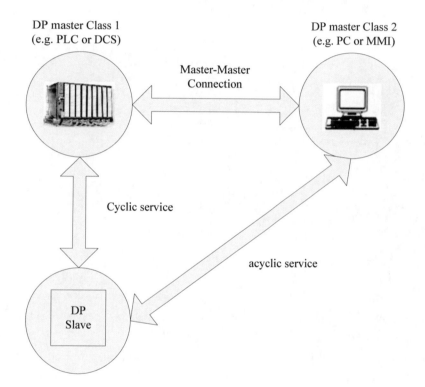

Figure 3.9. Mandatory and Optional Services between Class 1 and 2 Slave and Master.

3.1.3.7. Types of Devices

Each DP system may include three different types of devices:

- **CLASS - 1 DP MASTER (DPM1):** It is a main controller that exchanges information cyclically with the slaves. The programmable logic controllers (PLCs) are examples of the master devices.

- **CLASS - 2 DP MASTER (DPM2):** Are engineering stations used for configuration, monitoring or supervisory systems like, e.g., PROFIBUSView, AssetView, Simatic PDM, Commuwinll, Pactware, etc
- **SLAVE:** A DP slave is a peripheral device such as: I/O devices, actuators, IHM, valves, transducers, etc. There are also devices that have only one input, one output or combination of both. Here are included the PA slaves, as they are seen by the system as DP slaves.

The amount of input and output information depends on the type of device, being allowed up to 244 input bytes and 244 output bytes.

The data transmission between the DPM1 and the slaves is executed automatically by the DPM1 and is divided in three phases: parameterization, configuration and data transfer.

Safety and reliability are indispensable to add to PROFIBUS-DP the protective functions against parameterization errors or the transmission equipment failure. According to this effect, the monitoring mechanism is implemented in the DP master and the slaves too, monitoring the time specified during configuration.

The DPM1 Master monitors the slave data transmission with the Data Control Timer. A time counter is used for each device. The timer expires when a right data transmission does not happen within the monitoring time and the user is informed when this happens. If the automatic reaction to an error (Auto Clear = true) is enabled, the DPM1 master ends the OPERATION status and protects every slave output of and changes its status to "CLEAR." The slave uses the watchdog timer to detect failures on the master or on the transmission line. If no data is exchanged with the master within the watchdog timer interval, the slave will automatically change its outputs to the fail safe state.

The extended DP functions make possible acyclic reading and writing, and interruption recognition functions that may be executed in parallel and independently from cyclic data transmission. This permits the user to access the parameters in an acyclic way (via class-2 master) and that the measuring values of a slave may be accessed by supervision and diagnostics stations.

Currently these extended functions are widely used in the online operation of PA field equipments by engineering stations. This transmission has lower priority than the cyclic data transfer (one that requires high speed and high control priority).

3.1.3.8. PROFIBUS DP Response Time

The response time in a PROFIBUS DP system depends essentially on the following factors:

- MaxTSDR (response time which a station may respond);
- The communication rate that was selected;
- Min Slave Interval (time period between two polling cycles), when a slave may exchange data with a slave. It depends on the ASIC used, although in the market we can find ASICs with 100 µs intervals.

$$Tmc = 27 \ \mu s + N \ x \ 1.5 \ \mu s$$

For practical purposes, at 12Mbits/s we may assume that the time of message cycle (Tmc) that involves the *prompting telegram + TSDR +* slave response, where N is the number of slave inputs and outputs, is:

$$Tbc = 5 \ x \ 72 \ \mu s = 360 \ \mu s$$

For example: a master with 5 slaves and each slave with 10 input bytes and 20 output bytes, at 12Mbits/s would have a Tmc around 72µs/slave. The bus cycle time is obtained by the addition of all the message cycles:

More details about the system times can be consulted in the PROFIBUS Standards.

3.1.3.9. PROFIBUS PA

The use of PROFIBUS on typical devices and process control applications are defined in compliance with the PROFIBUS-PA profile, which defines the parameters of the field equipments and their typical behavior, independent from the manufactuer, and is also applicable to pressure and temperature transmitters, positioning devices. It is based on the functional blocks concept, as they are standardized in such a way to guarantee the interoperability between field equipments.

The measuring values and status, as well as the setpoint values received by the field equipment on the PROFIBUS-PA, are transmitted cyclically with the highest priority via class 1 master (DPM1). On the other hand, the parameters for visualization, operations, maintenance and diagnosis are transmitted by engineering tools (class 2 masters, DPM2) with low priority through the acyclic services via connection C2. Cyclically, a sequence of diagnostics bytes is also transmitted. The description of the bits of these bytes are on the equipment GDS file and depend on the manufacturer.

The approximate time of cycle (Tc) may be calculated as:

Tc $\geq$ 10 ms x number of equipments + 10 ms (acyclic class 2 master services) + 1.3 ms (for each set of 5 bytes cyclic values).

Think about a situation with 2 control loops with 5 pressure transmitters and 5 valve positioning devices. The cycle time would be around 110 ms.

3.1.3.10. PROFIBUS PA Network Elements

Basically, on a PROFIBUS network the following elements may be cited:

- Masters: the elements responsible for the bus control. They have two classes;

- Class 1: responsible for the cyclic operations (reading/writing) and the control of the open and closed loops of the control/automation (CLP) system;
- Class 2: responsible for the acyclic access to the PA equipment parameters and functions (engineering or operation station: PROFIBUSView, AssetView, Simatic PDM or Communwingll, FieldCare or Pactware);
- Couplers: they are devices used to translate the physical characteristics between PROFIBUS DP and PROFIBUS PA (H1: 31.25 kbits/s).

And also:

- They are transparent for the masters (with no physical address on the bus);
- They operate with safety applications (Ex) and (Non-Ex), by defining and limiting the maximum number of equipments on each PA segment. The maximum equipment number depends, among other factors, of the addition of the quiescent currents, the equipment failures (FDE) and the distances involved on cabling;
- They may be powered up to 24 Vdc, according to the manufacturer and area of classification;
- They may work with the following communication rates, depending on the manufacturer: P + F (93.75 kbits/s and SK2/SK3: up to 12Mbits/s) and Siemens (45.45 kbits/s).

- Link devices: They are devices used as slaves on PROFIBUS DP networks and master on PROFIBUS PA (H1: 31,25kbits/s). They are used to reach high speeds (up to 12Mbits/s) on the DP bus.

And furthermore:

- The have a physical address in the bus;

- They accept up to 5 couplers, but limit the number of equipments to 30 on each Non-Ex bus and 10 on each Ex bus. With that, they increase the DP network address capacity.

- Terminator: consists of a 1μF capacitor and one 100Ω resistor connecting each other and parallel to the bus, with the following functions:

- Shunt from current signal: the communication signal is transmitted as current, by is received as voltage. The conversion is made by the terminator;

- Protection against communication signal reflection: it must be located on the two bus terminations, one at the end and the other generally on the coupler.

- Cabling: it is recommended to use twisted cable 1 x 2, 2 x 2 or 1 x 4 shielded types, and also:

- Diameter: 0.8 mm² (AWG 18);

- Impedance: 35 to 165 Ohm on 3 to 20 Mhz;

- Capacitance: lower than 30 pF per meter.

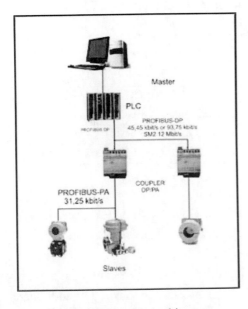

Connection diagram

Figure 3.10. Basic Coupler Architecture.

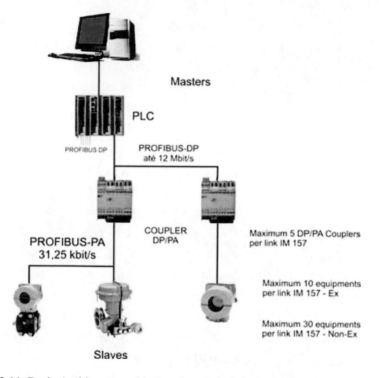

Figure 3.11. Basic Architecture with Couplers and Links (IM157).

Table 3.5. PROFIBUS PA Cables Data

Pair	Shield	Twisted Pair	Rail Gauge	Length	Type
Simple	Yes	Yes	0.8 mm² (AWG 18)	1900 m	A
Multi	Yes	Yes	0.32 mm² (AWG 22)	1200 m	B
Multi	No	Yes	0.13 mm² (AWG 26)	400 m	C
Multi	Yes	No	1.25 mm² (AWG 16)	200 m	D

3.1.3.11. PROFIBUS Network Addressing

Regarding to the addressing, there are two architecture to be analyzed where fundamentally stand out the couplers and the address attribution to the links devices, as seen on Figures 3.12 and 3.13.

In the Figure 3.13 the addressing capacity is significantly increased by the presence of the link devcices, as they are slaves for the DP and masters on the PA.

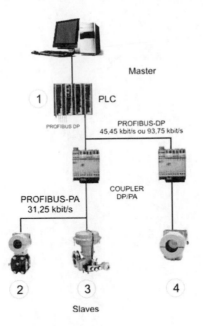

Figure 3.12. Addressing with Couplers.

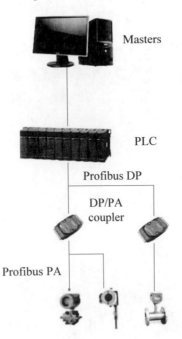

Figure 3.13. Addressing with Links.

Geng Liang, Wen Li and Guoping Liu

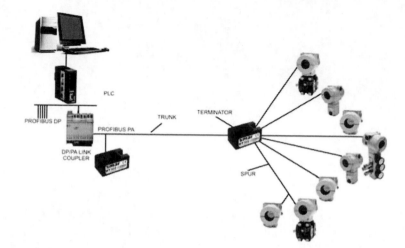

Figure 3.14. Tree topology.

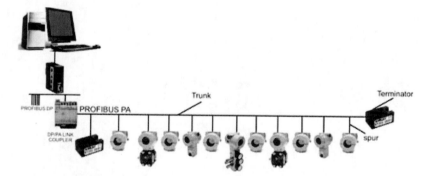

Figure 3.15. Bus topology.

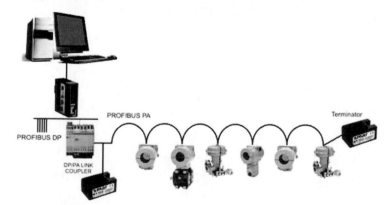

Figure 3.16. Point-to-point topology.

3.1.3.12. Topology

Regarding to the topology, there may be the following distributions: tree (Figure 3.14), bus (Figure 3.15) and point-to-points (Figure 3.16):

3.1.3.13. Integration with PROFIBUS Systems

In order to integrate an equipment on a PROFIBUS system, it is used the equipment GSD file. Each type of equipment has its own GSD file (electronic datasheet), which is a text file with hardware and software revision details, bus timing and information on the cyclic data exchange. See example on Figure 3.17.

In addition to the GSD file, it is commonly offered the Device Description files (DDs), where the parameters are detailed, methods and menus that will make possible to configure cyclically the field equipment. These files follow the EDDL standard defined by PROFIBUS International. Still there are the FDT and DTM standards for configuration, monitoring and calibration.

```
#Profibus_DP
GSD_Revision            =2
Vendor_Name             ="SMAR"
Model_Name              ="LD303"
Revision                ="1.0"
Ident_Number            =0x0895
Protocol_Ident          =0
Station_Type            =0
Bitmap_Device           =
"Src0895n"
FMS_supp                =0
Hardware_Release        ="3.0"
Software_Release        ="1.17"
31.25_supp              =1
45.45_supp              =1
93.75_supp              =1
187.5_supp              =1
MaxTsdr_31.25           =100
MaxTsdr_45.45           =250
MaxTsdr_93.75           =1000
MaxTsdr_187.5           =1000
Redundancy              =0
Repeater_Ctrl_Sig       =0
24V_Pins                =0
Freeze_Mode_supp        =0
Sync_Mode_supp          =0
Auto_Baud_supp          =0
```

```
Min_Slave_Intervall     =250
Modular_Station         =1
Max_Module              =2
Max_Input_Len           =10
Max_Output_Len          =2
Max_Data_Len            =12
Max_Diag_Data_Len       =14
Slave_Family            =12
User_Prm_Data_Len       =0
;
;Modules for Analog Input
Module  = "Analog Input (short) " 0x94
EndModule
Module  = "Analog Input (long)  "  0x42,0x84,0x08,0x05
EndModule
;
;Module for Totalizer
Module  = "Total"   0x41,0x84,0x85
EndModule
Module  = "Total_Settot"   0xC1,0x80,0x84,   0x85
EndModule
Module  = "Total_Settot_Modetot" 0xC1,0x81,0x84,0x85
EndModule
;
;Empty module
Module  = "EMPTY_MODULE"    0x00
EndModule
```

Figure 3.17. GSD file for the LD303 – pressure transmitter.

3.1.3.14. PROFIBUS-PA Profile 3.0

A PROFIBUS system may be operated and monitored independently of equipments and manufactures. This statement will be true if all of the functionalities and parameterizations, and the manner of access to this information are standardized. These standards are determined by the PROFIBUS-PA profiles.

These profiles specify how the manufacturers should implement the communication objects, variables and parameters, according to the class of work of the equipment. And there is also the parameters classification:

- Process dynamic values: those with respect to the process variables, whose information is described in the GSD (device data master) and will be read cyclically by the class 1 masters and also non-cyclically by the class 2 masters:

Class 1 Master: Class 1 – in charge of cyclic operations (readings/scripts) and control of open and closed loops in the system.

Class 2 Master: Class 2 – in charge of acyclic access of the parameters and PA equipments functions (engineering station like, for instance, PROFIBUSView, AssetView, Simatic PDM, ComuWinII, FieldCare, Pactware, etc.).

- Standard values of configuration/operation: those that are exclusively accessed for reading and writing, via acyclic services. There are parameters that are mandatory for implementation and others that are optional to manufacturers;
- Specific manufacturer parameters: those that are exclusive to the functionality for a manufacturer equipment and may be accessed in a non-cyclic way, as they are also defined in accordance with the profile structure standards.

Currently, the PROFIBUS-PA is defined according to the PROFILE 3.0 (since 1999), where exist information for the several types of equipment, like pressure and temperature transmitters, valve positioning devices, etc.

These equipments are implemented in accordance with the function blocks model, where parameters are grouped and ensure uniform and systematic access to the information.

Several blocks and functions are necessary, depending of the operational mode and phase. Basically, the following blocks may be cited:

- Analog input and output Functional Blocks: they describe, during the operation, functionalities like exchange of cyclic input and output data, alarm conditions, limits, etc;
- Physical Block: brings equipment I.D. information related to the hardware and software;
- Transducer Blocks: they pack sensor information that will be used by the functional blocks, and also receive information from these to shoot actuation in final control elements. Normally, an input equipment (e.g., a pressure transmitter) has a transducer block (TRD) linked to an analog input block (AI) through a channel, and an output equipment (e.g., a valve positioning device) and an analog output block (AO) that receives a setpoint value and enables it via channel to a transducer block (TRD) that will activate the final element (for example, positioning a valve).

Some equipment have several AI and AOs blocks that are called multi-channel equipments, where there must be several TRD blocks associated to the hardware.

The PROFIBUS-PA still differentiate the profiles in classes:

- Class A Equipment: includes information only from the physical and function blocks. In this class the equipment is limited to the basic necessary for the operation: process variable (value and status), unity and tag;
- Class B Equipment: stores extended functions from physical blocks, transducer and function blocks.

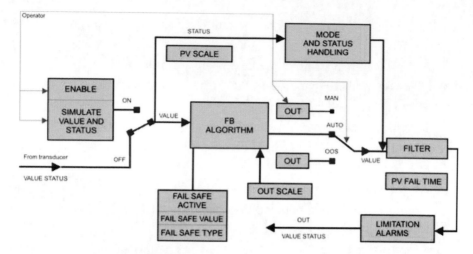

Figure 3.18. Analog Input Block AI.

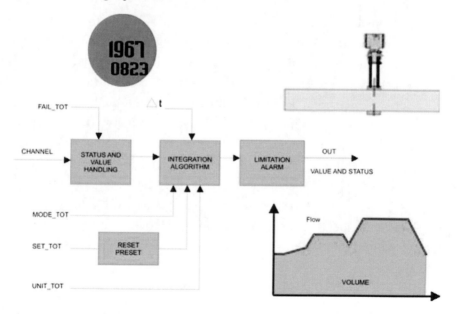

Figure 3.19. Totalization Block TOT.

A powerful feature supported by the PROFILE 3.0 is defining each segment in accordance with the GSD files. These files ensure that any PROFIBUS system is accepted by the equipment, regardless of its characteristics. By that, each manufacturer may develop his particularities as functional blocks, going further than what is defined on the profile. This adds value to the equipments and makes possible the development competition and offering additional features in the different equipments.

These specific equipment particularities may be accessed through standard interface concepts, with basis on EDDL (Equipment Descriptive Device Language) or FDT (Field Device Tool). These interfaces give the user configuration, parameterization, calibration versatility and flexibility, and mainly download and upload mechanisms in the phase of project planning and commissioning.

3.1.3.15. PROFISAFE: The Profile of Safety

The demand for more resources in the automation and process control area through the advent of digital technology and the fast expansion of Field-bus favored the development of the technology devoted to the diagnostics and treatment of safe failures. Mainly, aiming at the protection of people, equipments and the environment, always having for goal the ideal safety system.

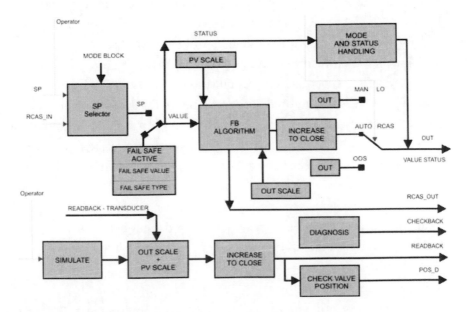

Figure 3.20. Analog Output Block AO.

This safe system requires, in other words, that the data and information may be validated in relation to its values and time domain, one that must be applicable to the system in its entirety. This implies ensuring that the data received was sent correctly and the sender is also de right transmitter. Furthermore, that this be the expected information, at a given moment and that the incoming information was sequentially correct, etc.

Currently, the most typical example of international safety standard, one that involves the most part of system developers and implementers with safety is the IEC 61508. This standard shows the activities involved in the entire life cycle of programmable electronic systems concerning safety. Therefore, it deals both to hardware and software requirements.

The danger with accidents in industrial processes is large and the probability of their happening depends on the probability of system failures. The implication of failures depends on the application's safety types and requirements.

The PROFIBUS "PROFISAFE" application profile – The Profile for a Safety Technology describes safety communication mechanisms between peripherals liable to fail-safe situations and safe controllers, like IEC 61508 and EN954-1, as well as in the experience of the manufacturers with fail-safe mechanisms and the community of PLC manufacturers.

Following, their main concepts will be presented.

This profile supports safe applications in a wide area of field applications. And, instead of using special buses for the safety functions, it permits the implementation of safe automation through an open solution in the PROFIBUS standard, which guarantees cost-effective cabling, consistency of the system regarding the parameterization and remote diagnostics functions.

It guarantees safe decentralized control systems through fail-safe communication and safe mechanism devices and equipments.

See below a few examples this safety profile application areas:

- Manufaturing Industry;
- Quick protection to persons, machines and environment;
- Emergency stop functions;

- Light barriers;
- Input control;
- Scanners;
- Drivers with integrated safety;
- Control of processes in general;
- Chemical and petrochemical areas;
- Public transportation;
- Others.

The PROFIBUS open technology meets a number of requirements, by the most varied applications in terms of safety according to PROFISAFE:

- Independency between relevantly safe communication and safe communication;
- Applicable to SIL3 (IEC61508), AK6 (DIN V 19250) levels and the control category 4 (KAT4) (EN 954-1);
- Redundancy is only used to increase trust ability;
- Any master or DP link may be used;
- Upon implementation, DP masters, ASICs, links and couplers must not be modified, as long as the safety functions are installed above the OSI layer 7, i.e., with no change or accommodation on the DP protocol;
- The implementation of safe transmission functions must be restricted to the communication between the equipments and should not restrict their number;
- It is always a communication relation 1:1 between the F devices;
- The transmission times must be monitored.

In practice, safe applications and standards share the PROFIBUS DP communication systems simultaneously. The safe transmission functions include every measure that may be deterministically found in possible dangerous failures. These may be added to the standard transmission system, aiming at minimizing its effects. They included, e.g., the random malfunctioning functions, EMI effects, systematic hardware or software failures, etc.

For instance, during communication it is possible that part of a frame is lost, part of it may be repeated, or yet, that it appears in the wrong order or even late.

On PROFISAFE, a few preventive measures may be taken, aiming at enclosing possible causes of failure or that these may happen with safety, should they occur.

- Consecutive numbering of every safe message: this minimizes the loss of communication, the insertion of bytes on the frame and the wrong sequence;
- Watchdog timer system for messages and their acknowledgment for controlling delays;
- A password between remittent and receptor, to avoid linking standard and safe messages;
- Additional telegram protection by including 2 to 4 CRC bytes, thus avoiding the corruption of user data and the linking of standard and safe messages.

These measures must be analyzed and taken on a single fail-safe data unit. See below the F message model.

PROFISAFE is a one-channel software solution that is implemented as an additional layer above layer 7 on the devices. A safe layer defines methods to increase the probability of detecting errors that may occur between two equipments/devices communicating in a field-bus.

A great advantage is that it can be implemented without changes, to protect the users investment.

On the physical means RS485 or H1 (31.25kbits/s) the cyclic communication mechanisms are used. The acyclic communication is used for irrelevant levels of data safety. It ensures very short response times, which are recommended in intrinsically safe manufactures and operations, in compliance with the requirements of the process control area.

PROFISAFE uses the error detecting mechanism to keep the desired safety levels. This profile detects communication errors such as duplicated frames, lost of frames, incorrect frame sequences, corrupted frames, frame delays and wrong frame addressing. The PROFISAFE profiles use the redundancy of information to validate the communication between two devices.

The relevant safe information is t is transmitted in conjunction with the process data, that is, this data is embedded in the PROFIBUS DP basic frame. This type of frame may deal with a maximum 244 bytes process data.

PROFISAFE reserves 128 bytes from this total for the safety data. Beyond that, 4 or 6 bytes are treated separately as status and control bytes, depending on the quantity of safe data transmitted. Always two control bytes are sent from each frame, one for status and the other with the frame sequence. The four remaining bytes are saved for the checksum generated to protect redundant safe information. A small amount of relevant safe data transmitted involves one 16-bit CRC and 4 bytes control. For transmissions over 12 safe data bytes (until 122), one 32-bit CRC is used with 6-byte control.

S	S	S	S	S	S

S=Standard Message

Sync Time	SD	LE	Ler	SD	DA	SA	FC	Data Unit	FCS	ED
33 bits	68H	...	...	68H	...	...	...	1···24 Bytes	...	16H

SD=Start Delimiter
LE=Length of Process Data
LEr=Repetition of Length
DA=Destination Address
SA=Source Address
FC=Function Code
Data Unit=Process Data
FCS=Frame Checking Sequence

Figure 3.21. Risk considerations according to IEC 61508.

Figure 3.21 shows the DP frame model that includes in the information the frame known to that frame, in addition to fail-safe data (a maximum 128 bytes in 244 bytes, due to its limitation of 64 words exchanged in a single time between the Host and the DP master), as well as the parity safety resources and FCS (Frame Checking Sequence).

Figure 3.22 shows the F message model (safe message), where may be seen the bytes for integrity control and error minimization previously described as preventive measures.

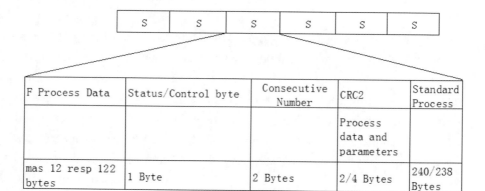

F Process Data	Status/Control byte	Consecutive Number	CRC2	Standard Process
			Process data and parameters	
mas 12 resp 122 bytes	1 Byte	2 Bytes	2/4 Bytes	240/238 Bytes

Figure 3.22. Typical system using default and security communication sharing the same bus and protocol.

Table 3.6. PROFISAFE Architecture

Bit 7	Bit 6	Bit 5	Bit 4	Bit 3	Bit 2	Bit 1	Bit 0
tbd	res	res	Fail safe values (FV) activated	Communi-cation failure: WD time-out	Communi-cation failure: CRC or consecutive number	Failure exists in F slave or F module	F slave has new i-parameter values assigned

The Table 3.6 shows details on how to deal with safe failure, communication, timer-outs, CRCs, message numbering, etc.

Through the monitoring and control of information between safe masters and slaves, such as: synchronization, F protocol cycle, watchdog timers, order of messages, frame repetitions, SIL monitor (one that counts corrupt messages in a given period of time), it is possible to guarantee safety to the integrity levels, as follows.

Table 3.7. SIL Monitor

SIL	CRC	Length of Process Data	Time Period (h)
3	16 Bit	<16 Bytes	10
2	16 Bit	<16 Bytes	1
3	32 Bit	<128 Bytes	0.1
2	32 Bit	<128 Bytes	0.01

3.1.3.16. GSD and PROFISAFE files

Equipments with the PROFISAFE features include in its GSD file the following key word:

F Device supp = 1; 1 = F device

This section in this chapter covered a few details about the PROFIBUS protocol, what it encloses in terms of resources and benefits to automation and the control of continuous and discreet processes. Its potentiality is outstanding at world level both in applications and the management of publicity and support jointly with Regional Associations and Competence Centers. Another detail is the concern by companies in the continuous offer of products according to the market demand and guarantee future investments with total interoperability and exchangeability.

3.2. HISTORY AND DEVELOPMENTS OF PROFIBUS

3.2.1. Origin of PROFIBUS

The history of PROFIBUS goes back to a publicly promoted plan for an association which started in Germany in 1986 and for which 21 companies and institutes devised a master project plan called "field-bus". The goal was to implement and spread the use of a bit-serial field-bus based on the basic requirements of the field device interfaces. For this purpose, member companies agreed to support a common technical concept for production (i.e., discrete or factory automation) and process automation. First, the complex communication protocol PROFIBUS FMS (Field-bus Message Specification), which was tailored for demanding communication tasks, was specified. Subsequently in 1993, the specification for the simpler and thus considerably faster protocol PROFIBUS DP (Decentralised Peripherals) was completed. PROFIBUS FMS is used for (non-deterministic) communication of data between PROFIBUS Masters. PROFIBUS DP is a protocol made for (deterministic) communication between PROFIBUS masters and their remote I/O slaves.

There are two variations of PROFIBUS in use today; the most commonly used PROFIBUS DP, and the lesser used, application specific, PROFIBUS PA:

- **PROFIBUS DP** (Decentralized Peripherals) is used to operate sensors and actuators via a centralised controller in production (factory) automation applications. The many standard diagnostic options, in particular, are focused on here.
- **PROFIBUS PA** (Process Automation) is used to monitor measuring equipment via a process control system in process automation applications. This variant is designed for use in explosion/hazardous areas (Ex-zone 0 and 1). The Physical Layer (i.e., the cable) conforms to IEC 61158-2, which allows power to be delivered over the bus to field instruments, while limiting current flows so that explosive conditions are not created, even if a

malfunction occurs. The number of devices attached to a PA segment is limited by this feature. PA has a data transmission rate of 31.25 K bit/s. However, PA uses the same protocol as DP, and can be linked to a DP network using a coupler device. The much faster DP acts as a backbone network for transmitting process signals to the controller. This means that DP and PA can work tightly together, especially in hybrid applications where process and factory automation networks operate side by side. In excess of 30 million PROFIBUS nodes were installed by the end of 2009. 5 million of these are in the process industries.

3.2.2. Technology

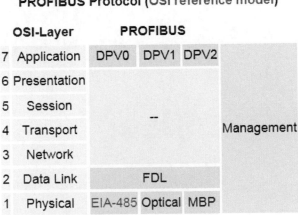

Figure 3.23. OSI reference model and PROFIBUS protocol.

3.2.2.1. Application Layer

To utilize these functions, various service levels of the DP protocol were defined:

- DP-V0 for cyclic exchange of data and diagnosis
- DP-V1 for acyclic data exchange and alarm handling

- DP-V2 for isochronous mode and data exchange broadcast (slave-to-slave communication)

3.2.2.2. Security Layer

The security layer FDL (Field-bus Data Link) works with a hybrid access method that combines token passing with a master-slave method. In a PROFIBUS DP network, the controllers or process control systems are the masters and the sensors and actuators are the slaves.

Various telegram types are used. They can be differentiated by their start delimiter (SD):

No data: SD1 = 0x10

Variable length data:
SD2 = 0 x 68

Fixed length data:
SD3 = 0 x A2

Token:
SD4 = 0 x DC

Brief acknowledgement:
SC = 0 x E5

SD
Start Delimiter
LE
Length of protocol data unit, (incl. DA, SA, FC, DSAP, SSAP)
LER

Repetition of length of protocol data unit, (Hamming distance = 4)

FC

Function Code

DA

Destination Address

SA

Source Address

DSAP

Destination Service Access Point

SSAP

Source Service Access Point

A Service Access Point (SAP) is an identifying label for network endpoints used in Open Systems Interconnection (OSI) networking.

The SAP is a conceptual location at which one OSI layer can request the services of another OSI layer. As an example, PD-SAP or PLME-SAP in IEEE 802.15.4 can be mentioned, where the Media Access Control (MAC) layer requests certain services from the Physical Layer. Service access points are also used in IEEE 802.2 Logical Link Control in Ethernet and similar Data Link Layer protocols.

When using the OSI Network Layer (CONS or CLNS), the base for constructing an address for a network element is an NSAP address, similar in concept to an IP address. OSI Application Layer protocols as well as Asynchronous Transfer Mode (ATM) can use Transport (TSAP), Session (SSAP) or Presentation (PSAP) Service Access Points to specify a destination address for a connection. These SAPs consist of NSAP addresses combined with optional transport, session and presentation selectors, which can differentiate at any of the three layers between multiple services at that layer provided by a network element.

The FCS is calculated by simply adding up the bytes within the specified length. An overflow is ignored here. Each byte is saved with an even parity and transferred asynchronously with a start and stop bit. There may not be a pause between a stop bit and the following start bit when the bytes of a telegram are transmitted. The master signals the start of a new telegram with a SYN pause of at least 33 bits (logical "1" = bus idle).

SAP (Decimal)	SERVICE
Default 0	Cyclical Data Exchange (Write_Read_Data)
54	Master-to-Master SAP (M-M Communication)
55	Change Station Address (Set_Slave_Add)
56	Read Inputs (Rd_Inp)
57	Read Outputs (Rd_Outp)
58	Control Commands to a DP Slave (Global_Control)
59	Read Configuration Data (Get_Cfg)
60	Read Diagnostic Data (Slave_Diagnosis)
61	Send Parameterization Data (Set_Prm)
62	Check Configuration Data (Chk_Cfg)

Note: SAP55 is optional and may be disabled if the slave doesn't provide non-volatile storage memory for the station address.

PDU: Protocol Data Unit (protocol data).

FCS: Frame Checking Sequence.

ED: End Delimiter (= 0x16 !).

3.2.2.3. Bit-Transmission Layer

Three different methods are specified for the bit-transmission layer:

- With electrical transmission pursuant to EIA-485, twisted pair cables with impedances of 150 ohms are used in a bus topology. Bit rates from 9.6 k bit/s to 12 M bit/s can be used. The cable length between two repeaters is limited from 100 to 1200 m, depending on the bit rate used. This transmission method is primarily used with PROFIBUS DP.

- With optical transmission via fiber optics, star-, bus- and ring-topologies are used. The distance between the repeaters can be up to 15 km. The ring topology can also be executed redundantly.

- With MBP (Manchester Bus Powered) transmission technology, data and field-bus power are fed through the same cable. The power can be reduced in such a way that use in explosion-hazardous environments is possible. The bus topology can be up to 1900 m long and permits branching to field devices (max. 60 m branches). The bit rate here is a fixed 31.25 K bit/s. This technology was specially established for use in process automation for PROFIBUS PA.

For data transfer via sliding contacts for mobile devices or optical or radio data transmission in open spaces, products from various manufacturers can be obtained, however they do not conform to any standard.

PROFIBUS DP uses two core screened cable with a violet sheath, and runs at speeds between 9.6K bit/s and 12M bit/s. A particular speed can be chosen for a network to give enough time for communication with all the devices present in the network. If systems change slowly then lower communication speed is suitable, and if the systems change quickly then effective communication will happen through faster speed. The RS485 balanced transmission used in PROFIBUS DP only allows 126 devices to be connected at once; however, more devices can be connected or the network expanded with the use of hubs or repeaters.

PROFIBUS PA is slower than PROFIBUS DP and runs at fixed speed of 31.2K bit/s via blue sheathed two core screened cable. The communication may be initiated to minimize the risk of explosion or for the systems that intrinsically need safe equipment. The message formats in PROFIBUS PA are identical to PROFIBUS DP.

Note: PROFIBUS DP and PROFIBUS PA should not be confused with PROFINET.

3.2.3. Profiles

Profiles are pre-defined configurations of the functions and features available from PROFIBUS for use in specific devices or applications. They are specified by PI working groups and published by PI. Profiles are important for openness, interoperability and interchangeability, so that the end user can be sure that similar equipments from different vendors perform in a standardised way. User choice also encourages competition that drives vendors towards enhanced performance and lower costs.

There are PROFIBUS profiles for Encoders, Laboratory instruments, Intelligent pumps, Robots and Numerically Controlled machines, for example. Profiles also exist for applications such as using HART and wireless with PROFIBUS, and process automation devices via PROFIBUS PA. Other profiles have been specified for Motion Control (PROFIdrive) and Functional Safety (PROFISAFE).

3.2.4. Standardization

PROFIBUS was defined in 1991/1993 in DIN 19245, was then included in EN 50170 in 1996 and, since 1999, established in IEC 61158/IEC 61784.

PROFIBUS is standardized in IEC 61158 – the foundation has therefore been laid for interoperability and compatibility. Furthermore the PROFIBUS PA profile allows the smooth cooperative working of process devices on the bus. The current PROFIBUS PA version V3.02 includes many functions, which make the handling of field devices even easier, e.g., in case of a device exchange.

When a field device is exchanged the new device automatically takes over the role of the predecessor device – therefore a device exchange can be carried out easily and without interruption of the system operation.

This automatic adaption is also possible with devices of different generations.

This means that standardization offers more flexibility and no limitation in your choice of supplier. Indeed, in the meanwhile there is a vast range of devices available that can be combined in almost any way. A focus on only one manufacturer is no longer given.

Even replacing devices later on is absolutely easy and with PROFIBUS new devices are always backward-compatible.

3.2.5. Organization

The PROFIBUS Nutzerorganisation e.V. (PROFIBUS User Organization, or PNO) was created in 1989. This group was composed mainly of manufacturers and users from Europe. In 1992, the first regional PROFIBUS organization was founded (PROFIBUS Schweiz in Switzerland). In the following years, additional Regional PROFIBUS & PROFINET Associations (RPAs) were added.

In 1995, all the RPAs joined together under the international umbrella association PROFIBUS & PROFINET International (PI). Today, PROFIBUS is represented by 25 RPAs around the world (including PNO) with over 1400 members, including most if not all major automation vendors and service suppliers, along with many end users.

3.3. PROFINET Technology

PROFINET (an acronym for Process Field Net) is an industry technical standard for data communication over Industrial Ethernet, designed for collecting data from, and controlling, equipment in industrial systems, with a particular strength in delivering data under tight time constraints (on the order of 1ms or less). The standard is maintained and supported by PROFIBUS & PROFINET International, an umbrella organization headquartered in Karlsruhe, Germany.

3.3.1. Related Technology

Three protocol levels are defined:

TCP/IP for non time-critical data and the commissioning of a plant [2] with reaction times in the range of 100 ms RT (real-time) protocol for PROFINET IO applications [2] up to 1 ms cycle times IRT (Isochronous Real-Time) for PROFINET IO applications in drive systems [2] with cycles times of less than 1 ms. The protocols can be recorded and displayed using an Ethernet analysis tool PRONETA [3] such as Wireshark.

3.3.2. Peripherals

Interfacing to peripherals is implemented by PROFINET IO It defines the communication with field connected peripheral devices. Its basis is a cascading real-time concept. PROFINET IO defines the entire data exchange between controllers (devices with "master functionality") and the devices (devices with "slave functionality"), as well as parameter setting and diagnosis. PROFINET IO is designed for the fast data exchange between Ethernet-based field devices and follows the provider-consumer model. Field devices in a subordinate PROFIBUS line can be integrated in the PROFINET IO system without any effort and seamlessly via an IO-Proxy (representative of a subordinate bus system). A device developer can implement PROFINET IO with any commercially available Ethernet controller. It is well-suited for the data exchange with bus cycle times of a few milliseconds. The configuration of an IO-System has been kept similar to PROFIBUS. PROFINET IO always contains the real-time concept.

A PROFINET IO system consists of the following devices:

- The IO Controller, which controls the automation task.
- The IO Device, which is a field device, monitored and controlled by an IO Controller. An IO Device may consist of several modules and sub-modules.
- The IO Supervisor is software typically based on a PC for setting parameters and diagnosing individual IO Devices

An Application Relation (AR) is established between an IO Controller and an IO Device. These ARs are used to define Communication Relations (CR) with different characteristics for the transfer of parameters, cyclic exchange of data and handling of alarms. Refer to PROFINET IO connection life-cycle for a more detailed description.

The characteristics of an IO Device are described by the device manufacturer in a General Station Description (GSD) file. The language used for this purpose is the GSDML (GSD Markup Language) - an XML based language. The GSD file provides the supervision software with a basis for planning the configuration of a PROFINET IO system.

3.3.3. IO Addressing

Every module within a PROFINET network has three addresses:

- MAC address
- IP address
- Device name, a logical name for the module within the total configuration

Because PROFINET uses TCP/IP a MAC and IP address are used. A MAC address changes if the device is replaced. An IP address is a form of dynamic addressing. Because there was a need for a fixed address a device name is used.

For allocation of the IP address, subnet mask and default gateway two methods are defined:

- DCP: Discovery and Configuration Protocol
- DHCP: Dynamic Host Configuration Protocol

3.3.4. Real-Time Characteristics

Within PROFINET IO, process data and alarms are always transmitted in real time (RT). Real time in PROFINET is based on definitions of IEEE and IEC, which allow for only a limited time for execution of real-time services within a bus cycle. The RT communication represents the basis for the data exchange for PROFINET IO. Real-time data are treated with a higher priority than TCP(UDP)/IP data. RT provides the basis for the real-time communication in the area of distributed periphery and for the

PROFINET component model. This type of data exchange allows bus cycle times in the range of a few hundred microseconds.

3.3.5. Isochronous Communication

Isochronous data exchange with PROFINET is defined in the isochronous real-time (IRT) concept. Devices with IRT functionality have switch ports integrated in the field device. They can be based e.g., on the Ethernet controllers ERTEC 400/200. The data exchange cycles are usually in the range of a few hundred microseconds up to a few milliseconds. The difference to real-time communication is essentially the high degree of determinism, so that the start of a bus cycle is maintained with high precision. The start of a bus cycle can deviate up to 1 µs (jitter). IRT is required, for example, for motion control applications (positioning control processes).

3.3.6. Profiles

Profiles are pre-defined configurations of the functions and features available from PROFINET for use in specific devices or applications. They are specified by PI working groups and published by PI. Profiles are important for openness, interoperability and interchangeability, so that the end user can be sure that similar equipments from different vendors perform in a standardized way.

There are PROFINET profiles for encoders, for example. Other profiles have been specified for motion control (PROFI drive) and Functional Safety (PROFI safe). A special profile for trains also exists.

Another profile is PROFIenergy which includes services for real time monitoring of energy demand. This was requested in 2009 by the AIDA group of German automotive Manufacturers (Audi, BMW, Mercedes-Benz, Porsche and VW) who wished to have a standardized way of actively managing energy usage in their plants. High energy devices and sub-systems such as robots, lasers and even paint lines are the target for this profile, which will help reduce a plant's energy costs by intelligently switching the devices into 'sleep' modes to take account of production breaks, both foreseen (e.g. weekends and shut-downs) and unforeseen (e.g. breakdowns).

3.3.7. Organization

PROFINET is defined by PROFIBUS and PROFINET International (PI) and backed by the INTERBUS Club and, since 2004, is part of the IEC 61158 and IEC 61784 standards.

3.4. PROFIBUS PROTOCOL

3.4.1. General Description

PROFIBUS was recently considered as one of the field-bus solutions of the General-Purpose Field-bus Communication System European Standard, EN 50170.

The PROFIBUS MAC mechanism is based on a token-passing procedure used by master stations to grant the bus access to each one of them, and a master–slave procedure used by master stations to communicate with slave stations. The PROFIBUS token-passing procedure uses a simplified version of the TT protocol. These MAC mechanisms are implemented at the layer 2 of the open systems interconnection (OSI) reference model, which, in PROFIBUS, is called field-bus data link (FDL). In addition to controlling the bus access and the token cycle time (a feature that will be later explained in Section II-B), the FDL is also responsible for the provision of data transmission services for the FDL user (e.g., the application layer). PROFIBUS supports four data transmission services: 1) send data with no acknowledge (SDN); 2) send data with acknowledge (SDA); 3) request data with reply (RDR); and 4) send and request data

(SRD). The SDN is an unacknowledged service used for broadcasts from a master station to all other stations on the bus.

Conversely, all other transmission services are based on a real dual relationship between the initiator (master station holding the token) and the responder (slave or master station not holding the token). An important characteristic of these services is that they are immediately answered, with a response or an acknowledgment. This feature, also called "immediate response," is particularly important for the real-time bus operation. In addition to these services, industrial applications often require the use of cyclical transmission methods. A centrally controlled polling method (cyclical polling) may be used to scan simple field devices, such as sensors or actuators. PROFIBUS enables a poll list to be created at the FDL layer, allowing the execution of cyclical polling services based on RDR and SRD services.

An important PROFIBUS concept is the message cycle. A message cycle consists of a master's action frame (request or send/request frame) and the associated responder's acknowledgment or response frame. User data may be transmitted in the action frame or in the response frame.

All the stations, except the token holder (initiator), shall, in general, monitor all requests. The acknowledgment or response must arrive within a predefined time, the slot time, otherwise the initiator repeats the request. At the network setup phase, the maximum number of retries, before a communication error report, must be defined in all master stations.

The message cycle duration must include the time needed to transmit the action frame and receive the related response, and also the time needed to perform the allowed number of message retries.

3.4.2. Medium Access Control Mechanism in PROFIBUS

One of the main functions of the PROFIBUS MAC is the control of the token cycle time. After receiving the token the measurement of the token rotation time begins. This measurement expires at the next token arrival and results in the real token rotation time (T_{RR}). A target token rotation time (T_{TR}) must be defined in a PROFIBUS network. The value of this parameter is common to all masters, and is used as follows.

When a station receives the token, the token holding time (TTH) timer is given the value corresponding to the difference, if positive, between and PROFIBUS defines two categories of messages: high priority and low priority. These two categories of messages use two independent outgoing queues. If, at the arrival, the token is delayed, that is, the real rotation time was greater than the target rotation time, the master station may execute, at most, one high-priority message cycle. Otherwise, the master station may execute high-priority message cycles while TTH > 0. TTH is always tested at the beginning of the message cycle execution. This means that once a message cycle is started, it is always completed, including any required retries, even if expires during the execution. We denote this occurrence as an overrun. The low-priority message cycles are executed if there are no high-priority messages pending, and while TTH > 0 (also evaluated at the start of the message cycle execution, thus leading to a possible overrun).

Apart from distinguishing high- and low-priority message cycles, the PROFIBUS MAC differentiates three subtypes of low-priority message cycles: poll list, non-cyclic low priority (application layer and remote management services), and gap list message cycles. The gap is the address range between two consecutive master addresses, and each master must periodically check the gap addresses to support dynamic changes in the logical ring.

After all high-priority messages have been carried out, poll list message cycles are started. If the poll cycle is completed within TTH, the requested low-priority noncyclical messages are then carried out, and a new poll cycle starts at the next token arrival with available TTH. If a poll cycle takes several token visits, the poll list is processed in segments, without inserting requested low-priority noncyclical messages. Low priority noncyclical message cycles are carried out only at the end of a complete poll cycle. At most, one gap address is checked per token visit, if there is still available, and there are no pending messages. Figure 3.24 synthesizes the PROFIBUS MAC message handling procedures, where stands for the length of the poll list.

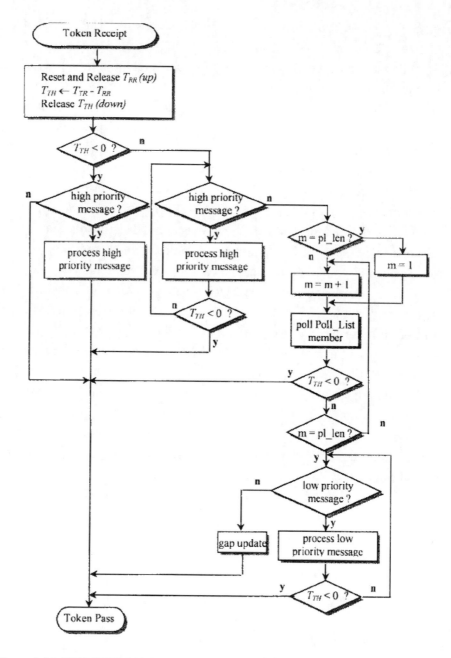

Figure 3.24. PROFIBUS MAC message handling procedures.

The procedures can be described as the following pseudo code.

```
/* initialisation procedure */
At each station k, DO:
TTH ← 0;
TRR ← 0;
Release TRR;
/* run-time procedure */
At each station k, at the Token arrival, DO:
TTH ← TTR - TRR;
TRR ← 0;
Release TRR; /* count-up timer */
IF TTH > 0 THEN
Release TTH /* count-down timer */
ENDIF;
IF waiting High priority messages THEN:
Execute one High priority message cycle
ENDIF;
WHILE TTH > 0 AND pending High priority
Message cycles DO
Execute High priority message cycles
ENDWHILE;
WHILE TTH > 0 AND pending Low priority
Message cycles DO
Execute Low priority message cycles
/* this includes poll list and */
/* GAP list message cycles */
ENDWHILE;
Pass the token to station (k + 1) (modulo k);
```

3.4.3. Real-Time Characteristics of the PROFIBUS

Compared to the TT protocol [9], the main difference of the PROFIBUS token passing consists in the absence of synchronous bandwidth allocation.

The basic idea of the Timed Token protocol was presented by Grow. In this protocol, messages are distinguished in two types. One concerns the synchronous messages, which are periodic messages that come to the system at regular intervals and have delivery time constraints. The other concerns asynchronous messages, which are non-periodic messages that have no time constraint measured at least in units that are large relative to the token rotation time. In the Timed Token Protocol, the time between two consecutive token arrivals at a specific station is bounded by 2 x *TTR* and the average token rotation time is no more than *TTR*.

In the TT protocol, this is a relevant station parameter, since it specifies the amount of time a station has to transfer its real-time traffic. In PROFIBUS, if a master receives a late token (was greater than) only one high-priority message may be transmitted. As a consequence, in PROFIBUS, low-priority traffic may drastically affect the high-priority traffic capabilities. In fact, if the low-priority traffic is not constrained when a master receives an early token (smaller than), the master may use all the available time to process low-priority traffic, delaying the token rotation. In this case, the subsequent masters may be limited to only one high priority message transmission when holding the token. Figure 3.25 illustrates this situation.

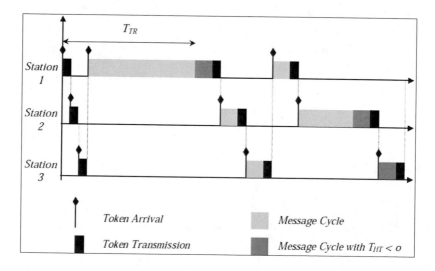

Figure 3.25. PROFIBUS token use.

In PROFIBUS, the absence of synchronous bandwidth allocation prevents the use of the traditional TT real-time analysis. In fact, real-time solutions for networks based on the TT protocol rely on the possibility of allocating specific bandwidth for the real-time traffic.

In order to guarantee high priority message deadlines, the bounded token rotation time is a necessary but not sufficient condition. A node with inadequate synchronous capacity may be unable to guarantee message deadlines, and, on the other hand, allocating excess amount of synchronous capacities to the nodes increases TTR, which may also cause message deadlines to be missed. Therefore, synchronous capacities must be properly allocated to individual nodes. As a consequence, synchronous capacities allocated to the nodes must satisfy two constraints: a protocol constraint and a deadline constraint. The protocol constraint states that the total sum of the allocated synchronous capacities should not be greater that the available portion of TTR, i.e.:

$$\sum_{i=1}^{n} H_i \leq TTRT - \tau$$

Theoretically, the total available time to transmit real-time traffic, during a complete token rotation, can be as much as *TTR*. However, factors such as ring latency and other protocol or network overheads reduce the total available time to transmit real-time traffic. We denote the portion of *TTR* unavailable for transmitting synchronous messages by ♦.

The deadline constraint states that the allocation of the synchronous capacities to the nodes should be such that the synchronous messages are always guaranteed to be transmitted before their deadlines. A message set can be guaranteed by an allocation scheme once the protocol and the deadline constraints are satisfied. Several allocation schemes have been proposed in. it can be found a first analysis on the message schedule ability in PROFIBUS networks. Based on the Timed Token Protocol, these results were later improved and presented in [Vas96]. The work here by described is a step forward in the analysis of message schedule ability in PROFIBUS networks.

3.4.4. PROFIBUS Timing Analysis

Despite the absence of synchronous bandwidth allocation, it is possible to guarantee the real-time behavior of the high-priority traffic with the PROFIBUS protocol. The two following approaches can be used:

- an *unconstrained low-priority traffic* profile, where realtime traffic requirements are satisfied even when only one high-priority message is transmitted per token visit, independent of the low-priority traffic load;
- a *constrained low-priority traffic* profile where, by controlling the number of low-priority message transfers, all pending real-time traffic is transmitted at each token visit. The analysis will demonstrate that the first profile is a suitable approach for more responsive systems (tighter deadlines), while the second allows for an increased non-realtime traffic throughput.

The following assumption as the basis for the analysis: the transmission of one high-priority message per token arrival is always guaranteed, independent of the low-priority traffic load. Under this assumption, the queuing of outgoing messages will very much impact the real-time properties of the system. We will consider in our analysis both priority-based queuing and first-in–first-out (FIFO) queuing. The latter is the one normally used in PROFIBUS implementations. The analysis is based on the definition of a deadline constraint and, using that deadline constraint, the definition of an upper bound for the parameter. In this context, the deadline constraint is defined as the condition that must be satisfied in order to guarantee that all real-time messages are transmitted before their deadlines, i.e., before the end of the minimum inter-arrival time between two consecutive message arrivals.

We consider a bus topology containing n master stations. A special frame (the token) circulates around the logical ring formed by the masters (from node k to nodes $k + 1$, ... until node n, then to nodes 1, 2, ...). We denote the logical ring latency (token walk time, including node latency delay, media propagation delay, etc) as ♦. Message cycles generated in the system at run-time may be classified as either high priority or low priority messages. To each k master node we assume that there are $nh(k)$ high priority message streams and $nl(k)$ low priority message streams. A message stream corresponds to a message cycles sequence related with, for instance, the reading of the value of a process variable.

We denote the *ith* (i = 1, 2, ... $nh(k)$) high priority stream associated to a master node k as *Shi (k)*. Similarly low priority streams will be denoted as *Slj (k)* (j = 1, 2, ..., $nl(k)$). A message stream *Si* is characterized as *Si* = (*Ci, Di*). *Ci* is the maximum amount of time required to transmit a message in a stream. In PROFIBUS this time should also include possible message retries. *Di* is the messages relative deadline, which is the maximum amount of time that may elapse between a message arrival and completion of its transmission. We consider that, in the worst case, the deadline can be seen as the minimum inter-arrival time between two consecutive messages in the same stream. The following notation will then be used:

$$Sh_i^{(k)} = \left(Ch_i^{(k)}, Dh_i^{(k)} \right)$$
$$Sl_i^{(k)} = \left(Cl_i^{(k)} \right)$$

$$(3.1)$$

As a consequence, in PROFIBUS, low priority traffic may drastically affect the high priority traffic capabilities. In fact, if a station receives an early token (*TTR – TRR (k)* > 0) and the low priority traffic is not constrained in that station, subsequent stations may have an initial value for *TTH* < 0.

Considering that we have only one high priority stream in a k master station, we must guarantee that after being produced, a message can be transmitted before the end of its deadline. To guarantee this, the token inter-arrival time to the station must be lower than the deadline. If we denote the maximum time between consecutive token visits to a station k by *Tcycle (k)*, this deadline constraint can be formulated as:

$$\frac{Dh_1^{(k)}}{Tcycle^{(k)}} \geq 1, \forall_k$$

$$(3.2)$$

If we now consider having $nh(k)$ high priority streams in the k station, $Tcycle\ (k)$ may be constrained as follows:

$$\sum_{i=1}^{nh^{(k)}} \frac{1}{Dh_i^{(k)}/Tcycle^{(k)}} \leq 1$$

$$(3.3)$$

The expression can be explained with a simple example. If we have only one high priority message stream in a k station, which deadline is 40ms, then the token should visit that station, at least, each 40ms. If the same station has 2 high priority message streams of 40 ms deadlines then, the token should visit that station, at least, each 20 ms. We should remember that we are supposing the worst case of only one high priority message transmitted per token visit, which is always guaranteed by PROFIBUS, independently of the token delay. As we will see, expression (3.3) will only stand for deadline constraint if the outgoing messages are put in a priority queue or, which is not reasonable, all the streams in the station k have equal deadlines. This can also be shown with a simple example. If a station k has two streams of 40 ms deadlines, from (3.3) $Tcycle\ (k)$ should be equal to 20ms. Lets denote this as scenario A. If the same station has two streams, one with a 40ms deadline and the other with a 20ms deadline, then, from expression (3-3), we will have for $Tcycle\ (k)$ the value of 13,3(3)ms. This will be denoted as another scenario.

Assuming expression (4.2) for the deadline constraint, we need to estimate a value for $Tcycle\ (k)$. Consider the following scenario, within which none of the three stations transmitted any message in the previous token cycle. When station 1 receives the token it can send messages during a $(TTR - \tau)$ time length. In fact it can hold the token by this amount plus the time corresponding to the transmission of the longest message issued by that station (including the non real-time messages). This may happens because once PROFIBUS starts to send a message it will proceed till the end of the message cycle even if *THT (k)* time has elapsed. For simplification we can derive the expression for *Tcycle (k)* using the maximum length for a message in the network (including high and low priority traffic):

$$Tcycle^{(k)} = T_{IR} + n \times C_{max} . \forall_k \qquad (3.4)$$

Chapter 4

NETWORKED CONTROL SYSTEM BASED ON FF FIELD-BUS WITH ITS APPLICATION IN INDUSTRY

4.1. INTRODUCTION OF FOUNDATION FIELD-BUS

The FOUNDATION field-bus can be flexibly used in process automation applications. The specification supports bus-powered field devices as well as allows application in hazardous areas. The Field-bus FOUNDATION's slogan '... dedicated to a single international field-bus' expresses the organization's claim to establishing an international, interoperable field-bus standard.

Field-bus technology replaces the expensive, conventional 4 to 20 mA wiring in the field and enables bidirectional data transmission. The entire communication between the devices and the automation system as well as the process control station takes place over the bus system, and all operating and device data are exclusively transmitted over the field-bus (see also Lit./4/). The communication between control station, operating terminals and field devices simplifies the start-up and parameterization of all components.

The communication functions allow diagnostic data, which are provided by up-to-date field devices, to be evaluated. The essential objectives in field-bus technology are to reduce installation costs, save time and costs due to simplified planning as well as improve the operating reliability of the system due to additional performance features. Field-bus systems are usually implemented in new plants or existing plants that must be extended. To convert an existing plant to field-bus technology, the conventional wiring can either be modified into a bus line, or it must be replaced with a shielded bus cable, if required. Note: To ensure trouble-free operation, the communication system must be designed and configured by experts.

4.1.1. History and Development

In 1992 an international group, the ISP – 'Interoperable Systems Project,' was founded with the intention to create an internationally uniform field-bus standard for use in hazardous environments. At the same time, the manufacturers and users of the French FIP (Flux Information Processus; previously: Factory Instrumentation Protocol) established the international user organization WorldFIP. Together with the FIP North America, they were a strong counterweight to the ISP consortium.

In 1994, for technical, economic and political reasons, the ISP and the WorldFIP merged to form the Field-bus FOUNDATION. The aim of the Field-bus FOUNDATION was and is to create a single, international field-bus standard for hazardous environments which will find widespread use as IEC standardized field-bus. The same goal is pursued by the PROFIBUS user organization with its PROFIBUS PA field-bus. While the PROFIBUS PA has its roots and its largest user community in Europe, the FOUNDATION field-bus manufacturers and users are concentrated in America and Asia.

The Field-bus FOUNDATION utilized some elements from the FIP for the specification of their FOUNDATION field-bus (FF) as well as – similar to PROFIBUS PA – details from the ISP specification. This is why the physical bus design of both field-bus systems is the same. Also, the device interface for application, which is based on function blocks, exhibits many common features. This is due to the fact that both systems have similar ambitions. However, when taking a closer look and comparing the system functions, it can be seen that there are also great differences.

4.1.2. Performance Features

The FOUNDATION field-bus provides a broad spectrum of services and functions compared to other field-bus systems:

- intrinsic safety for use in hazardous environments
- bus-powered field devices
- line or tree topology
- multi-master capable communication
- deterministic (predictable) dynamic behavior
- distributed data transfer (DDT)
- standardized block model for uniform device interfaces (inter-operability, inter-changeability')
- flexible extension options based on device descriptions

The characteristic feature of distributed data transfer enables single field devices to execute automation tasks so that they are no longer 'just' sensors or actuators, but contain additional functions.

For the description of a device's function(s) and for the definition of a uniform access to the data, the FOUNDATION field-bus contains predefined function blocks (see 'User application' on page 29). The function blocks implemented in a device provide information about the tasks the device can perform. Typical functions provided by sensors include the following:

'Analog Input' or
'Discrete Input' (digital input).

Control valves usually contain the following function blocks:
'Analog Output' or
'Discrete Output' (digital output).

The following blocks exist for process control tasks:

Proportional/Derivative (PD controller) or
Proportional/Integral/Derivative (PID controller).

If a device contains such a function block, it can control a process variable independently.

The shift of automation tasks – from the automation level down to the field results in the flexible, distributed processing of control tasks. This reduces the load on the central process control station which can even be replaced entirely in small-scale installations. Therefore, an entire control loop can be implemented as the smallest unit, consisting only of one sensor and one control valve with integrated process controller which communicate over the FOUNDATION field-bus.

The enhanced functionality of the devices leads to higher requirements to be met by the device hardware and comparably complex software implementation and device interfaces.

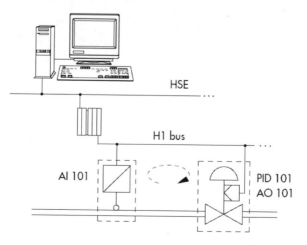

Figure 4.1. Complete control loop based on the FOUNDATION field-bus.

4.2. PROTOCOL MODEL

The FOUNDATION specification is based on the layered communications model and consists of three major functional elements:

- Physical Layer
- Communication "Stack"
- User Application

The User Application is made up of function blocks and the device description. It is directly based on the Communication Stack. Depending on which blocks are implemented in a device, users can access a variety of services. System management utilizes the services and functions of the User Application and the application layer to execute its tasks (Figures 3b and 3c). It ensures the proper cooperation between the individual bus components as well as synchronizes the measurement and control tasks of all field devices with regard to time.

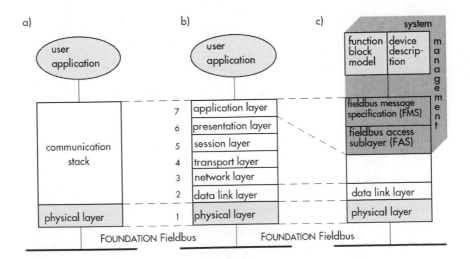

Figure 4.2. Structure and description of the FF communication layers.

The FOUNDATION field-bus layered communications model is based on the ISO/OSI reference model. As is the case for most field-bus systems, and in accordance with an IEC specification, layers three to six are not used. The comparison in Figure 4.2 shows that the Communication Stack covers the tasks of layers two and seven and that layer seven consists of the Field-bus Access Sub-layer (FAS) and the Field-bus Message Specification (FMS).

4.2.1. Physical Layer

The specification of the FOUNDATION Field-bus is not yet completed at this stage. However, it is certain that the topology of a FF system complies with the IEC Field-bus model in many aspects.

The IEC field-bus solves pending communication tasks by using two bus systems, the slow, intrinsically safe H1 bus and the fast, higher-level H2 bus with 1 to 2.5 M bit/s.

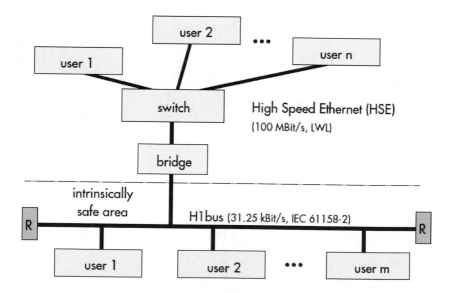

Figure 4.3. Structure of the FOUNDATION field-bus.

The physical design of the H1 bus of the FOUNDATION field-bus complies exactly with the specifications of the IEC field-bus model. The specification of the H2 bus is not yet completed and the publication of the preliminary specification (PS) has been announced. However, it is certain that the High Speed Ethernet (HSE) will be used.

4.2.1.1. H1 Bus

The following summary gives a brief overview of the basic values and features of the H1 bus. For more details, refer to the various 'Application Guides' of the Field-bus FOUNDATION (e.g., AG 140, AG 163). The H1 bus specification is based on the IEC 61158-2 (see Lit./2/):

- Manchester coding is used for data transfer. The data transfer rate is 31.25 K bit/s.
- Proper communication requires that the field devices have enough voltage. Each device should have minimum 9 volts. To make sure that this requirement is met, software tools are available which calculate the resulting currents and terminal voltages based on the network topology, the line resistance and the supply voltage.
- The H1 bus allows the field devices to be powered over the bus. The power supply unit is connected to the bus line in the same way (parallel) as a field device. Field devices powered by supply sources other than the bus, must be additionally connected to their own supply sources.
- With the H1 bus it must be ensured that the maximum power consumption of current consuming devices is lower than the electric power supplied by the power supply unit.
- Network topologies used are usually line topology or, when equipped with junction boxes, also star, tree or a combination of topologies. The devices are best connected via short spurs using tee connectors to enable connection/disconnection of the devices without interrupting communication.

- The maximum length of a spur is limited to 120 meters and depends on the number of spurs used as well as the number of devices per spur.

- Without repeaters, the maximum length of an H1 segment can be as long as 1900 meters. By using up to four repeaters, a maximum of 5*1900 m = 9500 m can be jumpered. The short spurs from the field device to the bus are included in this total length calculation.

- The number of bus users per bus segment is limited to 32 in intrinsically safe areas. In explosion-hazardous areas, this number is reduced to only a few devices due to power supply limitations (see EEx-i instrumentation below).

- Various types of cables are useable for field-bus (Figure 4.4). Type A is recommended as preferred field-bus cable, and only this type is specified for the maximum bus length of 1900 m.

- Principally, there need to be two terminators per bus segment, one at or near each end of a transmission line.

- It is not imperative that bus cables be shielded, however, it is recommended to prevent possible interferences and for best performance of the system.

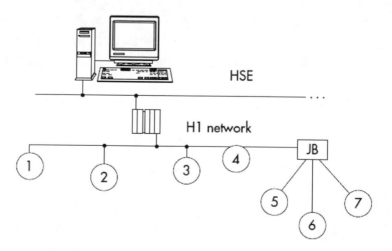

Figure 4.4. Mixed topology for an H1 network.

No. of devices	1 device per spur	2 devices per spur	3 devices per spur	4 devices per spur
25-32	1 m	1 m	1 m	1 m
19-24	30 m	1 m	1 m	1 m
15-18	60 m	30 m	1 m	1 m
13-14	90 m	60 m	30 m	1 m
1-12	120 m	90 m	60 m	30 m

Figure 4.5. Length of spurs.

	Type A	Type B	Type C	Type D
Cable description	shielded twisted pair	single or multi-twisted pair with an overall shield	multi-twisted pair without shield	multi-core, without twisted pairs, without shield
Size	0.8 mm² (AWG 18)	0.32 mm² (AWG 22)	0.13 mm² (AWG 26)	1.25 mm² (AWG 16)
Max. length incl. spurs	1900 m	1200 m	400 m	200 m

Figure 4.6. Field-bus cable types and maximum bus lengths.

4.2.1.2. EEx-i Instrumentation

The H1 bus can be designed intrinsically safe (Ex-i) to suit applications in hazardous areas. This requires that proper barriers be installed between the safe and the explosion hazardous area. In addition, only one device, the power supply unit, must supply the field-bus with power. All other devices must always, i.e., also when transmitting and receiving data, function as current sinks.

Since the capacity of electrical lines is limited in intrinsically safe areas depending on the explosion group – IIB or IIC – (see Figure 4.9), the number of de-vices that can be connected to one segment depends on the effective power consumption of the used devices.

Since the FOUNDATION field-bus specification is not based on the FISCO model (see Lit./4/), the plant operator himself must ensure that intrinsic safety requirements are met when planning and installing the communications network. For instance, the capacitance and inductance of all line segments and devices must be calculated to ensure that the permissible limit values are observed.

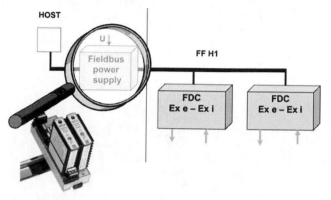

Figure 4.7. Application structure of H1.

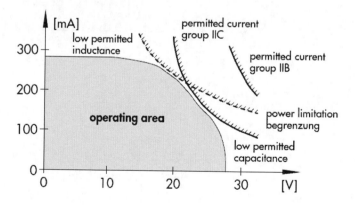

Figure 4.8. Limited operating area for Ex-i IIB and IIC installations.

Group	Co (Ca)	Lo (La)
IIC	165 nF	0.35 mH
IIB	1.14 µF	1.04 mH

Figure 4.9. Capacitance and inductance limit values for installation of Ex-i instrumentation.

4.2.1.3. High Speed Ethernet (HSE)

The HSE is based on standard Ethernet technology. The required components are therefore widely used and are available at low costs. The HSE runs at 100 M bit/s and cannot only be equipped with electrical lines, but with optical fiber cables as well.

The Ethernet operates by using random (not deterministic) CSMA bus access. This method can only be applied to a limited number of automation applications because it requires real-time capability. The extremely high transmission rate enables the bus to respond sufficiently fast when the bus load is low and devices are only few. With respect to process engineering requirements, real-time requirements are met in any case.

If the bus load must be reduced due to the many connected devices, or if several HSE partial networks are to be combined to create a larger network, Ethernet Switches must be used. A switch reads the target address of the data packets that must be forwarded and then passes the packets on to the associated partial network. This way, the bus load and the resulting bus access time can be controlled to best adapt it to the respective requirements.

4.2.1.4. Bridge to H1-HSE Coupling

A communications network that consists of an H1 bus and an HSE network results in a topology as illustrated in Figure 4.7. To connect the comparatively slow H1 segments to the HSE network, coupling components, so-called Bridges, are required. Similar to HSE, the specification of this bus component has not been completed up to now.

A Bridge is used to connect the individual H1 buses to the fast High Speed Ethernet. The various data transfer rates and data telegrams must be adapted and converted, considering the direction of transmission. This way, powerful and widely branched networks can be installed in larger plants.

4.2.2. Protocol Stack

The field devices used with the FOUNDATION field-bus are capable of assuming process control functions. This option is based on distributed communication which ensures that

- each controlling field device can exchange data with other devices (e.g., reading measuring values, forwarding correction values),
- all field devices are served in time ('in time' meaning that the processing of the different control loops is not negatively influenced),
- two or more devices never access the bus simultaneously. To meet these requirements, the H1 bus of the FOUNDATION field-bus uses a central communication control system.

4.2.2.1. Link Active Scheduler – LAS

The Link Active Scheduler (LAS) controls and schedules the communication on the bus (see page 19: Communication control). It controls the bus activities using different commands which it broadcasts to the devices. Since the LAS also continuously polls unassigned device addresses, it is possible to connect devices during operation and to integrate them in the bus communication.

Devices that are capable of becoming the LAS, are called 'Link Master.' 'Basic devices' do not have the capability to become LAS. In a redundant system containing multiple Link Masters, one of the Link Masters will become the LAS if the active LAS fails (fail-operational design).

4.2.2.2. Communication Control

The communication services of the FF specification utilize scheduled and unscheduled data transmission. Time-critical tasks, such as the control of process variables, are exclusively performed by scheduled services, whereas parameterization and diagnostic functions are carried out using unscheduled communication services.

4.2.2.3. Scheduled Data Transmission

To solve communication tasks in time and without access conflicts, all time-critical tasks are based on a strict transmission schedule. This schedule is created by the system operator during the configuration of the FF system. The LAS periodically broadcasts a synchronization signal (TD: Time Distribution) on the field-bus so that all devices have exactly the same data link time. In scheduled transmission, the point of time and the sequence are exactly defined. This is why it is called a deterministic system.

Device	Type	Action	Offset
1	Sensor	Execution AI (1) Transmission AI (1) of data	0 20
2	Sensor	Execution AI (2) Transmission AI (2) of data	0 30
3	Control valve	Execution PID (3) Execution AO (3)	40 62

Figure 4.10. Schedule for processing function blocks.

Figure 4.11 presents the schedule for a system with two sensors and two control valves. The schedule determines when the devices process their function blocks (AI, A0, PID) and when it is time to transmit data. Each activity to be executed has been scheduled for a certain time. This time is defined by an offset value which reflects the delay referred to the start of the schedule. Based on this schedule, a transmission list is generated which defines when a specific field device is prompted to send its data. Upon receipt of the message, the respective device ('publisher') broadcasts the data in the buffer to all devices on the field-bus which are configured to receive the data ('subscriber'). This type of data transmission is therefore called the 'publisher-subscriber' method.

The LAS cyclically transmits the data according to the list for all data buffers in all devices. Each cyclical data transmission is explicitly activated by the LAS:

- If a device (e.g., device 1: Sensor) is prompted to publish its measured data, the LAS issues the Compel Data (CD) command to the device.
- Upon receipt of the CD, the device publishes the data in the buffer.
- The 'subscribers' of this message (e.g., device 3: Control valve) can read and evaluate this data accordingly.

Each field device receives a separate schedule. This enables system management to know exactly what task is to be executed when and when data must be received or sent.

Example: For the above mentioned schedule, the following time sequence of actions results as shown in the following figures.

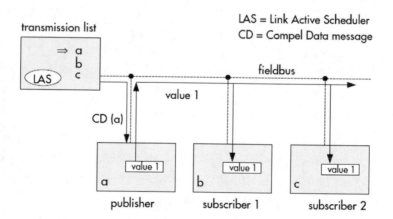

Figure 4.11. Scheduled data transmission according to the transmission list.

- at zero time, sensors (1) and (2) start their measurements;
- at time 20, the LAS prompts the sensor (1) to send its measuring data so that it can be read by the PID controller of the associated control valve (3);
- at time 30, the LAS prompts the sensor (2) to send its measuring data so that it can be read by the PID controller of the associated control valve (4);

- at time 40, both control valves are processing their PID function blocks;
- at time 57, control valve 4 starts its travel process;
- at time 62, control valve 3 starts its travel process;
- at 140 time increments, the same actions are repeated.

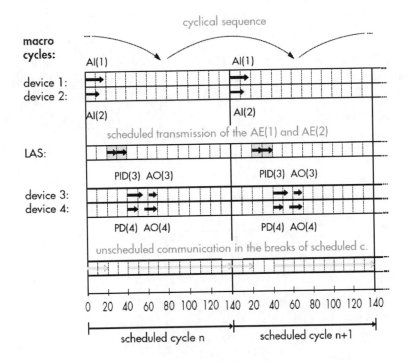

Figure 4.12. Scheduled transmission and unscheduled communication.

Each control loop accesses the bus only once for a short time. Therefore, the bus could be used for many more control loops as well as for other activities. This shows that the distributed control strategy reduces the number of data transmissions over the bus to a minimum.

4.2.2.4. Unscheduled Transmission

Device parameters and diagnostic data must be transmitted when needed, i.e., on request. The transmission of this data is not time-critical.

For such communication tasks, the FOUNDATION field-bus is equipped with the option of unscheduled data transmission.

Unscheduled data transmission is exclusively restricted to the breaks between scheduled transmission. The LAS granted permission to a device to use the field-bus for unscheduled communication tasks, if no scheduled data transmission is active.

Permission for a certain device to use the bus is granted by the LAS when it issues a pass token (PT command) to the device. The pass token is sent around to all devices entered in the 'Live List' (Figure 4.14) which is administrated by the LAS. Each device may use the bus as long as required until it either returns the token, or until the maximum granted time to use the token has elapsed.

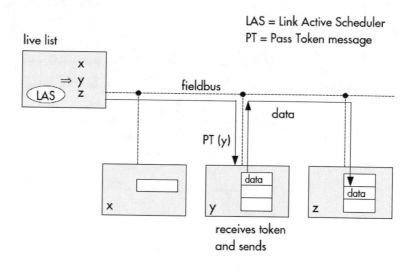

Figure 4.13. Unscheduled data transmission with token.

The Live List is continuously updated by the LAS. The LAS sends a special command, the Probe Node (PN), to the addresses not in the Live List, searching for newly added devices. If a device returns a Probe Response (PR) message, the LAS adds the device to the Live List where it receives the pass token for unscheduled communication according to the order submitted for transmission in the Live List. Devices which do not respond to the PT command or return the token after three successive tries are removed from the Live List.

Whenever a device is added or removed from the Live List, the LAS broadcasts these changes to all devices. This allows all Link Masters to maintain a current copy of the Live List so that they can become the LAS without the loss of information.

4.2.2.5. Communication Schedule

The LAS follows a strict schedule (Figure 4.14) to ensure that unscheduled communication using the token as well as the TD or PN commands do not interfere with the scheduled data transmission.

Before each operation, the LAS refers to the transmission list to check for any scheduled data transmissions. If this is the case, it waits (idle mode) for precisely the scheduled time and then sends a Compel Data (CD) message to activate the operation.

In case there are no scheduled transmissions and sufficient time is available for additional operations, the LAS sends one of the other commands. With PN it searches for new devices, or it broadcasts a TD message for all devices to have exactly the same data link time, or it uses the PT massage to pass the token for unscheduled communication. Following this, the sequence starts all over again with the above mentioned check of the transmission list entries.

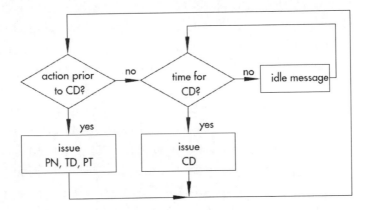

Figure 4.14. LAS communication control.

Client/Server	Report Distribution	Publisher/Subscriber
Operator communication	Event notification, alarms, trend reports	Data publication
Set point changes Mode and device data changes Upload/download Adjusting alarm values Access display views Remote diagnostics	Send process alarms to operator consoles Send trend reports to data historians	Send actual value of a transmitter to PID block and operator console

Figure 4.15. Virtual Communication Relationships of the FAS.

It is obvious that this cycle gives scheduled transmission the highest priority and that the scheduled times are strictly observed, regardless of other operations.

The Field-bus Access Sub-layer (FAS) and Field-bus Message Specification (FMS) layer form the interface between the data link layer and the user application. The services provided by FAS and FMS are invisible for the user. However, the performance and functionality of the communication system considerably depends on these services.

Field-Bus Access Sub-layer (FAS)

FAS services create Virtual Communication Relationships (VCR) which are used by the higher-level FMS layer to execute its tasks. VCRs describe different types of communication processes and enable the associated activities to be processed more quickly. FF communication utilizes three different VCR types as follows (Figure 4.15).

- The Publisher/Subscriber VCR Type is used to transmit the input and output data of function blocks. As described above, scheduled data transmission with the CD command is based on this type of VCR. However, the Publisher/Subscriber VCR is also available for unscheduled data transmission; for instance, if a subscriber requests measuring or positioning data from a device.

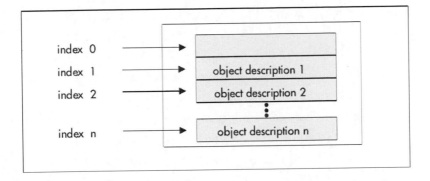

Figure 4.16. Access to the object dictionary using indices.

- The Client/Server VCR Type is used for unscheduled, user-initiated communication based on the PT command. If a device (client) requests data from another device, the requested device (server) only responds when it receives a PT from the LAS.

- The Client/Server communication is the basis for operator initiated requests, such as set point changes, tuning parameter access and change, diagnosis, device upload and download, etc.

- Report Distribution communication is used to send alarm or other event notifications to the operator consoles or similar devices. Data transmission is unscheduled when the device receives the PT command together with the report (trend or event notification). Field-bus devices that are configured to receive the data await and read this data.

Field-Bus Message Specification (FMS)

FMS provides the services for standardized communication. Data types that are communicated over the field-bus are assigned to certain communication services. For a uniform and clear assignment, object descriptions are used. Object descriptions contain definitions of all standard transmission message formats, but also include application specific data. For each type of object there are special, predefined communication services.

Object descriptions are collected together in a structure called an object dictionary.

- Index 0, called the object dictionary header, provides a description of the dictionary itself.
- Indices between 1 and 255 define standard data types that are used to build more complex object descriptions.
- The User Application object descriptions can start at any index above 255.

The FMS defines 'Virtual Field Devices' (VFD) which are used to make the object descriptions of a field device as well as the associated device data available over the entire network.

The VFDs and the object description can be used to remotely access all local field device data from any location by using the associated communication services.

User Application

An important criterion for a field-bus system to be accepted by the market is the interoperability of the devices. Interoperability is the capability of devices of different manufacturers to communicate with each other. In addition, it must be ensured that a component from one manufacturer can be substituted with that of another, also called interchangeability.

This requires an open protocol specification which defines uniform device functions and application interfaces. Other devices on the network and application programs can use these interfaces to access the functions and parameters of the field devices. The FOUNDATION field-bus makes these definitions based on blocks and device descriptions.

4.2.2.6. Block Model

The FOUNDATION field-bus assigns all functions and device data to three different types of blocks.

The assignment depends on the device's type of function. Depending on its functionality, it is described as follows:

- Resource block
- One or multiple function blocks
- Several transducer blocks, if required

The resource block describes characteristics of a field-bus device, such as the device name, manufacturer, serial number, hardware and firmware version, etc.

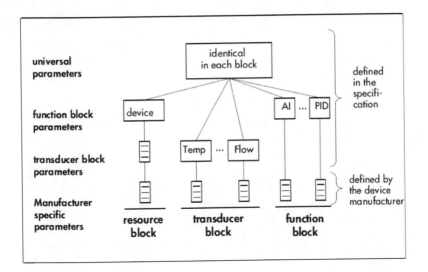

Figure 4.17. Division of field device data in resource, function and transducer block.

Function blocks describe a device's functions and define how these can be accessed. The transmission schedules of scheduled data transmission are based on these function blocks. Each block has a certain task including the associated inputs and outputs. Each device is equipped with one function block minimum.

The FF specification has defined sets of standard function blocks which can be used to describe all basic functions. These are listed below:

AI: analog input
AO: analog output
B: bias
CS: control selector
DI: discrete input
DO: discrete output
ML: manual loader
PD: proportional/derivative
PID: proportional/integral/derivative
RA: ratio

Transducer blocks expand the complexity and application possibilities of a device. Their data enables the input and/or output parameters of a function block to be influenced. They can be used to calibrate and reset measuring and positioning data, linear characteristics or convert physical units using additional process data.

Besides the three block types, the following additional objects are defined in the block model.

- So-called Link Objects define the links between different function blocks, internal to the field device as well as across the field-bus network.
- Alert Objects allow reporting of alarms and events on the field-bus.
- Trend Objects allow trending of function block data for access and analysis from higher-level systems.
- View Objects are predefined groupings of data and block parameter sets that can be used to view and display these quickly according to their tasks: process control, configuration, maintenance, and additional information.

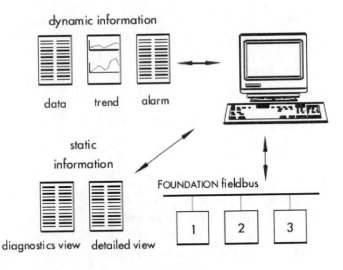

Figure 4.18. View objects group functions block data.

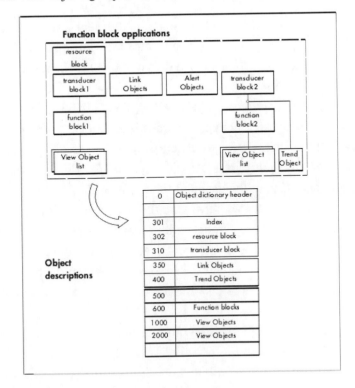

Figure 4.19. Assignment of block model data to an object dictionary.

The grouping of parameters in Trend and View Objects accelerates access to this data. If required, the operating program simply accesses the object which contains the predefined, desired data group.

The entire block model of a field device with two function blocks (e.g., AO and PID) consists of the elements depicted in Figure 4.19. The data structure of the blocks is accessed via the associated object dictionary.

4.2.2.7. Device Description

During start-up and maintenance as well as when performing diagnostic functions, an open communication system must ensure that higher-level control computers or the control system

- can access all field device data and
- have the proper controls to achieve this

The device descriptions (DDs) contain the necessary information to fulfill these requirements. They provide the information needed to understand the meaning of the device data and display them correctly at the operator console.

For the basic functions of the devices, the FOUNDATION field-bus uses different standard function and transducer blocks. For this purpose, predefined device descriptions (standard DDs) are available that can be obtained from the Field-bus FOUNDATION (FF). FF operating devices can interpret and display the data and functions of these standard blocks as well as providing the user with them via the operating interface.

If a device supplier implements additional functions and parameters in a device, he must define the contents, access and representation in an extended device description. Only when the device manufacturer supplies a device description tailored to his product, can it be operated and applied to the full extent.

The device description is written using the Device Description Language (DDL) to generate a text file. This file is then converted with the help of a 'Tokenizes' and distributed on diskette or via Internet download. If the manufacturer has registered his device with the associated device description with the FF, the DD can be also obtained there.

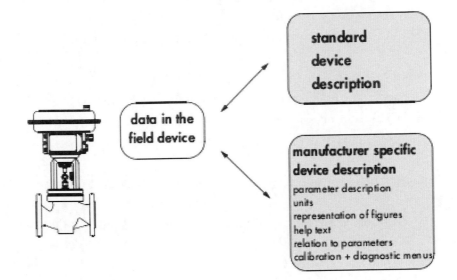

Figure 4.20. Device description extends the description of all objects in the virtual field device.

device description with DDL:

```
VARIABLE ProcessVariable
{  LABEL "MEASURED_VALUE"
   TYPE FLOAT
   {  DISPLAY_FORMAT "3.11";
      MAX_VALUE 110.0;
      MIN_VALUE  0.0; }
}
```

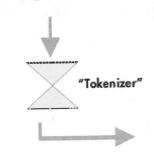

"Tokenizer"

converted device description

009	101
002	"MEASURED_VALUE"
001	010
061	"3.11"
021	006 220 000 000
020	000 000 000 000

Figure 4.21. Creating a device description.

4.2.2.8. System Management

The system management of each device has the following tasks:

- Synchronization of the relevant device activities in time, i.e., according to the predefined transmission schedule (see page 25).
- Cyclical processing of the transmission list (LAS only) within the predefined time schedule (page 19).

Further tasks performed by system management are the following

- Automatic assignment of the LAS function to another Link Master, if the active LAS fails.
- Application clock synchronizations.
- Automatic address assignment for new devices on the communications network.

The automatic assignment of device addresses enables a device to be as-signed a unique network address while the process is active. For the software controlled address assignment, special default addresses are reserved over which the new devices can be accessed. After the internal physical device tag as well as a unique and new bus address have been assigned to the new device, it is integrated in the communications network. The 'default address' is then available again for the assignment of more devices.

4.2.2.9. System Configuration

Scheduled communication as well as all field-bus devices must be parameterized before the first start-up. A configuration tool, e.g., the NI-FBUS configuration by National Instruments, is required for this purpose.

The device description of all used devices must be entered into the configuration device. The software must either be able to access the DDs in predefined libraries, or they must be loaded via external data carriers (e.g., via diskette).

The configuration software determines how and with which devices the measurement and control tasks of a plant are processed by interconnecting the function blocks of the field devices. This job can be easily performed by means of a graphical user interface. All that needs to be done is to connect the inputs and outputs of the corresponding block symbols.

The following figure shows an example of cascade control where the sensor output value is connected to a PID function block. This block can be implemented, for instance, in a control valve's positioning device. The positioning device output acts locally on the analog output of the final controlling element, so that no data has to be transmitted via the field-bus. The configuration shown corresponds to the control loop.

Besides connecting the function blocks, the network configuration device also configures the individual loop execution rate. Based on this data and the wiring diagram, the configuration tool generates the information needed to control the devices and the communication.

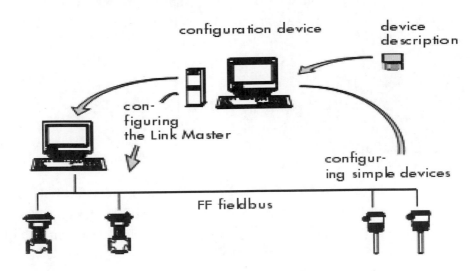

Figure 4.22. System configuration by means of a configuration device.

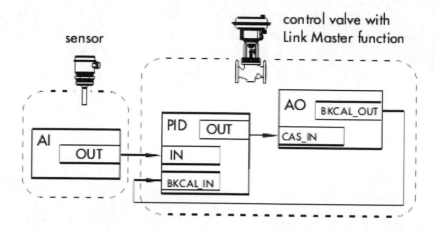

Figure 4.23. Connection of function blocks for cascade control (via software).

Finally, this data is entered into the individual field devices. During this process, the LAS is configured and all Link Masters receive the current transmission list for scheduled data transmission.

The system configuration is now complete so that the system management of the LAS and of the other field devices can take control over the system.

4.3. Performance Analysis for FF

4.3.1. Introduction

In FF, the Link Active Scheduler (LAS) node assigns the right of medium access to the local nodes in the medium. The LAS transmits Pass Token (PT) and Compel Data (CD) frames to the local nodes for token passing and scheduling services, respectively. In the token-passing service, the LAS transmits a PT frame to the local nodes in the medium according to a predefined order which is called the Token Circulation List (TCL). The token-passing service constitutes a priority mechanism. Each node can transmit messages whose priorities are greater than or equal to the priority of the PT frame. When the LAS completes one cycle of transmitting the PT frame to all of the nodes in the TCL, it measures the Actual Token Rotation Time (ATRT). The LAS compares the ATRT with the Target Token Rotation Time (TTRT), a network parameter maintained by the LAS. When a new token begins circulation, the LAS raises (or lowers) the priority of the PT frame as required if the ATRT is larger (or smaller) than the TTRT.

The token-passing service of the FF DLL provides a priority mechanism for the transmission of urgent, normal, and time- available data to offer more opportunities for transmitting high- priority messages. Some effort has been directed toward developing analytical models for token-passing systems and evaluating their performance.

4.3.2. Analytical Model

The priorities of time-critical and time-available data are assigned as 0 and 1, respectively. Time-critical and time-available data arrive according to an independent Poisson process. The length of the transmission times of time-critical and time-available data is fixed, and the traffic load of the same priority class is identical at all nodes. The FF is assumed to operate on a single-service discipline, i.e., each transmitter queue transmits one dataset at a time. In the token-passing system, the ATRT is dependent upon the previous ATRTs. It is very difficult to express the exact mathematical relationship of the ATRTs in a single-service token-passing system. It is assumed that the ATRT is an independent and identically distributed (iid.) random variable, and developed approximate analytical models. Herein, the ATRT is also assumed to be i.i.d. The notation used in this paper is as follows:

N_i : the number of priority i queues
L_i : the transmission time of priority i data
λ_i, : the arrival rate of priority i data
R : the token overhead time (processing time and propagation delay) during one complete circulation of a token

p_{ij} : the probability that priority **i** data is served when the priority of the token is j

$T(t)$: the probability density function (pdf) of the ATRT

$\overline{T}$: the expected value of the ATRT

$TR(t)$: the distribution function of the ATRT

P_i : the probability that the priority of the token is i

$T_i (t)$: the pdf of the ATRT when the priority of the token is i.

μ_i: the probability that the ATRT is less than the TTRT when the priority of the token is i

$r(t)$: the residual time of ATRT

$q_i(t)$: the pdf of the delay of the *i-th* time-critical data in the transmitter queue

d : average delay of time-critical data

D_a : the allowable average delay of time-critical data

D_m : the maximum allowable delay of time-critical data

p_f: the probability that the delay of time-critical data

p_a : the design constraint which is defined as the probability that time-critical data fails to be delivered within *Dm*

Schematic diagram of the analytical model for the token-passing and scheduled services is shown as Figure 4.24.

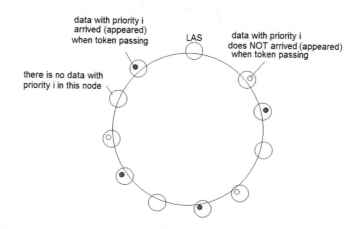

Figure 4.24. Schematic diagram of the analytical model for the token-passing and scheduled services.

Here in this Schematic diagram, the circle inside the node means the data with priority i. In this single service mode, there is only one data with priority i in any node. It is possible that the data with priority i appeared or does not appeared when token passing the node it belongs to. The circle filled with red color inside the node meant data appeared (arrived) when token was passing the node it belongs to. The empty circle inside the node means data did NOT appear (arrive) when token was passing the node it belongs to.

Actually, the location of data in nodes has nothing to do with the analytical results. The data can locate in any node in the network, i.e., maybe 3 data in node 1, 2data in node 2, and x data in node y and etc. So here we can ignore network nodes and just consider the data.

The amount of data with priority i is specified as N_i. Not necessarily every node has a data with priority i. Maybe only some nodes have data with priority i, just as shown in Figure 4.24.

Therefore, all possibilities of the data with priority i arrived when token passing were listed in the following table, which can lead to different ATRT value.

How many data with priority 0 arrived when token passing	How many Possibilities of this condition	Time consumed to serve these data	Probability under this condition
0	$\binom{N_0}{0}$	R	$(1-\rho_{00})^{N0}$
1	$\binom{N_0}{1}$	$R+L_0$	$\rho_{00}(1-\rho_{00})^{N_0-1}$
2	$\binom{N_0}{2}$	$R+2L_0$	$\rho_{00}^2(1-\rho_{00})^{N_0-2}$
...	...	...	...
i	$\binom{N_0}{i}$	$R+iL_0$	$\rho_{00}^i(1-\rho_{00})^{N_0-i}$
...	...	...	...
N_0	$\binom{N_0}{N_0}$	$R+N_0L_0$	$\rho_{00}^{N_0}$

If we add all the items inside the table we can get the following equation:

$$T_0(t) = \sum_{i=0}^{N_0} \binom{N_0}{i} \rho_{00}^i (1 - \rho_{00})^{N_0-i} \delta(t - (R + iL_0))$$

(1)

Also, we can explain the equation as follows.
The equation can be marked as equation (2).

$$T_0(t) = \sum_{i=0}^{N_0} \binom{N_0}{i} \underbrace{\rho_{00}^i (1 - \rho_{00})^{N_0-i}}_{<2>} \underbrace{\delta(t - (R + iL_0))}_{<1>}$$

<2>   <1>

(2)

In equation (2), all parts inside the dotted-line rectangle were summed. The content inside the dotted-line rectangle includes two parts: one part is the content underlined and numbered as <1>, which means the values in x-axis in a PDF curve (note: values in x-axis in a PDF curve meant various results of an event). The other part is the content underlined and numbered as <2> which means the values in y-axis in a PDF curve (i.e., the value of PDF, it was a probability value).

For example, if i = 1 then that means only 1 data arrived (appeared) when token passing and the only 1 data was transmitted, then the probability can be expressed as:

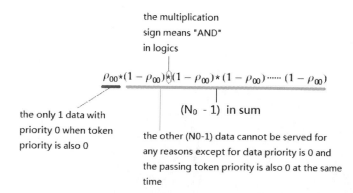

Therefore, the PDF can be expressed as:

$$P_{00}(1 - P_{00})^{N_o-1} \delta(t - (R + L_0))$$

The amount of the condition like above is $\binom{N_0}{1}$, therefore it can be expressed as:

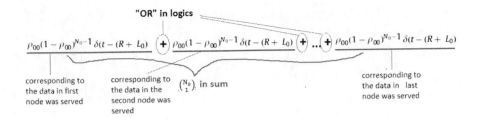

Therefore, it can be further expressed as:

$$\binom{N_0}{1} P_{00}(1 - P_{00})^{N_o-1} \delta(t - (R + L_0))$$

Then if i = 2 (means 2 data in with priority 0 2 nodes were served when token is passing), the corresponding PDF can be expressed as

$$\binom{N_0}{2} P_{00}^2 (1 - P_{00})^{N_o-2} \delta(t - (R + 2L_0))$$

The rest can be done in the same manner.
Therefore, the whole PDF can be summarized as:

$$T_0(t) = \sum_{i=0}^{N_0} \binom{N_0}{i} P_{00}^i (1 - P_{00})^{N_o-i} \delta(t - (R + iL_0))$$

Here, $T_0(t)$ means the pdf of the ATRT when the priority of the token is 0.

In a word, the essence of the PDF is the collocation of the following 3 elements:

- data has some priority;
- token has some priority
- data appeared when token is passing;

different collocation of the 3 elements lead to different elements in $T_0(t)$ expression. The $T_0(t)$ expression can cover all the possibilities in real data occurrence environment.

We can simplify it further by just understanding the process as selecting $0 \sim N_0$ data to be served from the data set.

When the priority of the token is 1, both priority 0 and 1 data are serviced. Thus, $T_1(t)$ is expressed as:

$$T_1(t) = \sum_{i=0}^{N_0} \sum_{j=0}^{N_1} \binom{N_0}{i} \rho_{10}^i (1-\rho_{10})^{N_0-i} \binom{N_1}{j} \rho_{11}^j (1-\rho_{11})^{N_1-j} \, \delta(t-(R+iL_0+jL_1))$$

The expression can be partly expanded as:

$$\binom{N_0}{i} \rho_{10}^i (1-\rho_{10})^{N_0-i} \binom{N_1}{j} \rho_{11}^j (1-\rho_{11})^{N_1-j} \, \delta(t-(R+iL_0+jL_1))$$

Then it was expanded into the following:

$$\left(\rho_{00}(1-\rho_{00})^{N_0-1} \underset{\text{"OR"}}{+} \rho_{00}(1-\rho_{00})^{N_0-1} \cdots \right) \underset{\text{"AND"}}{*} \left(\rho_{11}(1-\rho_{11})^{N_1-1} \underset{\text{"OR"}}{+} \rho_{11}(1-\rho_{11})^{N_1-1} \cdots \right)$$

It is equivalent to:

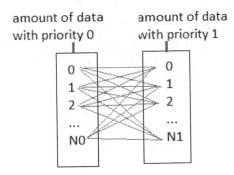

Figure 4.25. Complete collocation between the amount of data with priority 0 and that with priority 1.

It is a complete collocation between the amount of data with priority 0 and that with priority 1.

The following figure is a snapshot of one of all the conditions:

The $T_1(t)$ expression can cover all the conditions in real data occurrence environment.

The data in the priority 0 (time-critical) queue can be transmitted when the priority of the token is 0 or 1. Since the data arrival time is Poisson-distributed, ρ_{00} and ρ_{01} can be expressed as

$$\rho_{00} = \rho_{01} = \lambda_0(P_0\bar{T}_0 + P_1\bar{T}_1).$$

Here λ_0 represented the arrival rate of data with 0-priority. P_0 and P_1 represented the probability that the priority of the token is 0 and 1. $\bar{T}0$ and $\bar{T}1$ represent the expected value of the ATRT when the priority of the token is 0 and 1.

The dimension of $\bar{T}0$ or $\bar{T}1$ is time "second". λ_0 means the probability of arrival (appearance) of data with priority 0 in some time interval. So $\lambda_0 * \bar{T}0$ means probability of arrival (appearance) of data with priority 0 during ATRT when token priority is 0. $\lambda_0 * \bar{T}0$ also means that the data with priority 0 is kept alive (does not disappear) during $\bar{T}0$.

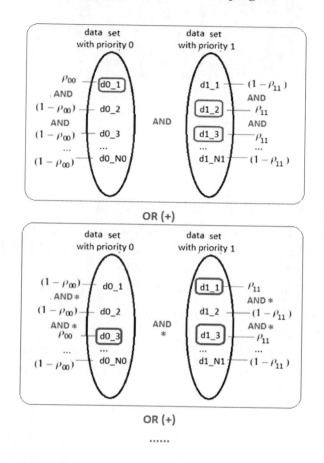

Figure 4.26. Snapshot of one of all the conditions.

The priority 1 (time-available) data can be transmitted only when the priority of the token is 1.

As for the calculation of ρ_{11}, researchers gave different solution. S. H. Hong thought ρ_{11} has nothing to do with anything about token with priority 0. So he gave the following equation.

$$\rho_{11} = \lambda_1 \overline{T_1}$$

This equation means that ρ_{11} has something to do with two things: 1) arrival (appearance) of data with priority 1 (represented by λ_1) and 2) time duration is that when the priority of token is 1 (represented by $\overline{T}1$).

If the priority of the current token is 0, the data must wait until the token priority is 1. Therefore, Y. H. Lee thought ρ_{11} related to not only token with priority 1, but also token with priority 0. So he gave the following equation.

$$\rho_{11} = \lambda_1 \sum_{n=0}^{\infty} P_0^n P_1 (n\overline{T}_0 + \overline{T}_1) = \lambda_1 \left(\frac{P_0 \overline{T}_0}{1 - P_0} + \overline{T}_1 \right).$$

However, we thought the equation should be revised as the following:

$$\rho_{11} = \lambda_1 \left(\sum_{n=0}^{\infty} P_0^n P_1 \, n\overline{T}_0 + \overline{T}_1 \right)$$

This equation included two parts:

$$\lambda_1 \sum_{n=0}^{\infty} P_0^n P_1 \, n\overline{T}_0 \qquad ② \quad \lambda_1 \overline{T}_1$$

The part ② is same with that proposed by S. H. Hong. The λ_1 in part ① means data with priority 1 kept alive during n (the n in part ①) circulations of token with priority 0 and last circulation of token when its priority became 0.

where

$$\overline{T}_0 = \int_0^{\infty} t \cdot T_0(t) \, dt \,, \quad \overline{T}_1 = \int_0^{\infty} t \cdot T_1(t) \, dt$$

The priority of the token is determined by comparing the TTRT and the ATRT. When the priority of the token is 0 and ATRT $>=$ TTRT, the priority remains at 0. However, if ATRT<TTRT, the priority of the token changes to 1.

4.3.3. Cyclic Communication and Scheduling of FF

The system manager of an FF network needs to specify two different types of scheduling: 1) FB and 2) LAS. FB scheduling is executed in the SMK of the user layer in each application process, whereas LAS scheduling is executed in the DLL of the LAS node that grants permission to a field device to use the field-bus medium.

4.3.3.1. Performance in LAS Scheduling

FB scheduling in the SMK supports the cooperative execution of FBs located on the same link. A message generated by an FB must be delivered before the next scheduled message is generated by that same FB. The execution of an FB is governed by the SMK of each IFD connected to the link, whereas the data transfer of messages generated by the FB is governed by the LAS node on the link. Thus, the scheduling of an FB, performed in the SMK of each IFD, must be synchronized with the data transfer that is separately scheduled and controlled by the LAS. One repetition of either schedule is called a "macro-cycle." Data transfers and FB execution times are synchronized by specifying their time offsets from the start of their respective macro-cycles. The appropriate portions of the FB schedule and its macro-cycle duration must be downloaded to the IFDs that are actually executing the FBs. The timing of the data transfers is defined in the LAS schedule, and this must be downloaded to the LAS. The LAS schedule contains a list of starting times and cycle periods for the data transfer for each FB. At precisely the scheduled time, the LAS sends a CD message to a specific IFD, specifying one of its data buffers. This IFD immediately broadcasts a message that contains the specified buffer data to all the IFDs on the field-bus. It is left up to the network designer to prepare an LAS schedule according to the characteristics of the FBs in the IFDs. This section presents our method of constructing the LAS schedule list based on the requirements for real-time communications of application systems, i.e., the scheduling of FBs.

4.3.3.2. Scheduling Methods

The LAS schedule list is constructed using the bandwidth allocation algorithm based on time division multiple access. The field-bus bandwidth is divided into time-division multiplexing intervals $T1$, each of which is further divided into scheduled (τs) and unscheduled (τt) intervals. During a scheduled interval, only one scheduled message packet is transmitted on the CD schedule. The length of τs is the time required to transmit one packet of periodic data (Ls) plus the LAS transaction time to execute a scheduled service (σ). On the other hand, unscheduled messages are transmitted during an unscheduled interval through the PT service. To reduce the delay of an unscheduled message that is transmitted between scheduled intervals, our bandwidth-allocation scheme uniformly distributes scheduled intervals across each $T1$.

Ti and φi are ordered according to increasing values (i.e., $Ti \leq Ti+1$, $\varphi i \leq \varphi i+1$). $T1$ and TNs are the minimum and maximum message-generation periods among Ns nodes, respectively. The basic concept of using the band width allocation scheme for our scheduling service is to schedule the message-generation time such that the number of scheduled messages generated during $T1$ does not exceed γ. That is, Ns buffers in the medium dynamically share the γ ($\gamma \leq Ns$) windows in $T1$ such that the number of scheduled messages transmitted during $T1$ does not exceed γ. Our scheduling method determines both ti ($i = 1$ to Ns) and Ti ($i = 1$ to Ns) of the scheduled messages for FB scheduling. ti and Ti are mapped to the schedule starting time si and the schedule period Si in the LAS scheduling list maintained by the LAS.

From the bandwidth-allocation scheme proposed by S. H. Hong, Ti is determined as follows:

$$T_1 = \phi_1$$

$$T_i = k_i T_1, \qquad k_i = 2^{\left\lfloor \log_2 \frac{\phi_i}{T_1} \right\rfloor}, \qquad \forall i = 2 \text{ to } N_s$$

When Ti is determined by (1) and (2), it does not exceed the predetermined maximum allowable delay φi. In our scheduling method, the values for Ti (i = 1 to Ns) are selected to be integer multiples of each other

$$\text{Rem}\left[\frac{T_j}{T_i}\right] = 0, \qquad \forall i, j \ (j \geq i)$$

Scheduling method repeats at intervals of TNs. The number of windows γ in $T1$ is determined by

$$\gamma = \lceil \alpha_K \rceil, \qquad \alpha_K = \sum_{i=1}^{N_s} \frac{T_1}{T_i}$$

where α_K is the average number of scheduled messages generated during $T1$.

The schedule of data traffic allows for communication between a given set of intelligent field devices (IFD) nodes. The schedule can be divided into two parts: 1) an FB schedule that determines when a block executes and 2) an LAS schedule that determines when data parameters are published over the field-bus. The FB schedule is downloaded to the round card IFD nodes that contain the block, and the LAS schedule is downloaded to the LAS station. Using the schedule configuration tool provided with the starter kit, the system manager of the FF network determines the execution order and timing of the schedule.

4.4. ANALYSIS AND PRACTICE ON PERFORMANCE IMPROVEMENT IN FF-BASED CONTROL SYSTEM

4.4.1. Nomenclature

ASIC	Application Specific Integrated Circuit
DCS	Distributed Control System
ERTEC	Enhanced Real-Time Ethernet Controller

EWS   Engineer Workstation
FB   Function Block
FF   Foundation Field-Bus
FFCS   Foundation Field-Bus Control System
HMI   Human Machine Interface
LAS   Link Activities Scheduler
MBCS   ModBus Control System
NCS   Networked Control System
NNE   Neural Network Estimator
OPC   OLE for Process Control
OWS   Operator Workstation
PLC   Programmable Logic Controller
UDFB-CM   User Defined Function Block for Control Moves
UDFB-DA   User Defined Function Block for Data Acquisition

4.4.2. Introduction

The development of communication network and technology has brought many remarkable changes to traditional control fashion in modern industries. IEC802.3 Ethernet and field based intelligent controls, which are combining communication and control technology closely, are playing an active role in modern industrial automation with greatly improved functions and performance but much reduced cost, offering more flexible and practical approaches to solve problems whose solutions were only be considered in theoretical ways in cybernetics before.

Field-bus is the foundation of field-based intelligent control with its highly reliable, deterministic real-time performance in communication between field instruments such as transmitters and actuators. Self-diagnosis, easy maintenance and reduction in cost and commissioning time are also its remarkable advantages. Among the field-bus technologies, Foundation Field-bus (FF) is one of the most popular field-bus widely used in industrial process control Two prominent features of FF lie in its Function Block (FB) scheme and cyclic scheduling strategy, enabling closed loop control and self-diagnosis be realized within field level and laying the foundation of entirely distributed control based on field. As for IEC802.3 Ethernet, high speed in communication, good compatibility and large covered area are its main advantages. It is a quite suitable communication fashion for higher levels in industrial automation architecture. Networked control system (NCS) is mainly based on it, in which closed loop controls are implemented in upper-level controller while data acquisition and device actuation are distributed in field. Communicates between the two levels are mainly over IEC802.3 Ethernet. However, non-determinism and time delay in communication transmission often cause degradation in control effects. Many researchers have explored and investigated improvement methods in perspective of control science, such as studies on maximum allowable transmission for control and various controller' parameters tuning algorithms. Joa˜o P. Hespanha etc. reviewed several recent results on estimation, analysis, and controller synthesis for NCSs. The results surveyed address channel limitations in terms of packet-rates, sampling, network delay, and packet dropouts. The above mentioned work are mainly focused on theoretical analysis and computation in terms of system stability and control algorithms. Issues of their practical effect and feasibility are not mentioned or addressed. In practical and theory-practice combined design, A. Fadaei presented a practical network platform to design and implement a networked-based cascade control system linking a Foundation Field-bus (FF) controller and a Siemens programmable logic controller through Industrial Ethernet to a laboratory pilot plant. The Smar OPC tag browser and Siemens WinCC OPC Channel provide the communicating interface between the two controllers. Fadaei also investigated the performance of a PID controller implemented in two different possible configurations of FF function block (FB) and networked control system (NCS) via a remote Siemens PLC. In the FB control system implementation, the desired set-point was provided by the Siemens Human-Machine Interface (HMI) software via an Ethernet Modbus link. The cascade loop was realized in remote Siemens PLC station and the final element set-point was sent to the FF station via Ethernet bus in the NCS implementation. Although Fadaei pointed out the causes of transmission delay in Field-bus and NCS approaches and presented experimental results of the delay effects on both approaches, the solution he proposed was a new fuzzy PID control strategy. That is to say, the ultimate means he proposed was also by improving control algorithms. Q. Li investigated delays associated with the use of FF H1 networks within control loops. A distributed control system (DCS) and a FF H1 workstation are used to implement test loops with the control-in-the-field architecture. Analytical and experimental evaluations are performed with a test loop using hardwired analog channels as a benchmark. Li identified three segments of FF-H1-network-induced delays and developed their analytical models. He provided suggestions to potentially reduce the delays in aspect of field-bus-specific properties such as macro-cycle design, setting of signal acquisition interval and elimination of idle time between some specific execution of FB and the communication. Y. Pang's research pointed out that the execution time of FBs and the margin time are dominant over communication delays in FF field-bus, and optimizing configuration by reducing the number of external links can contribute to increasing the control frequency. The work above mentioned demonstrated that appropriately matching network parameters can improve control performance, which also showed the variety and diversity of means to achieve that goal.

Actually, NCS is a complex composition including many different elements such as network hardware selection and deployment, software configuration, parameters setting etc.. Bottleneck in any part of the system can cause degradation of control performance. That can cancel the improvement by control algorithms. Therefore, not only control algorithm but also other performance-affecting elements of a NCS must be fully considered when a practically feasibly network based measurement and control system is designed and implemented.

In this chapter, we address the issue of improving control performance of a network based control system in a quite different perspective from control algorithms. Some important performance-affecting elements such as design of network architecture, configuration and delay compensation are investigated and some methods to improve control performance based on those are presented. Two different designs and implementations for a traditional cascade control system based on FF and IEC802.3 Ethernet respectively were presented. Differences between them were analyzed. Advantages of system implementation by field-bus were presented. Degradation in control effect of the networked control system caused by network transmission time delay was investigated. Improvement measures for control performance by reducing or compensating network transmission time delay in terms of network configuration and control algorithms were proposed. Experimental and on-site practice shows the proposed methodologies are effective in preventing performance degeneration in networked control system Based on FF Field-bus and IEC802.3 Ethernet. All the methods proposed here are proved practically feasible.

This chapter is organized as follows: In section 2, we introduced the general principles of control system implementation in FF field-bus and IEC802.3 Ethernet fashion respectively. In section 3, we present two experimental control systems based on FF and IEC802.3 Ethernet. Detailed analysis on the performance degeneration caused by transmission delay and methodologies for improvement are presented in section 4. Some conclusions, which are useful in design of networked control system, are given in the last part of the chapter.

4.4.3. Principles for Control System Implementation

4.4.3.1 Implementation in FF Fashion

When field-bus-based control fashion is applied, the whole system can be divided into 2 levels basically, which are field level and upper supervisory level. Various intelligent instruments, such as transmitters, valve positioning devices and actuators, deployed and interconnected with each other by FF in field level. Industrial PCs can serve as the upper supervisory level to monitor operation in field, display data from field and download some modified parameters such as setting point to field level. Some specific configuration software for programming control strategies implemented with FF instruments in field locally is installed in the supervisory computer called Engineer Workstation (EWS) while Human Machine Interface (HMI) software for users' supervision and control are installed in computer called Operator Workstation (OWS). A gateway, connected with supervisory level by Ethernet while with field level by field-bus, is used to connect the field and supervisory levels.

Function Block (FB) scheme is the foundation of control implementation. Function Blocks (FBs) are User Layer elements that encapsulate basic automation functions and consequently make the configuration of a distributed industrial application modular and simplified [14]. Distributed among the transmitters, the FBs have their inputs and outputs linked to other blocks in order to perform distributed closed control loop schemes. The Foundation Field-bus standardized a set of basic function blocks [15], a complementary set of eleven advanced control blocks [16], and a special flexible function block intended to be fully configurable, i.e., internal logic and parameter, by the user [17]. The standard and advanced block sets provide mathematical and engineering calculations necessary to configure typical industrial control loop strategies, while the flexible function block can be applied to custom or advanced controls or to complex interlocking logics based on ladder nets. FBs are distributed among the field intelligent instruments. Users can construct complete control strategies by selecting some specific FBs, setting parameters and connecting them through configuration platform provided in supervisory level.

When function blocks from different transmitters or actuators are linked together, a remote link is configured and mapped to a cyclic message. Considering that all cyclic messages should be released in a predetermined instant defined on a schedule table, and that they carry data generated by the FBs, it is adequate to synchronize the execution of the FB set on the system with the referred cyclic transmissions schedule table [18]. All field devices can be scheduled to execute the function blocks in a pre-determined sequence and publish the results at a pre-determined time. Function blocks, located in the other field devices, may use the results too. These function blocks will be executed only after the required inputs are scheduled to be available. To address the case, where a device providing an input becomes unavailable, the user can configure the number of consecutive communications that may be lost before the input status of the receiving device is set to the bad state and consequently the actual mode of the block using this input switches to manual [19, 20].

A typical implementation of control system with FF field-bus is shown in Figure 4.27.

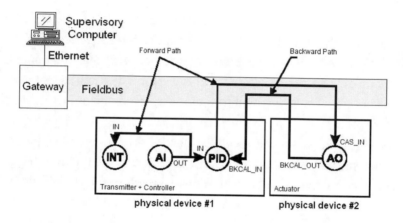

Figure 4.27. A typical control system implementation with field-bus.

4.4.3.2. Implemented in Ethernet Fashion

When IEC802.3 Ethernet based networked control fashion is applied, the whole system can be divided into 3 levels, which are field level, control level and supervisory level. Some intelligent field instruments or remote digital I/O modules serves as field level, only providing services such as data acquisition and control move actuation. Typically, a Programmable Logic Controller (PLC) executing communication with field level and closed loop control within serves as control level. The upper supervisory level is the same with field-bus based control fashion. A gateway, connected with control level by Ethernet while field level by field-bus, is used to connect the field and control levels. Supervisory level and control level are connected by IEC802.3 Ethernet by means of a hub. Various control strategies, which are configured in EWS by users, can be implemented within PLC.

The procedures of implementing control system with this fashion are approximately the same with that of field-bus based control system, which includes hardware and software configuration.

4.4.4. Experimental Control Systems

4.4.4.1. Architecture and Configuration of Experimental Control System

The control strategy of the pilot control system is chosen as typical cascade control. The testbed is as shown in Figure 4.28 involving 2 cascaded tanks. The first tank serves as the controlled plant, which is commonly used to represent many practical industrial processes. The water level in the first tank can be controlled. The water flow into both tanks can be controlled as well with water flow into the first tank as the control action while that into the second tank simulating disturbance. To keep water level in the tank stable is the main control objective of the cascade control system. In this system, an outer water-level loop is applied with a Level Detector LD302 and a primary PID control to keep level stable. An inner flow loop is applied with a flow transmitter, also in form of LD302, and a secondary PID control to keep the feeding water flow stable. The block diagram of the cascade control is shown in Figure 4.29.

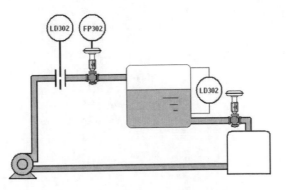

Figure 4.28. Test bed for a typical cascade control system.

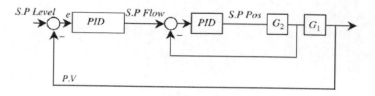

Figure 4.29. Block diagram for the cascade control system.

Figure 4.30. Pilot experimental plant.

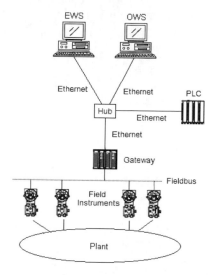

Figure 4.31. The proposed hybrid control system architecture involving FF subsystem and IEC802.3 Ethernet based networked subsystem.

The practical experimental plant is developed according to the test bed and employed for system analysis, as shown in Figure 4.30.

Based on the principles of control system implementation described above, here we presented a hybrid control system architecture involving FF subsystem and IEC802.3 Ethernet based networked subsystem at the same time, which provides a desired experimental plant for test and analysis of them. The system is shown as Figure 4.31.

FF subsystem was composed of upper supervisory computers, gateway module DFI302 from Smar Co. Ltd. and field intelligent instruments which were connected with each other by FF H1 field-bus. Intelligent field instruments from Smar Co. Ltd. including flow/level transmitter LD302 and field-bus-to-pressure converter FP302 were applied to the plant mentioned above. IEC802.3 Ethernet based networked subsystem was composed of supervisory computers, Siemens S7-300 series PLC, gateway, field intelligent instruments and FF H1 field-bus. The gateway served as a common intersection in topology by connecting FF intelligent instruments with supervisory computers and PLC. IEC802.3 Ethernet was used as a common transmission network as well shared by PLC and FF Control System (FFCS). Upper supervisory computers include EWS and OWS. FFCS control strategy configuration software Syscon from Smar Co. Ltd. and Siemens PLC configuration and programming software STEP7 are installed in EWS. HMI software such as WinCC or other brands is installed in OWS for process supervision. An Ethernet hub was applied in connecting supervisory computers, PLC and gateway module.

4.4.4.2. Implementation of Experimental Control System with FF Field-Bus

The procedures of implementing FFCS including hardware and software configuration have been summarized before. Two level transmitters LD302 detecting water level and flow respectively and a field-bus-to-pressure converter FP302, which converts field-bus digital signal to pneumatic pressure to actuate the valve, are used as the fundamental elements. Fields instruments are connected to the upper-level supervisory

OWS and EWS by means of field-bus-to-Ethernet gateway DFI302, as presented above.

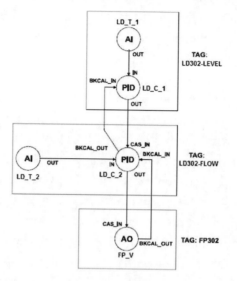

Figure 4.32. Function blocks configuration scheme I for cascade PID control.

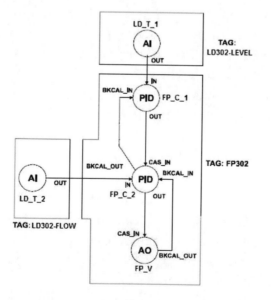

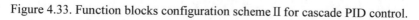

Figure 4.33. Function blocks configuration scheme II for cascade PID control.

All control strategies are implemented and executed entirely within field instruments by means of Function Block. The principal part of the implementation lies in the control strategy implementation with Function Block by configuration software Syscon installed in EWS. Two different kinds of function block scheme can be configured to fulfill the cascade PID control by field-bus intelligent instruments, as shown in Figure 4.32 and Figure 4.33.

From the figures, it can be seen that the all connections and parameters of function blocks involved keep the same while the distribution of the function blocks within the field instruments are quite different. In both figures, rectangular blocks represent different instruments with some function blocks included. No communication via field-bus network takes place when connected function blocks are within the same instruments, namely no network induced transmission delay happens for data exchange between these function blocks, and vice versa. For the former case, only some processor time, which is quite small and often ignored in calculation, is taken to achieve the data exchange within the host instruments. Therefore, configuration scheme shown in Figure 4.33, which make field-bus network transmission time less and consequently the control cycle shorter, are more efficient in control and preferable.

Some parameters in control such as proportion and integral values in PID, and setting point value can be obtained and modified in EWS or OWS. Various process parameters can be monitored in form of graphic or text display by HMI set up in OWS. Field-bus OPC server provided by the field-bus system manufacturer is essential in the implementation of data communication between the field and upper supervisory level by communicating with DFI302. OPC server is installed in EWS, and OWS at the same time to provide support for communication with OPC client, which is used by supervisory softwares to exchange data with OPC server in form of reading and writing. Data transmission process between field and supervisory levels are shown in Figure 4.34.

After the field-bus system is correctly configured and the validity of the connections between OWS/EWS, DFI302 and field instruments are confirmed, the level set-point is set to 50% to check the process response in this control fashion. The obtained response result is shown in Figure 4.35.

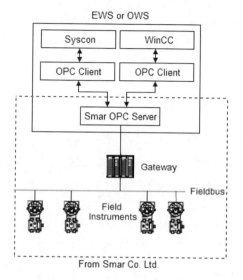

Figure 4.34. Data transmission process between field and supervisory levels.

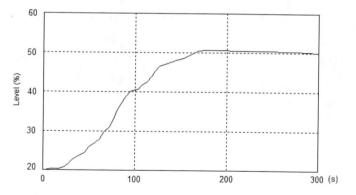

Figure 4.35. Step response for level set-point disturbance with field-bus control subsystem and function blocks configuration.

4.4.4.3. Implementation of Experimental Control System with IEC802.3 Ethernet

In the Ethernet based control system, it is the Siemens S7-300 series PLC that plays the main role with all control strategies implemented and executed within it. Field-bus intelligent instruments only serve as remote digital I/O modules for data acquisition and control move actuation. The communication between the PLC and DFI302 is via Ethernet Modbus link.

In this fashion, cascade PID control strategy is implemented in the Siemens S7-300 series PLC. Field data acquisitions, such as water level and flow here, are executed by field intelligent instruments in field-bus subsystem and control moves generated by PLC are sent back to FP302 for actuation. The essentially important part in this control fashion implementation is to achieve data exchange between PLC and field intelligent instruments serving as I/O modules. Some researchers proposed a method by exporting WinCC OPC tags into S7 protocol suite to provide I/O data interface for PLC control program. Here we propose a new solution based on Function Block MBCS provided by DFI302, which combines field-bus subsystem and PLC world closely in a simpler but more flexible way.

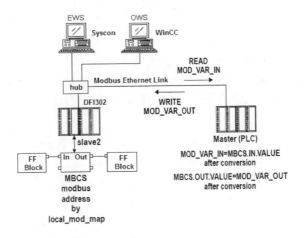

Figure 4.36. Architecture of the control system involving PLC, DFI302 and MBCS function block.

ModBus Control System (MBCS) block [21] generates a communication strategy between a Modbus master and a Field-bus Foundation slave. In this case, the slave is the Smar's linking device DFI302 that has slave behavior for the Modbus network. It allows Modbus variables to be associated with Field-bus variables and data between these two "worlds" to be exchanged through DFI302. The architecture of the control system involving PLC, DFI302 and MBCS function block is shown in Figure 4.36. Control strategies are located in PLC. Acquired field data by LD302 is sent to PLC and control move is sent by PLC to FP302 for actuation with function block MBCS as the data exchange interface.

The schematic of function block MBCS is shown in Figure 4.37.

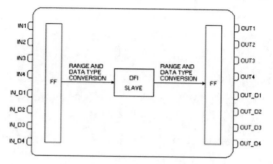

Figure 4.37. Schematic of function block MBCS in DFI302.

Some extra strategies need to be configured for Field-bus subsystem with Syscon in order to exchange I/O data with PLC by means of function block MBCS and Modbus Ethernet. The control strategies configuration for Field-bus subsystem based on MBCS provided by DFI302 is shown in Figure 4.38.

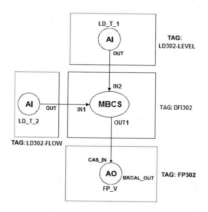

Figure 4.38. Control strategies configuration for Field-bus subsystem based on MBCS provided by DFI302.

The level set-point is set to 50% to check the process response under this control fashion. The obtained response result is shown in Figure 4.39.

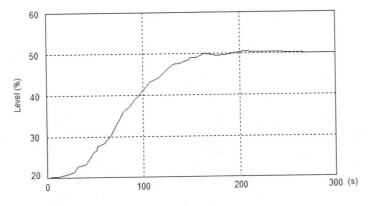

Figure 4.39. Step responses for level set-point disturbance with control system involving PLC, DFI302 and MBCS function block.

4.4.5. Analysis and Improvements

4.4.5.1. Analysis of Effects on Control by Time Delay in Transmission

As a matter of fact, data transmission time delay consists of two different parts: ① transmission time delay caused by microprocessors' data processing within computers or field instruments ② transmission time delay caused by data transmission over communication links. Generally, the former is often ignored for that the microprocessors' processing speed is much faster than ever before and much less when compared with the latter. Therefore, transmission time delay caused by communication links is the principal element.

4.4.5.1.1. FF Field-Bus Based Control System

From the control system implementation scheme based on field intelligent instruments, with distributed function blocks execution and bus scheduling as the main mechanism (see Figure 4.32 and Figure 4.33), it can be seen that each function block within control strategy is executed serially and deterministically in *chronological order* by scheduling since bus network media is unshared by any node at any time. This kind of mechanism makes sure that downstream function blocks will be executed only after the required data from upstream function blocks, no matter over network or inside instruments, are transmitted to them successfully. If not, the status values of function block inputs will indicate an error, which will trig an appropriate handling process by the function blocks. When distributed control strategies are scheduled, control moves sent to actuators are scheduled at the end of this cycle. Function block AI, by which outputs of plants are acquired, is scheduled at the beginning of the next cycle. As thus, control moves taking action is always prior to feedback from plant, which ensures the correct timing sequence in control.

Therefore, no mismatch and asynchrony between control moves taking real actions and feedback being generated exists in Field-bus-based control scheme thanks to its cyclic FB scheduling, by which the control moves and feedbacks are in deterministic sequence. Only some minor transmission time delay, which is deterministic and can be predicted based on the field-bus communication speed and numbers of FB to be scheduled, takes place over field-bus between two consecutive control moves.

4.4.5.1.2. IEC802.3 Ethernet Based Networked Control System

In this fashion, transmission delay is mainly caused by Ethernet. It occurs on 2 paths including downward path on which data are downloaded to the field and upward path on which data are uploaded to the controller. The two paths correspond to control channels and feedback channels respectively. Data transmission delay in control channels and feedback channels are represented as $e^{-t_c s}$ and $e^{-t_f s}$. non-determinism, which lies in that of transmission time itself and sequence in control causing mismatch and asynchrony between control moves and feedback and consequently degrade the control effect, is the main features of transmission over Ethernet.

Some researchers investigated the degradation of control effects caused by Ethernet transmission time delay and pointed out that increasing transmission delay reduces the rising time and degrades the steady state response for typical PID cascade control. The conclusion was based on the assumption that control moves are generated continuously despite of the delayed control moves actuation and feedback. Degradation of steady state response can be mainly attributed to asynchrony of control moves and feedback under circumstance of continuous control.

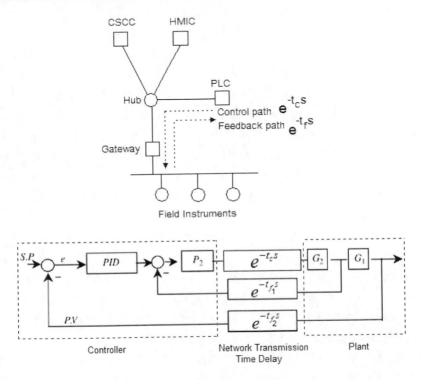

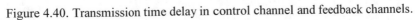

Figure 4.40. Transmission time delay in control channel and feedback channels.

4.4.5.2. Improvement Measures for Control Effects in IEC802.3 Ethernet Based Networked Control System

To improve control effects degraded with network transmission time delay in IEC802.3 Ethernet based case, 2 problems should be considered and solved. Firstly, the *asynchrony* between control moves and feedback caused by transmission delay should be reduced as much as possible. Secondly, network transmission delay itself should be reduced by means of hardware or network architecture improvements. Alternatively, some compensation methodologies in perspective of control theories can be applied in order to counteract the effect by the transmission delay.

4.4.5.2.1. Reducing Asynchrony between Control and Feedback Caused By Transmission Delay

As mentioned before, asynchrony between control moves and feedback mainly existed in NCS fashion. Therefore, the solutions proposed in this section are used for Ethernet based NCS fashion.

Synchronization control is necessary to reduce asynchrony between control moves and feedback caused by transmission delay. IEC61499, an international standard for fully distributed process control based on IEC61131, provides a synchronization control mechanism for NCS fashion [22]. Since it is based on event-triggered mode, some specific events can be correctly set for PID blocks in PLC to control the synchronization between control moves out of PID blocks and feedbacks into PID blocks. PLC programming compatible with IEC61499 is supported with some of the Siemens products. Here we propose a methodology to realize the synchronization control based on IEC61499.

Events need to be configured to control the synchronization between feedback data acquisition and control move actuation. To control the sequence between data acquisition and control algorithm execution, event signals in PID block need to be configured. The configured event in PID block will not be triggered until the feedback from the plant over Ethernet is fully available at the inputs of PID blocks by means of data acquisition block. The event is triggered by the data acquisition block upstream to PID block. Therefore, PID control algorithm will not be executed and no new outputs are generated if the event is not triggered. As for feedback, the acquisition of data from field will not be executed only if the generated control moves by PID blocks are sent to field. To achieve this, an event signal is dispatched to data acquisition block by control moves output block to control the sequence. Data acquisition block and control moves output block are user defined blocks which are very flexible and can be programmed with 5 standard languages specified in IEC61131-3. The schematic of the proposed methodology is shown in Figure 4.41.

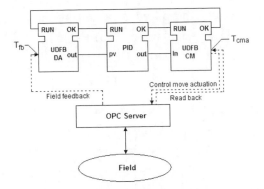

Figure 4.41. Schematic of the proposed methodology based on IEC61499.

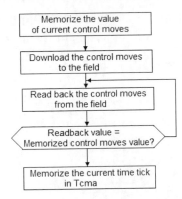

Figure 4.42. Flow chart of the proposed scheme based on IEC61499.

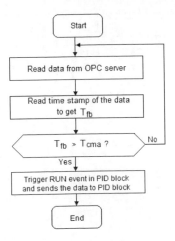

Figure 4.43. Execution control logics of UDFB-DA.

In configuration, the proposed scheme consists of a User Defined Function Block for Data Acquisition (UDFB-DA), a PID block compliant with IEC61499 and a User Defined Function Block for Control Moves (UDFB-CM). Two global time variables T_{fb} and T_{cma}, which represents the time tick when data from field is sampled and the control move is surely actuated in field respectively, need to be created to store the two time ticks. A scheme dealing with control moves download and a read-back is used to decide the time when the control move is surely actuated in field. The flow chart of the scheme is shown in Figure 4.42.

The main function of block UDFB-DA is to control the sequence of feedback acquisition and control move actuation to make it deterministic that control move actuation is prior to feedback acquisition in each execution of control strategy by means of global time variables T_{fb} and T_{cma}. The execution control logics of UDFB-DA are shown in Figure 4.43.

The execution control logics of PID are shown in Figure 4.44.

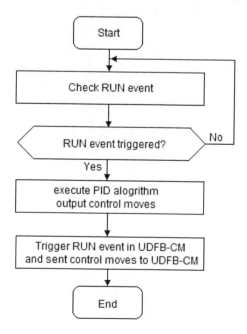

Figure 4.44. Execution control logics of PID.

The main functions of block UDFB-CM is to download the control move generated by PID block to field and record the time tick when the download and actuation is finished. Read-back check is used to make sure that the control move has been downloaded to the field successfully. The execution control logics of UDFB-CM are shown in Figure 4.45.

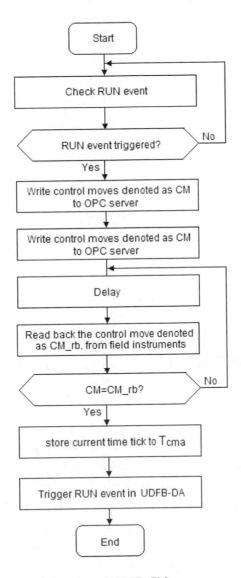

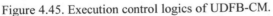
Figure 4.45. Execution control logics of UDFB-CM.

The level set-point is set to 50% to check the process response under this improved control fashion. The obtained response result is shown in Figure 4.46.

Some extra design and programming are necessary for those with which IEC61499 standard is not supported.

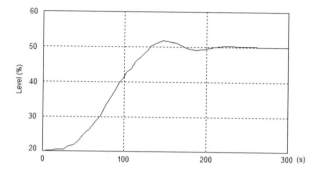

Figure 4.46. Step response for level set-point disturbance with the Ethernet based control system and PLC using the proposed control scheme based on IEC61499.

4.4.5.2.2. Using Output Estimation to Compensate for the Transmission Delay in Feedback

Transmission delay in feedback path will cause the feedback data from the plant field not updated within some time-span. It can be observed by upper supervisory workstation (OWS or EWS) by means of "time-stamp" property of data acquired by OPC server. Since the maximum time delay caused by the IEC802.3 Ethernet cannot be predicted while regulation must be continued to keep system stable, it is necessary to get estimation of the output of plants to take the role of the real output which is not available at current time tick. There are many ways to achieve the estimation. Here we proposed an output estimation scheme based on neural network since any non-linear mapping can be realized by means of it. Neural network are used to predict the output of plant. In this case, predicted output by neural network instead of the real one is used as inputs of block UDFB-DA to be sent to PID to generate control moves.

Schematic of output estimation with neural network was shown in Figure 4.47. In this scheme, a neural network estimator (NNE) with 1 input layer and 2 hidden layers and 1 output layer is used to estimate the output of plant in the case that the up-to-date output of plant cannot be obtained from OPC server within certain time limit T_{opc_max}. Control move $u(k-1)$ serves as input of NNE. $\hat{y}(k)$ is the estimated output of plant by NNE. Gradient descending algorithm is used to training NNE. The running of NNE is parallel to data acquisition by OPC server. At the same time, a switch is used. If field data from OPC server is up-to-date, which can be judged from "time-stamp" property of data acquired by OPC server, the output of plant by OPC server is switched to block UDFB-DA for further use. Otherwise, the estimated output by NNE is switched to block UDFB-DA. The switching algorithm is shown in Figure 4.47.

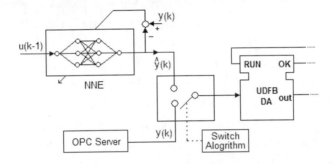

Figure 4.47. Schematic of output estimation with neural network.

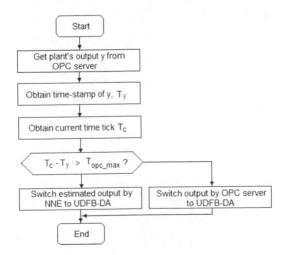

Figure 4.48. Flow chart of switching algorithm.

To be noted, the propose method has its own prerequisite in application. The advanced control function block such as the NNE and the output function block, which is directly linked to the analogue actuator, should be configured within the same module. It is feasible and practical with many networked control system such as FF system. Under such condition, no data transmission over network is needed. Data transmission is conducted within the configured module itself. Only measurements are transmitted over network to the controller. Otherwise, the action commands, produced by the controller, would have to travel through the same network to the actuators, so they would be subjected to the same delays and non-determinism as the measurements, so even if the correct control commands could be generated without the measurements, they would likely not reach the actuators in time to remedy the situation.

4.4.5.2.3. Reducing Network Transmission Delay Itself

1) By Improving Hardware and Network Architecture

Because the network communication over IEC802.3 Ethernet is CSMA/CD based, the time non-determinism of data communication between different nodes increases greatly with network traffic load, which is proportional to the number of nodes connected to the same network segments, to cause network transmission delay to different extent. Here we propose 3 principal ways to reducing network transmission delay itself by improving hardware and network architecture. Firstly, raising the whole network communication speed, especially the communication speed of PLC, DFI302 and hubs, by improving related hardware; secondly, leaving more bandwidth to communication between PLC and DFI302, which is more time critical, by properly dividing the whole network into different segments with routers to block broadcasting storm and other data communication unrelated to that between PLC and DFI302 from contention of bandwidth; thirdly, try to reduce the time in store-and-forward by related network components , such as routers.

① raising network communication speed.

Since the communication between PLC and DFI302 that exchanges I/O data with field instruments, is time critical, raising Ethernet network communication speed along the path between PLC and DFI302 quite contributes to reducing the network transmission delay. Three key components along this communication path, including PLC, hub and DFI302, are dealt with. Communication speed for each component must be raised simultaneously to achieve the overall communication speed increment. Any ignorance among the three will cause a bottleneck effect in communication speed increment. As for PLC and hub, faster Ethernet interface such as 100M instead of 10M should be selected to serve. Ethernet interfaces above100M is not available in DFI302 itself currently and a 10/100 Mbps Ethernet Switch- DF61 must be used to achieve the speed enhancement for DFI302. After connecting 10 Mbps port of DF61 with 10 Mbps port of DF51 using DF54 cable, the 100 Mbps port of DF61 is ready to be connected to a 100M hub. The connection schematic is shown in Figure 4.49. Since it is a peer-to-peer connection between DF61 and DFI302 and no bandwidth contention exists along the path between them, the bottleneck effect is much less remarkable.

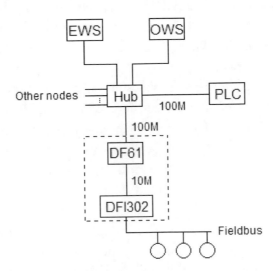

Figure 4.49. Schematic of network connection for enhancing the entire network speed.

In addition, a switch is more preferred to hub to raise network communication speed for its more efficient and faster data transmission speed.

② dividing Ethernet network into different segments based on time critical requirement rating to leave more bandwidth to time critical communication

Network bandwidth contention increases with the number of nodes connected when all the nodes are allocated in the same network segment. Available bandwidth for time critical communication, such as that between PLC and DFI302 here, is in reverse proportion to the number of nodes connected within the segment. However, priorities of communication among nodes are quite different within. Data transmission between PLC and DFI302 is quite time critical for its control function while that between OWS,EWS and PLC are not since only setting point data and some supervision-based data need to be exchanged. Therefore, communication between nodes should be grouped and rated based on their time critical requirements. And then divide the whole network into several different segments using router to allocate the nodes involved in different communication priorities into those segments. Traffic load within segment is lowered greatly and efficiently since bandwidth contention from nodes outside local segment is blocked. Besides, broadcasting data flow within the same segment, known as "broadcasting storm," is also effectively blocked and screened.

As far as the control system investigated in this chapter is concerned, communication between nodes can be classified into 2 groups based on their time critical requirements. One group is the non-time-critical communication including that between OWS, EWS, PLC and other computers. The other is the time-critical communication, namely data transmission between PLC and DFI302. The two groups are divided into 2 different network segments with different subnet mask and gateway configuration, by means of a router. Nodes in each segment are interconnected by means of a hub. The corresponding schematics of network structure and subsections according to the scheme proposed above are shown in Figure 4.50. The corresponding network configuration for each segment and node is shown in Table 4.1.

Obviously, it can be seen from Figure 4.50 that broadcast storms from other segments are blocked outside the segment 168.192.201.*, in which

PLC and DFI302 reside, by the router and no bandwidth contention from any node in segment 168.192.200.* or other segments comes up. Full bandwidth in segment 168.192.201.* is available to the communication between PLC and DFI302, which ensures the stable and reliable data exchange between them in turn.

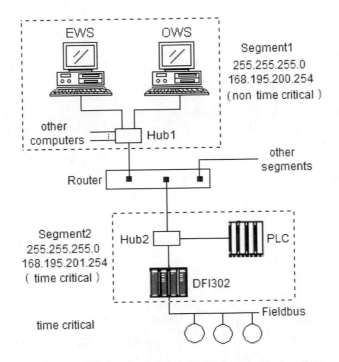

Figure 4.50. Schematics of network structure and subsections.

Table 4.1. Network configuration for segments and nodes

	Segment 1		Segment 2	
Mask	255.255.255.0		255.255.255.0	
Gateway	168.195.200.254		168.195.201.254	
Nodes IP	PLC	168.192.200.1	OWS	168.192.201.1
	DFI302	168.192.200.2	EWS	168.192.201.2

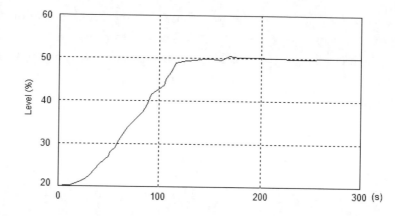

Figure 4.51. Step response for level set-point disturbance with Ethernet based control system using the proposed methodologies of improving network architecture.

The level set-point is set to 50% to check the process response under this improved control fashion. The obtained response result is shown in Figure 4.51. It can be seen that control effect in NCS fashion with improved network structure is better than that without any improvement in network structure with the same PID parameters since shorter control cycle can be achieved.

③ reducing transmission delay from store-and-forward by related network components.

With no sense of priority, an industrial telegram, which may be critical for operating some machine, might be delayed, sitting in some switch's store-and-forward buffer waiting for an IT telegram to pass through. The store and forward buffers in Ethernet switches are the source of the problem for industrial telegrams. First, as the telegram passes through the switch, it gets stored in a buffer until the entire message is received; only then it is forwarded out of the switch. Second, if the industrial message arrives at the switch at the same time the switch is processing an IT telegram, it must wait until the entire IT telegram passes through the switch before it can move on. Because a frame with a higher priority is always given precedence, automation frames are delayed if the queue buffers are filled with frames that have the same or higher priority. And, automation frames can be delayed for an unpredictable amount of time. There may also be congestion at the switch's output port: When the output port is filled with frames, high-priority frames have to wait until the port is available again. Some companies and organizations, such as Harting, have proposed some effective solutions to the problems. The solutions are to, first of all, pass all automation telegrams straight through the switch, bypassing the store-and-forward mechanism. Secondly, if an industrial telegram arrives at a switch while an IT telegram is being processed, that processing stops immediately and the industrial telegram is given clearance to pass through. After it has cleared the switch, the IT telegram is re-transmitted through the switch. This is called a "cut through" method. Experiments haves shown that the delay for the time critical industrial messages is over 2,000 microseconds with standard "store and forward" switching, but when the Fast Track Switching with the proposed solutions is turned on the maximum delay is only about 50 microseconds. Siemens has designed its ERTEC (Enhanced Real-Time Ethernet Controller) PROFINET chips to deal with the situation. These IEC802.3 Ethernet ASIC (Application Specific Integrated Circuit) are high-performance Ethernet controllers (based on 32-bit ARM 946 processors) that have integrated real-time switches especially developed for industrial use. The chips prioritize the isochronous real-time motion control telegrams and make sure they get to their destination in a timely fashion. Besides, Phoenix Contact has also announced a PROFINET enhancement to speed up industrial frames.

2) By Some Compensating Methodologies in Perspective of Control Theory
    In recent years, many researchers have focused on solution to the network transmission delay in Ethernet-based control system by means of control theoretical methods and many algorithms, such as fuzzy PID control strategy, augmented deterministic discrete-time model control, optimal stochastic control methodology, robust control methodology and end-user control adaptation methodology, were proposed, to compensate for or counteract the degradation in control effect caused by the Ethernet transmission delay. These control methodologies cover a large variety of systems and protocols. To design an NCS with a certain networked control methodology, a designer has to clearly understand an application whether

it is feasible, acceptable, and reliable enough to be controlled by the methodology under a selected network protocol. There are also additional factors of concern including the price for the network protocol, and the size and distance of the application. The premises and conditions under which these methodologies were used were summarized by Yodyium Tipsuwan and Mo-Yuen Chow.

4.4.6. Conclusion

The use of a multipurpose shared network to connect spatially distributed elements results in flexible architectures and generally reduces installation and maintenance costs. Consequently, Ethernet and field-bus based NCS have been finding application in a broad range of areas. Most of the recent research are mainly focused on theoretical analysis and computation in terms of system stability and control algorithms for NCS. Issues of their practical effect and feasibility are not mentioned or fully addressed. In this chapter, we address the issue of improving control performance of a network based control system in a quite different perspective from control algorithms. Some important performance-affecting elements are investigated and some methods to improve control performance based on those are presented. The main contribution of this chapter lies in that the proposed approaches to improve control performance for Ethernet and field-bus based network combines practical feasibility into the co-design of control and communication and proved practical usable. Through our research, it can be found out that:

- As for design and implementation of field-bus system, configuration scheme on allocating function block to different field instruments can notably affect the control performance and worth paying attention to. With the improved function block allocation and configuration scheme proposed in this chapter, shorter control cycle and thereby more efficient control can be achieved.

- As for the design of IEC802.3 Ethernet based system, function block MBCS provided by DFI302 combining field-bus subsystem and PLC world closely provide a simpler but more flexible way to implement a hybrid system.

- No essentially non-deterministic data transmission delay was involved and thereby no degradation caused by it in control when control strategies were implemented with field-bus control system with by means of function blocks and fully distribution in control was achieved, which demonstrated the apparent advantage over general networked control system. No mismatch and asynchrony between control moves taking real actions and feedback being generated exists in Field-bus-based control scheme thanks to its cyclic FB scheduling. Degradation of steady state response can be mainly attributed to asynchrony of control moves and feedback under circumstance of continuous control as far as the Ethernet based control system is concerned.

- Methodologies based on IEC61499 proposed in this chapter can be utilized to control the execution sequence of each function block in PLC controller with events and some specific action control logic. The proposed output estimation algorithm based on neural network can also compensate for the transmission delay in feedback effectively.

- It is an effective and efficient way to reduce network transmission delay itself by improving hardware and network architecture. 3 methods, which are raising network communication speed, dividing Ethernet network into different segments based on time critical requirement rating and reducing transmission delay from store-and-forward by related network components, are proposed to achieve this aim. When the network segmenting solution proposed in this chapter is applied, the control system can operates well without the proposed sequence control scheme. When the most adverse network structure is applied, namely without any improvement in network components and structure, the proposed sequence control scheme is quite preferred.

Consequently, as proposed and proved in this chapter, many problems existing in networked control, in which communication and control technologies involved at the same time, can be solved to great extent by means of network related methodologies, which provides alternative or most possibly comprehensive solutions.

Chapter 5

NETWORKED CONTROL SYSTEM BASED ON WORLDFIP WITH ITS APPLICATION IN INDUSTRY

5.1. INTRODUCTION TO WORLDFIP FIELD-BUS

5.1.1. History of FIP

The Factory Instrumentation Protocol or FIP originally was specified by the French and the Italian users at the beginning of the 1980's. In fact it was the reactions to the national market needs in those countries which lead towards the development of FIP protocol. From the beginning, the FIP was dedicated to serve both real-time distributed control requirements and the ordinary supervisory and instrumentation tasks [Beeston 96]. It was successfully adapted in many technical commercial products such as Electrical Power Generation programs, Road Systems, and the high speed train (TGV) along with many other international products.

The WorldFIP is standardization to the old field-bus Interoperable Protocol which was defined In France 1989 by the FIP (Factory standard NFC46). The CEGELEC proposed a European standard for three existing protocols, one of them was the WorldFIP.

Since the first French standard was launched, the new European standards EN 50170/3 and EN 50254/3 had no major changes except that at 1993 when it was the first adoption of physical layer IEC2 IS 61158-2.

In March 1993, the WorldFIP (Factory Instrumentation Protocol) was jointly created by Honeywell, A-B (Allen-Bradley), CEGELEC, and several other companies. In this thesis we will work on the latest available WorldFIP protocol standard which was updated in 19983. What is worth to state here is that we are going to use the words FIP and WorldFIP interchangeably throughout this thesis.

5.1.2. Use of WorldFIP

WorldFIP is a field-bus network protocol designed to provide links between levels zero (i.e., sensors and actuators) and one (i.e., controllers, PLC's, CNC's...) in automation systems [FIP 98]. WorldFIP is proposed so that it can be used with all types of automation, including the centralized, the synchronous and the asynchronous applications.

This particular field-bus protocol was not dedicated only for the real-time requirements but also for transferring the monitoring information from the plant and along the network to the supervisory equipments. This must be done without interfering with the basic real-time tasks of the protocol.

The WorldFIP protocol is relatively simple to learn in comparing to other protocols. It maximizes the use of international standards, such as the MME (Manufacturing Messaging Specification). What is worth adding here is that the true origin of the FIP protocol was proposed by the users of the automation in France.

5.1.3. Configuration of the WorldFIP

The FIP network consists of a 3-layer model in comparison with OSI 7-layer model.

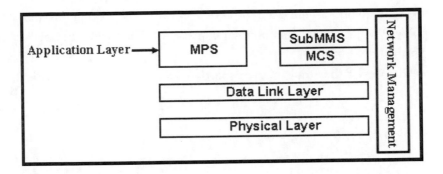

Figure 5.1. 3-layer model in comparison with OSI 7-layer model.

In the above figure, the MPS stands for Manufacturing Periodic/Non-periodic Services, Sub MMS stands for Subset of Manufacturing Messaging Services, and MCS is for application service element which offers high quality of MMS service exchange [Inter 99]. These three layers of the FIP are:

1. The Physical Layer
2. The Data link Layer
3. The Application Layer

In fact most of the existing Field-buses consisted of these same 3 layers as we Saw in chapter one of this thesis. For more information one can see standard protocol [FIP 98] other useful supplementary on the WorldFIP web page, where there the WorldFIP are also some materials.

Now we will go through the details of each one of these three layers of the WorldFIP protocol.

5.1.4. Physical Laver in WorldFIP

The function of WorldFIP's physical layer is to ensure the transfer of information bits from one node to all other nodes that are connected to the bus. The transmission medium can be shielded twisted pair wire or even optical fiber [FIP 98].

The network architecture of the WorldFIP is relying on the Bus topology, which means that all the devices on the network are attached to the same line (bus).

There exist four transmission speeds of the WorldFIP protocol; these are

- 31.25 K bps (low speed).
- 1 M bps (high speed).
- 2.5 M bps (high speed).
- 5.00 Mbps (high speed for fiber optic) [FIP 98].

The physical layer encodes the bits transmitted by the data link layer using the Manchester code. Each cable segment has a maximum of 64 nodes. The repeaters can connect up to four segments at the same time. Although the cable segment length depends on the data bit rate, the standard suggests that the ideal segment length is one km. Following figure shows an example of the overall configuration the physical connections of one FIP system with two main cables and one repeater.

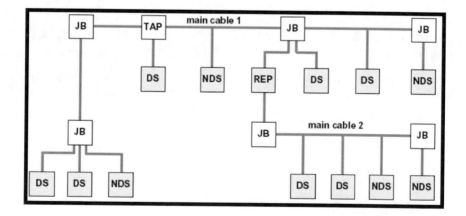

Figure 5.2. Overall configuration the physical connections of one FIP system.

Where JB is a Junction Box, TAP provides connection on the main cable, Repeater brings together two main cables to form the field-bus, DS stands for a locally disconnecting subscriber (i.e., a node or station), where NDS stands for a Non- locally disconnecting subscriber and the DB is a Diffusion or Broadcasting Box. The JB is a simple passive multiple tap and the DB brings together several terminal segments on the main cable.

In addition to that, the backup cable (bus) is an optional where it becomes a necessity in the new field-bus standards like the FlexRay one can refer to chapter 1 to see the FlexRay protocol.

5.1.5. Data Link Layer (DLL) in WorldFIP

The Data Link Layer of the WorldFIP utilizes the famous network producer/consumer model with a centralized bus scheduler. This centralized scheduler is called the Bus Arbitrator or BA.

5.1.5.1. The Data Link Layer Services

The FIP protocol basically supports two types of transmission services. These are:

- Exchange of Identified Variables.
- Message Transfers.

The WorldFIP supports both types of variables; the real-time or time-critical data and the non time-critical data. The real-time variables can be cyclic (i.e., periodic), or acyclic (i.e., non-periodic), that is, event based variables. In addition it supports asynchronous messages transferring between the nodes. For the exchange of messages transfer, they have two types either unacknowledged non-periodic message broadcasting, or acknowledged non-periodic message broadcasting.

There are other services that are associated to the WorldFIP's Data Link Layer like the interfaces between the data link layer and physical and the application layers.

5.1.5.2. Addressing of Variables and Messages

The transmission technique in FIP is basically based on broadcasting over the network medium (i.e., the Bus). So we need to know how the FIP is able to distinguish between variables. The same goes for the messages. Thus we need to know the variables, and messages addressing strategies of the FIP protocol. The WorldFIP has two distinct addressing spaces Variable Addressing Space, and Messages Addressing Space. Next we will demonstrate each addressing scheme in the next subsections.

5.1.5.2.1. Variable Addressing

In the WorldFIP protocol each variable in the system is associated with a unique identifier that is used to characterize that variable. There are 16 bits that are used to encode this address. In other words there are $216 = 65536$ variables that can have identifiers. These addresses variables can be used for both the periodic and non-periodic

We assume in this thesis that the non-periodic variables ID's are different from that of the periodic variables ID's (despite the FIP standard state that they both share the same ID domain). This means that any periodic variable cannot be invoked non-periodically or *vice versa.*

5.1.5.2.2. Message Addressing

In the WorldFIP the exchange of messages takes place in one of two ways; either point-to-point, or in a multi-point on a single segment. Each message transmitted contains the address of the transmitting and the destination entities. There are 24 bit that is used to code the addresses of the messages. This means that there were 16777216 addresses for the messages in the WorldFIP. The addressing scheme is based on addressing of Entities. Entity address contains the address of network segment as well as the address of the station (node) in this segment.

In the following figure, we show three samples of the WorldFIP data frames that are used to transfer periodic data and messages on the bus. These are the ID_DAT, the RP_DAT, and the RP MSG frames.

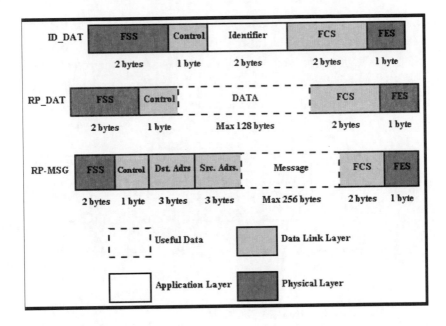

Figure 5.3. WorldFIP frames.

Where the FSS is the beginning of the frame or the Frame Start Sequence, the FES the end of the frame or the Frame End Sequence, and the FCS stands for the Frame Check Sequence which used to verify the integrity of the frame (is the result of error checking algorithm). It is quite obvious that Dst. Adrs., and Src. Adrs are the source, and the destination addresses of the message respectively. The Control byte is used by the network subscribers (nodes) to recognize the type of the frame that they are receiving. This control field is used to code variable transfer requests, and acknowledgement frames as we will see later.

5.1.5.3. The FIP Network Configuration

Any WorldFIP network is made up of stations or nodes that are attached via connectors over the network bus. There are two types of nodes in the WorldFIP standard. These are the Bus Arbitrating Node, and the Producer/Consumer Nodes. The Bus Arbitrating node, manage the accessibility to the transmission medium (Bus). We called it before the centralized scheduler that controls which node transmits at any specific time. The BA (the bus arbitrator) node has a table to scan the periodic variables at exact time intervals. This table is called the Bus Arbitrator Table or BAT. The Producer/Consumer Nodes are all the remaining nodes in the FIP. Any node can be either producer node or consumer node and sometimes it can be both types at the same time.

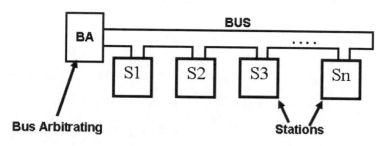

Figure 5.4. WorldFIP bus arbitrating.

5.1.5.3.1. The Bus Arbitrating Tables

The BA must have a scanning table or BAT in which a list of identifiers of periodic variables exit to be circulated or scanned along the bus at equal time intervals. When the system is configured, the Bus Arbitrator node is given the list of the periodic variables identifiers to be scanned and the periodicity associated with each one of these variables. Also the bus arbitrator must take the transfer time or the length of each variable data packet in order to estimate the required transmission time. The BAT consists of small scanning cycles that are called the micro-cycles, and bigger scanning cycles that is called the macro-cycles. The micro-cycle imposes the maximum rate at which the BA performs a set of scans (periodic and non-periodic).

The macro-cycle corresponds to a juxtaposition of specified number of elementary cycles.

The BA validates the system configuration to see whether the system will meet the time constraints or not. After validating the configuration, the BA will infinitely repeat the scanning mechanism until either we shut down the system or any failure occurred.

Now we will follow with the question: How the Bus Arbitrator can build the Bus Arbitrator Table? The WorldFIP scheduling algorithm is based on the Cyclic Executive Scheduling. The Cyclic Executive Scheduling constructs a fixed repeating schedule called a major cycle (macro-cycle), which consists of several minor cycles of fixed duration (micro-cycles). The minor cycle is less than or equal to the smallest period of the highest priority process that will be executed. Vahid et al. have another definition to the minor cycle "The minor cycle is therefore equal to the smallest age of the registers to be pre-fetched." This method was called the Highest Common Factor/Least Common Multiple (HCF/LCM) method. Other references used the fact that the WorldFIP is a cyclic executive protocol and proposed other methods to set up the BAT.

We will see these methods in the next chapter but here we will introduce the BAT setup formal standard method or the HCF/LCM.

5.1.5.3.2. Using HCF/LCM Methodology for Setting the BAT

In the beginning we would like to say that not only the Bus Arbitrator is responsible for scheduling the periodic traffic in the WorldFIP network, but also it has its responsibility towards managing the non-periodic traffic which includes the non-periodic variables and messages transfers.

First we will introduce the network model that we will use to formulate the bus arbitrator table.

Given network model as follows:-

n = the number of stations, one of them is the BA.

np = the number of periodic variables.

Sp_i = the Periodic Stream I {Cps, Tp, Dp;},   i =1, 2,...,np.

Cps = Maximum amount of time to periodic buffer transfer.

Tp_i = Periodicity of Sp;.

Dp_i = Deadline of the periodic stream Sp;.

N = Number of macro-cycles in the Macro-cycles.

μcy = time length of macro-cycle.

Mcy = time length of macro-cycle.

After we have demonstrated the WorldFIP network model we will introduce now how can we estimate both the elementary cycle, and the macro cycle.

The macro-cycle or the elementary cycle can be easily found as it is equal to the highest common factor of all the periodicities of the periodic variables. The following equation shows us the mathematical notation of the macro-cycle in terms of the periodicities of the periodic variables streams.

$$\mu cy = HCF(Tp_i), i = 1,.....,np \; ;$$

where HCF is the Highest Common Factor and i is running up from 1 to np or the number of the periodic variable streams.

But we need the macro-cycle to be integer multiple of any periodicity of the periodic variables [FIP 98]. Equation (2.2-a) shows to us how we can achieve this.

$$\mu cy = \max \{ \Omega \}, \Omega \in \aleph$$

where Ω is the positive integer number set; while Tpi/Ω is calculated by as the HCF using the equation (2.2-b) as follows:

$$Tp_i / \Omega = \lfloor Tp_i / \Omega \rfloor, i = 1, ..., np$$

Now after we have calculated the macro-cycle interval, we will find the macro-cycle of the BAT. From the network model above, the macro-cycle simply equals to N integer multiple of the macro-cycle.

$$Mcy = N * \mu cy$$

The problem is to find the integer number N. following equation shows how this integer quantity can be found.

$$N = \min \{ \Phi \}, \Phi \in \aleph$$

where $"\aleph"$ is the positive integer number set; while "Φ" is calculated as the LCM using the equation (2.4-b) as follows:

$$\Phi /(Tp_i / \mu cy) = \lfloor \Phi /(Tp_i / \mu cy) \rfloor i = 1,....,np$$

Thus we have just calculated the integer number "N" using LCM or the Least Common Multiple of the periodic variables periodicities.

Now after finding the two key parameters of the BAT we must build the BAT itself. Here we will use the Rate Monotonic scheduling algorithm. In this algorithm the BA assigns fixed priorities to the periodic variables based on the periodicities of these variables. The BA then fills the BAT with the periodic variables from the highest priority to the lowest variable priority.

5.1.5.3.3. The BA Periodic Variable Scanning Mechanism

The main task of the Bus Arbitrator is to transmit the question frame ID-AT over the Bus. This frame or packet contains the identifier of any specific periodic variable. All the Data Link Layers of the stations in this Bus will record this frame. But there is only one station that will recognize itself as the producer of this variable and one or many nodes know that they need the value of this variable (i.e., consumers). This station will respond with the response frame RP-AT and broadcast it along the bus. This value will be captured and consumed by the consumer nodes. The Bus Arbitrator will go to the next periodic variable in the list and continue to the end of the BAT then repeat it infinitely [FIP 98].

We will give now a numerical example of how to set the BAT.

5.1.5.3.4. Numerical Example of BAT

Suppose now we have list of six periodic variables as shown in Table 5.1. And we want to build a FIP BAT to map these variables to be used in

FIP system. Here the Cp; represents the time that is taken to complete sending the variable to its destination.

Table 5.1. BAT example

Variable	Periodicity (ms)	Cp_i (μs)
A	5	170
B	10	178
C	15	418
D	20	194
E	20	194
F	30	290

We apply the algorithm we mention before to calculate the macro-cycle length and the macro-cycle length. We will find that the macro-cycle is equal to 5 milliseconds, and the macro-cycle is equal to 12 macro-cycles or 60 milliseconds.

Then we apply the rate monotonic scheduling algorithm in order to find the table itself. Here is an example of how is the shape of the FIP traffic load would appear in the first 15 elementary cycles in the following figure.

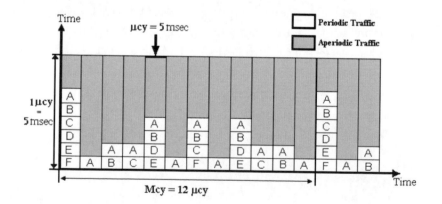

Figure 5.5. The shape of the FIP traffic load.

We have some notes that we would like to add on Figure 2.5. First the vertical axis is corresponding to the scanning windows 4 time for one elementary (macro-cycle) cycle. This means that the vertical axis is a time axis. We choose this method to save the space that we could use if tried to represent the scanning windows horizontally. Second the horizontal axis corresponds to the flow of elementary cycles in time. This axis is supposed to go infinitely. Third there is no elementary cycle that can go beyond its 5 millisecond limit. In other words, when the BA finishes all the periodic traffic in one macro-cycle and there still some time in this macro-cycle, the BA then can switch and use remaining time to fulfill requests for non-periodic transfers or message. If no requests are made for the non-periodic traffic, the BA transmits padding frames until end of this elementary cycle. We have shaded the empty scanning windows with light gray which means that these windows are available to be used by the non-periodic traffic.

The following figure shows that each macro-cycle consists of four unequal windows. The first window is for the periodic traffic.

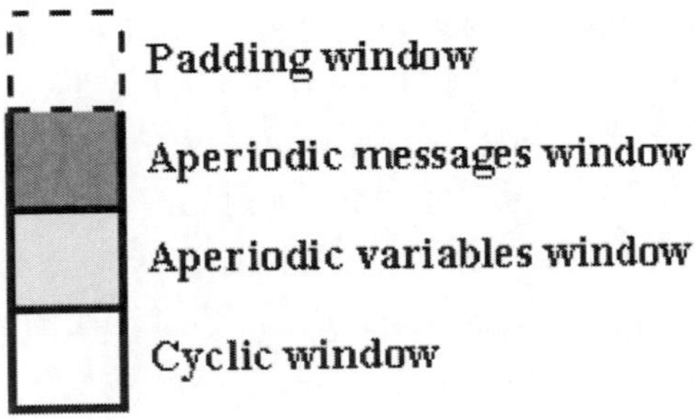

Figure 5.6. Each macro-cycle consists of four unequal windows.

The second window is for non-periodic variable transaction for both types; the urgent and normal non-periodic variables. These non-periodic variables are mainly used to initiate alarms in critical situation or system failure. The third window is dedicated for non-periodic message transfer with its two types, the acknowledged, and the unacknowledged messages. Finally the fourth window is the padding window which is used to maintain the synchronization of the macro-cycles. Again the only constraint here on the macro-cycle is that there always must be time to finish the periodic load, then if there is any extra time it can be used for non-periodic load.

5.1.5.4. Modes of Operation of the WorldFIP

WorldFIP field-bus has several modes of operation in what Concerns synchronization of the macro-cycles and the macro-cycles. Here we talk mainly about three of them.

One of the most common modes is the Synchronous mode. The main feature of this mode is that the macro-cycles always have a constant duration that must be found at the beginning of the BAT configuration. Another important feature in this synchronous mode is that the next scan of the BAT starts immediately upon the termination of the current scan. In this mode it is always possible to assure the periodic variables with only a little time fitter (as we'll see in the next chapters). When the exchange of one periodic variable is going to take less time than the macro-cycle duration, then the BA will transmit padding frames up to the end of that macro-cycle (that in case there is no pending non-periodic traffic). When this synchronous mode is used, the macro-cycle duration is typically set to the highest common factor (HCF) of the variables' scanning periods.

There are other modes that the WorldFIP can use. For example, the no-pad mode is when the BA allows the start of the next macro-cycle as soon as the transactions of the current macro-cycle is terminated (i.e., there is no insertion of padding frames). In this case the macro-cycle time duration is not constant.

Yet another example, the Asynchronous mode is when the next BAT scan can be triggered by an external event, independently of the termination of the current scan (e.g., case system failure or special system state for supervisory or maintenance).

There will be only one mode that will be addressed throughout this thesis; that is the Synchronous mode.

5.1.5.5. Medium Allocation Mechanism for Non-Periodic Variables

After we saw how bus arbitrator deals with the periodic variables and how it allocates them using the BA tables or BATS. One of our main goals in this thesis is to try to find a way to estimate the worst case response time of any periodic or non-periodic variable in the FIP network. So we need to look at the way the BA allocates these non-periodic variables into the medium or the bus.

Not all the variables in the FIP network are included in the BAT; in fact only the periodic variables. The mechanism that the BA used to accomplish the non-periodic variable transactions is divided into three stages. These stages are:

Stage One

Suppose that the BA broadcasts a question frame concerning the periodic variable A as can be seen in Figure 5.7A. This is done in the usual way as we see before and in the cyclic window of any macro-cycle. The producer of the variable A responds with the corresponding value of variable A and sets the non-periodic request bit in the control field of the response frame ID_RQ.

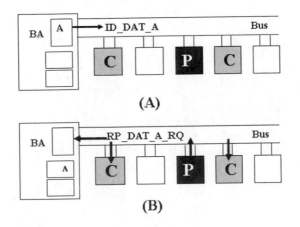

Figure 5.7. Stage one.

When the producer of variable A sets the non-periodic bit it means that it requests non-periodic variable transfer. There are two priority levels of such non-periodic transfer request, and the station must determine which level it wants. These levels are called Urgent and Normal non-periodic requests. It's clear that the Urgent level than the Normal priority level. The

BA lists the variable A queues of the requests for the non-periodic variable transfer which are Normal queues have higher priority in one of the two the Urgent and the

Stage Two

During the window of the non-periodic traffic, the BA sends an identification request frame IDs RQ to the producer of the variable A to transmit its request.

The producer of variable A will respond with an RPs RQ frame which contains the list of non-periodic variable identifiers another queue by the BA. This list is then stored in there are two queues one for each priority levels. The maximum size of list is 64 identifiers and it must contain at least one identifier.

The bus arbitrator may transmit the identification request frame IDs RQ soon after the request is noted, or later in any empty macro-cycle. The delay depends on the periodic traffic load and other requests of higher priority levels that are being served by the BA at this time.

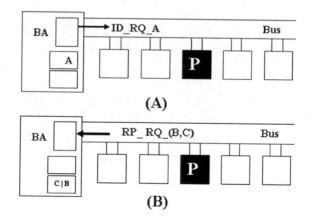

Figure 5.8. Stage two.

Stage Three

At last, the BA starts fulfilling the requests for non-periodic variable transfers that are stored in its queues starting with the Urgent queue then the Normal queue. The BA uses the same mechanism for fulfilling these non-periodic variables requests as it do with the periodic variables (i.e., it sends a polling frame requesting the non-periodic variable value, then the producer of that variable will respond with the required value). The BA fulfills one or more requests depending on the time available in the window of the macro-cycle that assigned for this non-periodic variables traffic.

We have some remarks that we would like to state here about this allocation scheme of the non-periodic variables. Firstly, any node can only request non-periodic variables transfer in response to periodic variable that it produces (i.e., if the node that is not a producer of any periodic variables, it can't ask a non-periodic variable transfer). In addition to that, the station that requests a non-periodic variable transfer can be the producer of that variable, the consumer, or the producer and consumer at the same time. Also at sometimes this node or station can be neither the producer, nor the consumer or what we call third party nodes or the supervisory nodes.

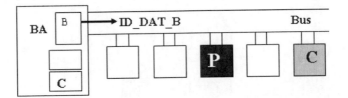

Figure 5.9. Stage three.

The same scenario can be applied for both types of non-periodic variables (i.e., urgent or normal non-periodic variables), so no need to demonstrate the Normal non-periodic variables allocation mechanism. The variables either periodic or non-periodic are not the only traffic that supported by the FIP network; in addition, there are the Messages which in turn has two types; the Acknowledged and the Unacknowledged. The messages are the only traffic type can be transferred point-to-point in addition to the usual way by broadcasting.

5.1.5.6. Medium Allocation of the Non-periodic Messages

The scheme that is used for non-periodic message transfer requests is similar to that of a non-periodic variable transfer request as we will see. Again the non-periodic messages are of the lowest priority in the WorldFIP transactions. There are two types of messages as we mention before. Here we will deal with both types of message (Unacknowledged, and Acknowledged) transfer each one alone.

5.1.5.6.1. Unacknowledged Message Transfer Request

First Stage

Suppose that the BA calls for periodic variable B. The producer node of variable B replies with the newest value B, using the frame ID_DAT and sets in this frame the MSG bit in the control field. This means that the station has a request for message transfer as indicated in the following figure. The BA then will store the identifier B in a special queue (the message request queue).

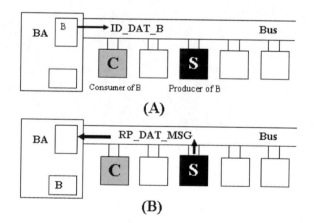

(A)

(B)

Figure 5.10. Stage one.

Second Stage

In the window of the non-periodic traffic and after the BA finishes the non-periodic variables, the BA checks to see if there is no more non-periodic variable requests, it turns to process the message requests.

The BA gives the producer of variable B right to send the message. In other words the bus arbitrator leaves the bus to the station; by sending a frame IDs MSG B to the producer node of variable B.

The message frame must include both the sender and the destination addresses and it is of the type RPs MSG NOACK. This is clearly shown in Figure 5.11 which indicated this scenario.

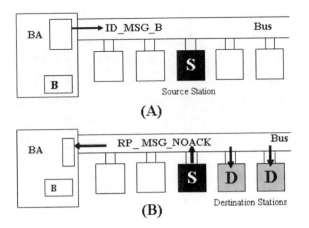

Figure 5.11. Stage two.

Third Stage

The BA waits until it receives a frame which indicates that the message transfer transaction has been successfully finished. This frame as can be seen in Figure 5.12 is called RP_FIN. After that, the BA will once again take over the control of the bus and start to send and receive frames from the producers of the variables along the bus.

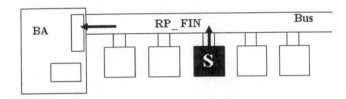

Figure 5.12. Stage three.

When the BA gives the station the right to send its message, it does not know in advance whether this message is acknowledged or not acknowledged. So the BA must make sure that the time that remains in the non-periodic window of the micro cycle is enough to both types for fulfilling any request. The BA sets a timer to avoid waiting forever for the RP_FIN frame. If this timer expires, the BA will seize the bus and starts to transmit the periodic variables.

5.1.5.6.2. Acknowledged Message Transfer Request

WorldFIP's data link layer also provides acknowledged message transfer services, which makes the point-to-point data exchanges more reliable. The same mechanism used in the unacknowledged message transfer used for the acknowledged message transfer, but with some modifications. In stage two, instead of the station respond with frame RP_MSG_NOACK it responds with RP_MSG_ACK frame shown in the following figure. These two frames and their differences are demonstrated in detail.

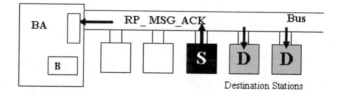

Figure 5.13. RP_MSG_NOACK.

The receiving station must responds with an acknowledgement frame of type RP_ACK which is received by the sender station of the message indicating ending the message transaction as we see in the following figure.

At the end, the sender of the message sends "RP_FIN" packet to BA to finish the transaction. This service uses a module-2 message numbering mechanism that allows the destination station to detect the loss or duplication of a message. When the message is lost, the sender repeats sending it using the numbering technique we refer to it above. The number of repetitions in case of an acknowledgment absence is between 0 and 2. This parameter (i.e., the number of repetitions) is global operating parameter of the FIP network.

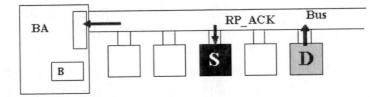

Figure 5.14. RP_ACK.

5.1.6. Application Laver in WorldFIP

Now we will demonstrate the key features of the WorldFIP Application layer protocol. WorldFIP's application layer provides users with local/remote variable read/write services to place variables values in buffers or remove variables values from buffers. These services generate no traffic on the bus. From Figure 5.9 one can see that the variables are accessible through the MPS interface. As for the messages; they are accessible via the Sub-MMS interface. There are several services that are attached to both the MPS and the Sub-MMS. Take the MPS as an example; it's supposed to provide the user with local/remote read/write services, variables successful transmission/reception indicators, and information on the freshness, the spatial and temporal consistencies of data. These last services will be referred in the next chapter. In chapter 3 we will discuss the FIP clock synchronization using the existing application layer services and timers; such as the freshness and promptness of the data.

While reading a variable value at the application layer, we can know some qualitative information about how fresh is that variable. The WorldFIP protocol called this information as Promptness status and the Refreshment status. These statuses are boolean (i.e., True or False) and usually used to synchronize the processes in application layer between the producer node and the consumer node(s). These two statuses can be asynchronous, or synchronous. We will show these services in detail.

5.1.6.1. Asynchronous Refreshment

Refreshment statuses are estimated by the application layer of the producers of variables. For each periodic variable produced it should be indicated whether or not a refreshment status is provided. If the variable has a refreshment status, then the period of production (i.e., the production delay) associated with the variable must also be indicated. The following figure shows an example indicating the asynchronous refreshment mechanism.

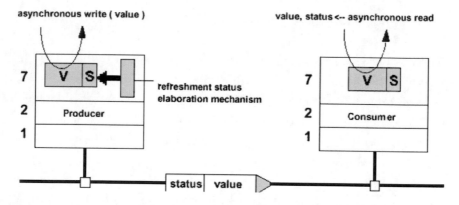

Figure 5.15. An example indicating the asynchronous refreshment mechanism.

The producer node (the node to the left) produces (i.e., writes) the new variable values in its application layer buffer. With each new write operation the producer's application layer uses the production delay to calculate a refreshment status. A "true" status indicates the producer's application process is functioning properly. The consumers of this variable (like the node to the right) consume an object consists of a value V and a refreshment status S. These consumers use the refreshment status to make sure that the producer respects the production delay of this variable. The following figure shows the timing diagram of this example.

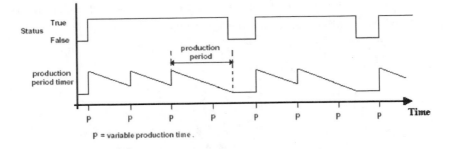

Figure 5.16. Timing diagram of this example.

Whenever a new value of a variable is written; the application layer of the producer sets the refreshment timer which is associated with that variable with the value of the production period. Status will be "true" as long as long as this timer has not expired.

5.1.6.2. Synchronous Refreshment

If a synchronous refreshment status mechanism is to be done for any periodic variable, then the production period and the synchronization variable (one can refer to [FIP 98] for more information about the synchronization variables) for estimating the refreshment status must be both indicated. Each time a synchronization variable is received the refreshment timer is reset with the value of the production period and the refreshment status becomes "false." Figure 5.17 showed an example to the synchronous refreshment mechanism.

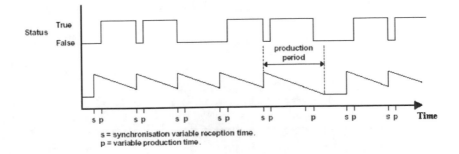

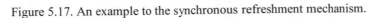

Figure 5.17. An example to the synchronous refreshment mechanism.

If the refreshment timer has not expired when the application layer writes new variable value the refreshment status becomes "true". It remains "true" until the refreshment timer expires or a new synchronization variable is received.

5.1.6.3. Promptness

As we said before, the Promptness status is one of the two statuses that indicate the freshness of the variables values at the application layer. The promptness status is also an indicator that the BA respects the periodic variables periods.

5.1.6.4. Asynchronous Prompting

Unlike the refreshment statuses, the asynchronous promptness statuses are calculated by the application layers of the variables consumer nodes rather than by producer nodes. For each variable it must be decided, whether it will have a promptness status or not. If a promptness status is required, then the consumption period associated with the variable must also be indicated. When an asynchronous promptness status is true it means that the buffer transfer mechanism is correctly working. Figure 5.18 shows an example of asynchronous promptness mechanism.

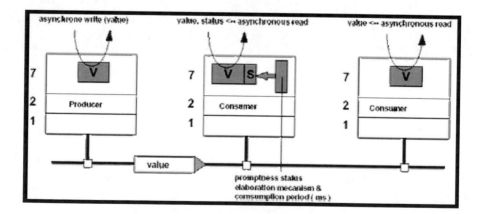

Figure 5.18. Example of asynchronous promptness mechanism.

In this example one consumer station (in the middle) estimates an asynchronous promptness status for a variable and the other (to the left) does not. When the first station reads the value it obtains both the value of the variable and the promptness status. Since the value is made up of the [value, refreshment status] or (V, S) pair, the station knows whether or not the producer has respected the period of production and whether or not the buffer transfer mechanism is functioning correctly.

In Figure 5.19, one can see the corresponding timing diagram of the previous asynchronous promptness example.

When the consumer station's application layer receives a new variable value it sets the asynchronous promptness timer associated with the variable consumed with the value of the consumption period. The promptness status becomes "true" and remains so until the timer expires.

At the end, we see that when the producer station wants to assure the whether or not the BA respect the periods of periodic variables, it uses the refreshment status. When the consumer station wants to make sure that the BA respects the periods of the periodic variables, then it uses the promptness status.

Now after we done our survey in this chapter about the WorldFIP protocol standard and specifications, we will move on to chapter 3 of this thesis in which we will comment on the previous real-time analysis work that were done on the FIP protocol.

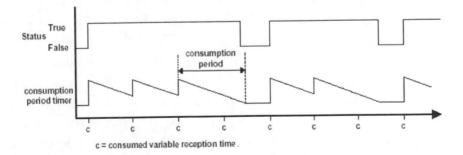

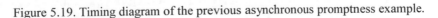

Figure 5.19. Timing diagram of the previous asynchronous promptness example.

5.2. Performance Analysis of WorldFIP Field-Bus

5.2.1. PDC Communication Model

In WorldFIP, the exchange of identified variables is based on a producer/distributor/consumer (PDC) model, which relates producers and consumers within the distributed system. In this model, for each process variable there is one, and only one producer, and one or more consumers. For instance, consider the variable associated with a process sensor. The station that provides the value of the variable will act as producer and its value will be provided to all the consumers of the variable (e.g., the station that acts as process controller for that variable or the station that is responsible for building an historical data base). In order to manage transactions associated to a single variable, a unique identifier is associated to each variable. The WorldFIP data link layer (DLL) is made up of a set of produced and consumed buffers, which can be locally accessed (through application layer (AL) services) or remotely accessed (through network services).

The AL provides two basic services to access the DLL buffers: L_PUT.req, to write a value in a local produced buffer, and L_GET.req to obtain a value from the local consumed buffer. None of these AL services generate activity on the bus. Produced and consumed buffers can be also remotely accessed through a network transfer (service also known as buffer transfer). The bus arbitrator broadcasts a question frame ID_DAT, which includes the identifier of a specific variable. The DLL of the station that has the corresponding produced buffer, responds with the value of the variable, using a response frame RP_DAT. The DLL of the station that contains the produced buffer then sends an indication of transmission to the AL (L_SENT.ind). The DLL of the station(s) that has the consumed buffers accepts the value contained in the RP_DAT, overwriting the previous value and notifying the local AL with a L_RECEIVED indicator.

A buffer transfer implies the transmission of a pair of frames: ID_DAT, followed by RP_DAT. We denote this sequence as an elementary transaction. The duration of this transaction equals the time needed to transmit the ID_DAT frame, added to the time needed to transmit the RP_DAT frame, and added to twice the turnaround time (tr). The turnaround time is the time elapsed between any two consecutive frames. Every transmitted frame is encapsulated with control information from the physical layer (PL). Specifically, an ID_DAT frame has always 8 bytes (corresponding to a 2 bytes identifier plus 6 bytes of control information), whereas a RP_DAT frame has also 6 bytes of control information plus up to 128 bytes of useful data. The duration of a message transaction is

$$C = \frac{\text{len}(ID\_DAT) + \text{len}(RP\_DAT)}{\text{bps}} + 2 \times t_r$$

where bps stands for the network data rate and len is the length, in bits, of frame.

For instance, assuming a variable with a 4 bytes data field, if tr =20 μs and the network data rate is 2.5 Mbps then, the duration of an elementary transaction will be $(64 + 80)/2.5 + 2* 20\mu s$.

5.2.2. Bus Scheduling Mechanism

In WorldFIP networks, the bus arbitrator table (BAT) regulates the scheduling of all buffer transfers.

The BAT imposes the timings of the periodic buffer transfers, and also regulates the non-periodic buffer transfers.

Assume a distributed system within which six variables are to be periodically scanned, with scan rates as shown in Table 5.20. The WorldFIP BAT must cope with these real-time requirements.

Two important parameters are associated with a WorldFIP BAT: the micro-cycle (elementary cycle) and the macro-cycle. The micro-cycle imposes the maximum rate at which the BA performs a set of scans. Usually, the micro-cycle is set equal to highest common factor (HCF) of the required scan periodicities. Using this HCF rule, and for the example of

Table 5.20, the value for the micro-cycle is set to 1 ms. A possible schedule for all the periodic scans is illustrated in Figure 5.20, where we consider

$C = 97.6\ \mu s$ for each elementary transaction.

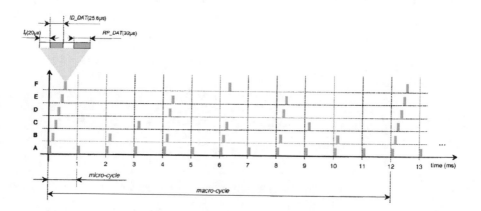

Figure 5.20. A possible schedule for all the periodic scans.

It is easy to depict that, for this example, the sequence of micro-cycles is repeated after each 12 micro-cycles. This sequence of micro-cycles is said to be a macro-cycle, and its length is given by the lowest common multiple (LCM) of the scan periodicities. The HCF/LCM approach for building the WorldFIP BAT has the following properties:

1. The scanning periods of the variables are multiples of the micro-cycle.
2. The variables are not scanned at exactly regular intervals. For the given example, only variables A and B are scanned exactly in the same "slot" within the micro-cycle. All other variables suffer from a slight communication jitter. For instance, concerning variable F, the interval between macro-cycles 1 and 7 is (1-5*0:098)+5+ 3*0:098=0.58 ms, whereas the interval between micro-cycles 7 and 13 is (1- 3* 0:098) +5+.5* 0.098=6.2 ms.
3. The length of the macro-cycle can induce a memory size problem, since the table parameters must be stored in the BA. For instance,

if scanning periodicities of variables E and F were, respectively, 5 and 7 ms, the length of the macro-cycle would be 420 micro-cycles instead of only 12.

Both the communication jitter and memory size problems have been addressed in the literature. In the authors discuss different methodologies for reducing the BAT size, without penalizing the communication jitter. The idea is very simple, and it basically consists on reducing some of the scan periodicities in order to obtain a harmonic pattern. The problem of table size has also been addressed in, however in a different perspective. In the referred work, the authors discuss an online scheduler (instead of storing the schedule in the BA's memory), which is not directly applicable to the WorldFIP case.

It is also worth mentioning that the schedule shown in Figure 5.20 represents a macro-cycle composed of synchronous micro-cycles, that is, for the specific example, each micro-cycle starts exactly 1 ms after the previous one. Within a micro-cycle, the spare time between the end of the last scan for a periodic variable and the end of the micro-cycle can be used by the BA to process non-periodic requests for buffer transfers, message transfers and padding identifiers. A WorldFIP BA can also manage asynchronous micro-cycles, not transmitting padding identifiers at the end of the micro-cycle. In such case, a new macro-cycle starts as soon as the periodic traffic is performed and there are no pending non-periodic buffer transfers or message transfers. Initial periodicities are not respected, since identifiers may be more frequently scanned.

5.2.3. Non-Periodic Communication Mechanism

In a WorldFIP system, not all the variables are to be included in the BAT. Some may only be occasionally exchanged, and thus do not need to be periodically scanned. Typically such exchanges will concern application events or alarms, which by their own nature do not occur with a periodic pattern. Therefore, it is preferable to map these variables into non-periodic buffer transfers, in order to reduce the network load. In the context of this paper, we consider that non-periodic requests use the urgent priority level.

The BA handles the non-periodic buffer transfers after processing the periodic traffic in a micro-cycle. The portion of the micro-cycle reserved for the periodic buffer exchanges is denoted as the periodic window, whereas the time left after the periodic window is denoted as the non-periodic window. The non-periodic buffer transfers take place in three stages (Figure 5.2):

1. A station with a pending non-periodic request must wait for its next periodic buffer transfer (say periodic variable X) to notify the BA, setting an non-periodic request bit in the RP_DAT frame. The bus arbitrator stores the indication of a yet not identified non-periodic request in a queue of requests for variable transfers. At the end of this interval, the BA is aware of a pending request in the station that produces periodic variable X.

2. In a subsequent non-periodic window, the BA asks the producer of the variable X (ID_RQ frame) to transmit the list of its pending non-periodic requests. The producer of X responds with a RP_RQ (list of identifiers) frame. This list is placed in another BA's queue, the ongoing non-periodic queue. At the end of this interval the BA knows what requested identifiers are.

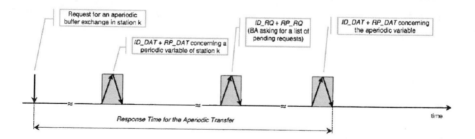

Figure 5.21. Timings for transactions associated with the processing of one non-periodic variable.

3. Finally, the BA processes requests for non-periodic transfers that are stored in its ongoing non-periodic queue. For each transfer, the BA uses the same mechanism as that used for the periodic buffer transfers (ID_DAT followed by RP_DAT).

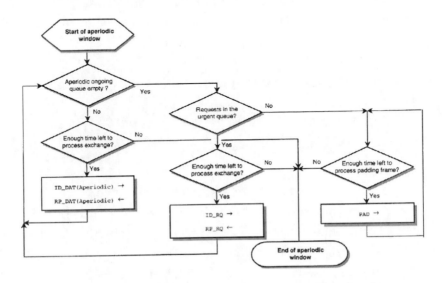

Figure 5.22. Non-periodic buffer transfer mechanisms of the WorldFIP protocol.

It is important to note that a station can only request non-periodic transfers using responses to periodic variables that it produces and which are configured in the BAT. Finally, it is important to stress that the urgent queue in the BA is only processed if, and only if, the BA's ongoing non-periodic queue is empty. As it can be depicted from Figure 5.22, traffic concerning the non-periodic buffer transfers (transactions ID_RQ/RP_RQ or ID_DAT/RP_DAT) can only be carried out if there is time left in a specific micro-cycle to completely process them.

5.2.4. Construction of Bus Scheduling Table

In WorldFIP networks, the *bus arbitrator table* (BAT) regulates the scheduling of all buffer transfers. In practice, two types of buffer transfers can be considered: periodic and non-periodic (sporadic). The BAT imposes the timings of the periodic buffer transfers, and also regulates the non-periodic buffer transfers.

Assume a distributed system within which 6 variables are to be periodically scanned, with scan frequencies as shown in Table 5.2. The WorldFIP BAT must be set in order to cope with these timing requirements.

Table 5.2. A distributed system within which 6 variables

Identifier	A	B	C	D	E	F
Periodicity (ms)	1	2	3	4	4	6

Two important parameters are associated with a WorldFIP BAT: the *macro-cycle* (elementary cycle) and the *macro-cycle*. The macro-cycle imposes the maximum rate at which the BA performs a set of scans. Usually, the macro-cycle is set equal to *highest common factor* (HCF) of the required scan periodicities. Using this rule, and for the example shown in Table 5.20, the value for the macro-cycle is set to 1ms. A possible schedule for all the periodic scans can be as illustrated in the following figure, where we consider $C = 97,6\mu s$ for each elementary transaction.

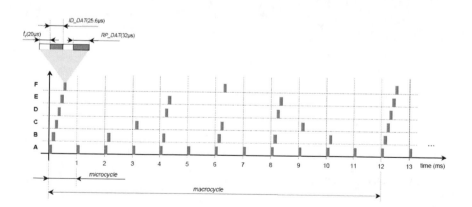

Figure 5.23. Scheduling diagram.

It is easy to depict that, for this example, the sequence of macro-cycles repeats each 12 macro-cycles. This sequence of macro-cycles is said to be a macro-cycle, and its length is given by the *lowest common multiple* (LCM) of the scan periodicities. Thus, the setting of the WorldFIP BAT for the given example is as follows:

<length of macro-cycle> = 1ms;
<length of macro-cycle> = 12;
<identifiers in each of the 12 macro-cycles>
<macro-cycle 1>: A, B, C, D, E, F;
<macro-cycle 2>: A;
<macro-cycle 3>: A, B;
<macro-cycle 4>: A, C;
<macro-cycle 5>: A, B, D, E;
<macro-cycle 6>: A;
<macro-cycle 7>: A, B, C, F;
<macro-cycle 8>: A;
<macro-cycle 9>: A, B, D, E;
<macro-cycle 10>: A, C;
<macro-cycle 11>: A, B;
<macro-cycle 12>: A;

The HCF/LCM approach for building a WorldFIP BAT has the following properties:

1. The scanning periods of the variables are multiples of the macro-cycle;
2. The variables are not scanned at exactly regular intervals. For the given example, only variables A and B are scanned exactly in the same "slot" within the macro-cycle. All other variables suffer from a slight communication jitter. For instance, concerning variable F, the interval between macro-cycles 1 and 7 is 5.8048ms, whereas the interval between macro-cycles 7 and 13 is 6.1952ms.

3. The length of the macro-cycle can induce a memory size problem, since the table parameters must be stored in the BA. For instance, if the scanning periodicities of variables E and F were, respectively, 5ms and 7ms, the length of the macro-cycle would be 420 macro-cycles instead of only 12.

Both the communication jitter and memory size problems have been addressed in the literature. Some researchers discuss different methodologies for reducing the BAT size, without penalising the communication jitter problem. The idea is very simple, and it basically consists on reducing some of the scan periodicities in order to have a harmonic pattern. The problem of table size has also been addressed in other works, however, in a different perspective. In the referred work, the authors discuss an online scheduler (instead of storing the schedule in the BA's memory), which is not directly applicable to the WorldFIP case.

It is also worth mentioning that the schedule shown in Figure 5.23 represents a macro-cycle composed of synchronous macro-cycles, that is, for the specific example, each macro-cycle starts exactly 1ms after the previous one. Within a macro-cycle, the spare time between the end of the last scan for a periodic variable and the end of the macro-cycle can be used by the BA to process non-periodic requests for buffer transfers, message transfers and padding identifiers4. A WorldFIP BA can also manage asynchronous macro-cycles, not transmit padding identifiers at the end of the macro-cycle. In such case, a new macro-cycle starts as soon as the periodic traffic is performed and there are no pending non-periodic buffer transfers or message transfers. Initial periodicities are not respected, since identifiers may be more frequently scanned.

The real-time requirements of the WorldFIP periodic traffic can be easily guaranteed since the BAT implements a static schedule for the periodic buffer transfers. In this section, we present three different algorithms to build the BAT schedule: two adapted algorithms from the well-known Rate Monotonic (RM) and Earliest Deadline First (EDF) algorithms , respectively, and also a third algorithm which we denote as the Deferred Release (DR) algorithm. Building the BAT schedule with either the RM or the EDF algorithms has several advantages, since it allows for the use of well-known schedule ability analysis theory.

Considering the RM scheduling algorithm, variables are scheduled according to their periodicity: the variable with the smallest periodicity will have the highest priority. If several variables have the same periodicity, the higher priority is given to the variable with the smaller identifier. A detailed algorithm for building the BAT using the RM algorithm is presented as follows. The algorithm indicates whether all traffic is schedulable or not.

Considering the WorldFIP characteristics, the BAT can be built as follows: 1. From variable with the shortest period until variable with the longest period 1.1 If the load in each cycle plus the variable's length (buffer transfer length) is still shorter than the value of the macro-cycle, then schedule a scan for that variable in each one of the macro-cycles (of a macro-cycle) multiple of the period of the variable. Update the value of the load in each concerned macro-cycle.

If the load in some of the macro-cycles does not allow schedule a scan for that variable, try to schedule it for the first of the subsequent macro-cycles up to the macro-cycle in which a new scan for that variable should be made. If this is not possible, the variable set is not scheduled. For the example of Table 5.2 (Cpi = 0.0976ms, "i) and considering the RM algorithm, the BAT is:

Table 5.3. BAT (using RM) for Example of Table 5.2

	Microcycle											
	1	2	3	4	5	6	7	8	9	10	11	12
bat[A.cycle]	1	1	1	1	1	1	1	1	1	1	1	1
bat[B.cycle]	1	0	1	0	1	0	1	0	1	0	1	0
bat[C.cycle]	1	0	0	1	0	0	1	0	0	1	0	0
bat[D.cycle]	1	0	0	0	1	0	0	0	1	0	0	0
bat[E.cycle]	1	0	0	0	1	0	0	0	1	0	0	0
bat[F.cycle]	1	0	0	0	0	0	1	0	0	0	0	0

where $bat[i, j]$ is a table of booleans with i ranging from 1 up to np, and j ranging from 1 up to N (number of macro-cycles in a macro-cycle).

Below, we give a detailed description of an algorithm for building the BAT using the RM algorithm is presented. In the algorithm, the vector *load* [ ] is used to store the load in each macro-cycle as the traffic is scheduled. It also assumes that the array $Vp[,]$ is ordered from the variable with the shortest period ($Vp[1,]$) to the variable with the longest period ($Vp[np,]$). Note that by using the RM algorithm some of the variables with longer periods can be scheduled in subsequent macro-cycles, thus inducing an increased communication jitter for those variables. For example, if the network data rate is 1Mbps instead of 2.5 Mbps ($Cpi = (64 + 80)/1 + 2*20 = 184\mu s$), the BAT would be as shown in Table 5.4, since a macro-cycle is only able to schedule up to 5 periodic buffer transfers (the following figure).

Table 5.4. BAT if the network data rate is 1Mbps instead of 2.5 Mbps

	Microcycle											
	1	2	3	4	5	6	7	8	9	10	11	12
Bat[*A,cycle*]	1	1	1	1	1	1	1	1	1	1	1	1
Bat[*B,cycle*]	1	0	1	0	1	0	1	0	1	0	1	0
bat[*C,cycle*]	1	0	0	1	0	0	1	0	0	1	0	0
bat[*D,cycle*]	1	0	0	0	1	0	0	0	1	0	0	0
bat[*E,cycle*]	1	0	0	0	1	0	0	0	1	0	0	0
bat[*F,cycle*]	0	1	0	0	0	0	1	0	0	0	0	0

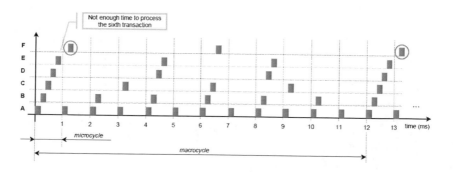

Figure 5.24. Schedule table.

An alternative to the use of the RM algorithm to build the BAT schedule is the EDF algorithm. When compared to the RM scheduling, one of the known advantages of the EDF scheduling is that it allows a better utilization. Considering the EDF algorithm, variables are scheduled according to the earliest deadline (we assume deadlines equal to periods and thus the variable with the earliest deadline is the one with the earliest end of period). If several variables have the same deadline (priority tie), the higher priority is given to the variable with the earliest request. The increased utilisation allowed by the EDF scheduling algorithm is emphasized, considering the set of periodic buffer transfers shown in Table 5.4 (utilization equal to 90%). Considering the RM algorithm, the request for V_{PF} would miss its deadline (Table 5.4). In fact, there is no empty slot for variable V_{PF} in the first three macro-cycles, since each micro-cycle is only able to schedule up to three buffer transfers.

5.3. COMMUNICATION PERFORMANCE ANALYSIS FOR WORLDFIP

5.3.1. Introduction

WorldFIP field-bus is increasingly applied in process control, manufacturing industry, power system automation and traffic information integration. It is unparalleled with its dual-bus redundancy techniques ensuring communication reliability in process control to great extension. Distributed intelligent control network based on WorldFIP technology is completely distributed in function, high in reliability and intelligence. Bus schedule algorithm and patterns for data exchange between nodes in WorldFIP network is quite meaningful in improving its communication performance. In bus schedule algorithm, structure, algorithm and scale of schedule table were studied to great extension. Response-time-based schedulability analysis for the real-time traffic was presented in some literature. Control performance and schedule issues for periodic message with sequence constrain were also delved into. Methodology ensuring real-time constrain for non-periodic message in FF field-bus, which is similar with WorldFIP technologically, was researched and approaches to improve protocol was presented as well. Performance in schedule for non-periodic message in WorldFIP and FF were analyzed and compared. Stability of inquiry system based on multi-inputs and single server was discussed.

In this chapter, two patterns for data exchange between nodes in WorldFIP Field-bus network were presented. Effects on communication performance of WorldFIP network with number of bits in user effective data and turn-around time at different network speed under both patterns were analyzed. Effects on communication performance of WorldFIP network with number of bits in user effective data and turn-around time at different network speed under periodic message transmission pattern using acknowledged and non-acknowledged message approaches were analyzed. Communication performance under both patterns were analyzed and compared.

5.3.2. Communication Patterns for WorldFIP

Centralized medium control strategy is used in WorldFIP network, which is a controlled communication system based on schedule. Two kinds of nodes, which are Link Activity Scheduler (LAS) and elementary nodes, are included in WorldFIP network. Variable exchange and message transmission are all supported in data exchange between nodes in the network [10].

Variable exchange is an effective pattern for communication over network, which can implement data transmission from 1 node to n nodes. All nodes requiring the data from the same produced variable can obtain the data in form of consumed variables in a data transmission cycle. Addressing is used in message transmission to implement data exchange between any 2 peer nodes. m message transmission cycles are used if the same data is required by m nodes, which make it less efficient than variable exchange pattern in communication performance. The 2 patterns were shown in Figure 5.25 and Figure 5.26.

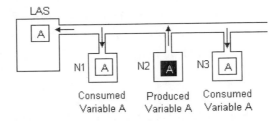

Figure 5.25. Data exchange by Produced/Consumed Variable between 1 node and n nodes.

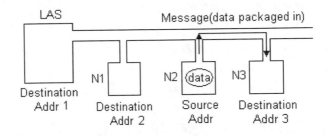

Figure 5.26. Data exchange by message transmission between 2 peer nodes.

Data exchange patterns between nodes were related closely to the type of communication controller used in nodes over network. 2 types of communication controller used in WorldFIP, which are FULLFIP2 and MICROFIP. Bus communication schedule is implemented with FULLFIP2, which supports any kind of periodical/non-periodical variables exchange and direct addressing messages transmission. FULLFIP2 provides interface between data link layer and application layer and user. MICROFIP cannot schedule bus communication and is designed for elementary nodes needing little communication and no bus scheduling. MICROFIP supports periodical/non-periodical variables exchange between LAS, elementary nodes and direct addressing messages transmission. Generally, FULLFIP2 is used in LAS and MICROFIP used in elementary nodes.

Limited by the number of identifiers, nodes using MICROFIP as communication controller are not able to exchange data directly with variable exchange pattern, which can be achieved by FULLFIP2. However, cost of nodes with FULLFIP2 is much higher than that of nodes with MICROFIP.

In data exchange between nodes using MICROFIP, 2 kinds of pattern can be used as followed.

1. WorldFIP variable exchange and LAS forwarding pattern. For 2 nodes with MICROFIP cannot exchange data directly with variable exchange pattern, LAS using FULLFIP2 served as data forwarding node thereby. 2 variable exchanges were included in data exchange between 2 peer elementary nodes: ① variable exchange between node N holding source data and LAS ② variable exchange between LAS and node M as data receiver.
2. WorldFIP periodic message direct data exchange pattern

Data exchange between 2 peer nodes is supported by MICROFIP and FULLFIP2, by which direct data exchange can be implemented over network.

The assumed condition of variable exchange application in pattern 1 is that the number of destination nodes was 1, i.e., data in produced variable is consumed by only 1 node.

5.3.3. Communication Performance Analysis for WorldFIP by Variable Exchange

5.3.3.1. WorldFIP Variable Exchange and LAS Forwarding Pattern

Assumed that number of field intelligent nodes, in all of which MICROFIP were used, was n. FULLFIP2 was used in LAS with physical address $0xa$. Node N with address $0xn$ was required to transmit periodic data to node M with address $0xm$. LAS forwarding pattern was used in the transmission. Address of LAS, N and M conform to the expression (1).

$$a < N, a < M \tag{1}$$

A produced variable $0x02n$ was configured in N; a consumed variable $0x01m$ was configured in M; a consumed variable $0x02n$ was configured in LAS to receive data from N; a produced variable $0x01m$ was configured in LAS to forward data received from N to M. Communication flow was described as followed.

1. Periodic data inquiry frame ID_DAT($0x02n$) was broadcast by LAS;
2. Response frame RP_DAT(*data*) was sent by N as response to frame ID_DAT($0x02n$). After this step, data in N was transmitted to variable $0x02n$ in LAS;
3. Data in consumed variable $0x02n$ in LAS was copied to produced variable $0x01m$ by internal program of LAS;
4. Periodic data inquiry frame ID_DAT($0x01m$) was broadcast by LAS;
5. Reply frame RP_DAT(*data*) was sent by LAS itself as response to frame ID_DAT($0x01m$) as LAS was the producer of variable $0x01m$. After this step, data in produced variable $0x01m$ in LAS was transmitted to consumed variable $0x01m$ in node M.

Formats for the related frames in the data transmission cycle were shown in Figure 5.27.

ID_DAT frame:

FSS	Control	Identifier	FCS	FES
(2)	(1)	(2)	(2)	(1)

RP_DAT frame:

FSS	Control	User Data	FCS	FES
(2)	(1)	(1~128)	(2)	(1)

Figure 5.27. Frame format by variable exchange.

In above communication, the cycle time for the data transmission was different when the network speed was different even if the number of bits in data was the same. To make evaluation convenient, the number of bits in data but not the time consumed in data transmission was used here to analyze and evaluate communication performance of the network. Therefore, the concept-bus efficiency was introduced here.

Bus efficiency λ was defined as: the ratio between number of bits in user data, which was specified as N_{data}, and number of bits in all frames in a data transmission cycle, which was specified as N_{all}, in a specified time-span to implement a effective data transmission between nodes over WorldFIP network, i.e.:

$$\lambda = \frac{N_{data}}{N_{all}} \tag{2}$$

In a data transmission involving frame ID_DAT and RP_DAT, N_{data} was user data packaged in RP_DAT, which conformed to the rule $N_{data} \leq 128$ according to WorldFIP specification; N_{all} was the sum of the number of all bits in frame ID_DAT and RP_DAT, i.e.:

$$N_{all} = N_{ID\_DAT+RP\_DAT} \tag{3}$$

5.3.3.2. Performance Analysis for Single Data Exchange between Nodes

In case of single data exchange between nodes,

$$N_{all} = N_{ID\_DAT(0x02n)} + N_{RP\_DAT(data)} + N_{ID\_DAT(0x01m)} + N_{RP\_DAT(data)}$$
$$= 8 + (6+n) + 8 + (6+n) = 2n + 28 \tag{4}$$

where, n was for number of bits in user data packaged in RP_DAT, $n \leq 128$.

Then the bus efficiency

$$\lambda = \frac{n}{2n + 28} \tag{5}$$

Turn-around time T_r in WorldFIP network, which represents the time span between receiving prior frame and sending next frame, was considered and converted into number of bits of data in communication, i.e.:

$$N_{tr} = T_r \times \beta \tag{6}$$

where β was for WorldFIP network speed with unit *bps*.

Therefore, expression (4) was modified as

$$N_{all} = N_{ID\_DAT(0x02n)} + N_{RP\_DAT(data)} + N_{ID\_DAT(0x01m)} + N_{RP\_DAT(data)} + 4N_{tr}$$
$$= 8 + (6 + n) + 8 + (6 + n) + 4N_{tr} = 2n + 28 + 4N_{tr}$$

Then bus efficiency

$$\lambda = \frac{n}{2n + 28 + 4N_{tr}} \tag{7}$$

Relation between network communication speed β and turn-around time T_r was described as

$$T_r = \begin{cases} 22.4 \sim 320\mu s, \beta = 31.25 Kbps \\ 10 \sim 70\mu s, \quad \beta = 1 Mbps \\ 4 \sim 28\mu s, \quad \beta = 2.5 Mbps \end{cases} \tag{8}$$

Then $N_{tr} = T_r . \beta$ could be obtained as

$$N_{tr} = \begin{cases} 0.7 \sim 10, \beta = 31.25 Kbps \\ 10 \sim 70, \quad \beta = 1 Mbps \\ 10 \sim 70, \quad \beta = 2.5 Mbps \end{cases} \tag{9}$$

For N_{tr} has to evaluated as integer, expression (9) was modified as

$$N_{tr} = \begin{cases} 1 \sim 10, \quad \beta = 31.25 Kbps \\ 10 \sim 70, \quad \beta = 1 Mbps \\ 10 \sim 70, \quad \beta = 2.5 Mbps \end{cases} \tag{10}$$

Then bus efficiency was analyzed by different cases.

Case 1: $\beta = 31.25 Kbps$, number of bits in user data $n \in [1,128]$, communication efficiency λ varied with $N_{tr} \in [1,10]$ as shown in Figure 5.28.

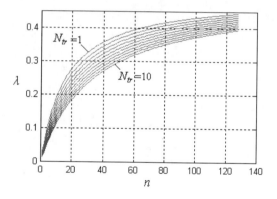

Figure 5.28. λ varied with $N_{tr} \in [1,10]$ under $\beta = 31.25 Kbps$ and single data exchange.

When $N_{tr} = 1$ and $n \in [1,128]$, λ took maximum $\lambda_{max} = 0.44$; when $N_{tr} = 10$, $n \in [1,128]$, λ took minimum $\lambda_{min} = 0.395$.

Case 2: $\beta = 1Mbps, 2.5Mbps$, number of bits in user data $n\in[1,128]$, communication efficiency λ varied with N_{tr} in interval $[10,70]$ as shown in Figure 5.29.

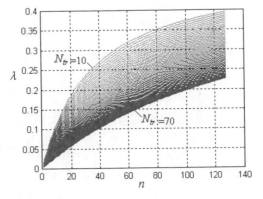

Figure 5.29. λ varied with $N_{tr} \in [10,70]$ under $\beta = 1Mbps, 2.5Mbps$ and single data exchange.

When $N_{tr}=10$ and $n \in [1,128]$, λ took maximum $\lambda_{max} = 0.395$; when $N_{tr}=70$, $n \in [1,128]$, λ took minimum $\lambda_{min} = 0.227$.

Therefore, in case that single data exchange between nodes, it was inverse ratioed between λ and β. When network communication was in lower speed, bus efficiency was higher. Meantime, number of bits in user data also affected bus efficiency to relatively great extension. Bus efficiency varied greatly with $n\leq50$; Increment in bus efficiency was reduced gradually with $n>50$. When network communication was in higher speed such as $\beta = 1Mbps, 2.5Mbps$, bus efficiency took linear relation with N_{tr}.

5.3.3.3. Performance Analysis for Data Exchange between Nodes with Maximum Communication Cycles

Assumption:

Number of all nodes in the whole network was m.

In case that each of m nodes required data from other one node among the all m nodes. Then m communication cycles, which were the maximum, were required to implement all tasks of data transmission, i.e.:

$$N_{all} = \sum_{a=1}^{m} D_{ij} = \sum_{a=1}^{m} (2n_{ij} + 28 + 4N_{tr}) \tag{11}$$

$$i \neq j, \quad D_{ij} \neq D_{ji}$$

where N_{all} representing number of bits of all data transmission in m communication cycles; D_{ij} representing data sent from node i to node j; n_{ij} representing number of bits of user data packaged in various frames.

Then the bus efficiency in this case was

$$\lambda = \frac{\sum_{a=1}^{m} n_{ij}}{N_{all}} = \frac{\sum_{a=1}^{m} n_{ij}}{\sum_{a=1}^{m} (2n_{ij} + 28 + 4N_{tr})} = \frac{\sum_{a=1}^{m} n_{ij}}{2 \times \sum_{a=1}^{m} n_{ij} + 28m + 4mN_{tr}} \tag{12}$$

where $\sum_{a=1}^{m} n_{ij}$ representing sum of number of bits in user data in the m communication cycles.

Therefore, bus efficiency λ was function of variable m, $\sum_{a=1}^{m} n_{ij}$ and N_{tr}. Obviously, $\lambda \propto \frac{1}{m}$. Relation of λ and $\sum_{a=1}^{m} n_{ij}$, N_{tr} was analyzed as followed.

Case 1: $\beta = 31.25 Kbps$, $m = 1$ for easing computation. Communication efficiency λ varied with $N_{tr} \in [1,10]$ as shown in Figure 5.30.

It could be seen that bus efficiency was affected greatly with $\sum_{a=1}^{m} n_{ij} \in [40,100]$; bus efficiency kept relatively stable and was affected by N_{tr} much less on the whole with $\sum_{a=1}^{m} n_{ij} > 400$.

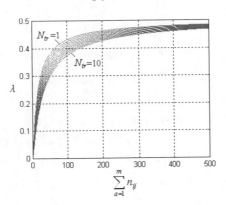

Figure 5.30. λ varied with $N_{tr} \in [1,10]$ under $\beta = 31.25 Kbps$ and maximum communication cycles.

Case 2: $\beta = 1 Mbps, 2.5 Mbps$, $m = 1$. Communication efficiency λ varied with $N_{tr} \in [1,10]$ as shown in Figure 5.31.

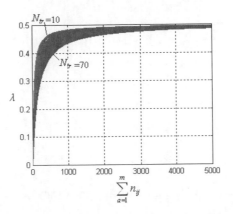

Figure 5.31. λ varied with $N_{tr} \in [1,10]$ under $\beta = 1 Mbps, 2.5 Mbps$ and maximum communication cycles.

It could be seen that bus efficiency was affected greatly with $\sum_{a=1}^{m} n_{ij} \in [20,2000]$; bus efficiency kept relatively stable and was affected by N_{tr} much less on the whole with $\sum_{a=1}^{m} n_{ij} > 5000$.

5.3.4. Communication Performance Analysis for WorldFIP by Periodic Message

5.3.4.1. WorldFIP Periodic Message Direct Data Exchange Pattern

Assumed that number of field intelligent nodes, in all of which MICROFIP were used, was n. FULLFIP2 was used in LAS with physical address $0x$a. Node N with address $0x$n was required to transmit periodic data to node M with address $0x$m. Periodic message direct data exchange was used in the transmission. A produced variable needed to be configured in node N. No configuration of variables were needed for node M. User data was packaged in message frames and addressing was used to implement direct data transmission between 2 peer nodes. Communication flow could be described as followed.

- **Non-acknowledged message used**

① Periodic message inquiry frame ID_MSG($0x$02n) was sent by LAS;
② Response frame RP_MSG_NOACK(*msg*) was sent by N to respond to frame ID_MSG($0x$02n). User data was packaged in *msg*. After this step, data in N was transmitted to M;
③ Frame RP_FIN() was sent by N to finish the message transmission.

- **Acknowledged message used**

① Periodic message inquiry frame ID_MSG($0x$02n) was sent by LAS;
② Response frame RP_MSG_ACK(*msg*) was sent by N to respond to frame ID_MSG($0x$02n). User data was packaged in *msg*. After this step, data in N was transmitted to M;

③ Message response frame RP_ACK() was sent by N;
④ Frame RP_FIN() was sent by N to finish the message transmission.

Formats for the frames included in the message transmission pattern were shown in Figure 5.32.

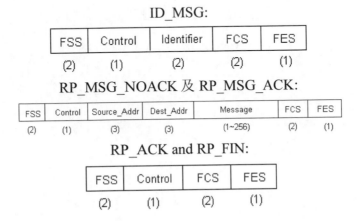

Figure 5.32. Formats for the frames included in the message transmission pattern.

5.3.4.2. Performance Analysis for Single Data Exchange between Nodes

1) Non-acknowledged message used

$$N_{all} = N_{ID\_MSG(0x02n)} + N_{RP\_MSG\_NOACK(msg)} + N_{RP\_FIN()} \qquad (13)$$
$$= 8 + (12 + n) + 6 = n + 26$$

Number of bits in user data $N_{data}=n$, which really was *msg* packaged in frame RP_MSG_NOACK, $n \in [1,256]$.

Then bus efficiency

$$\lambda = \frac{N_{data}}{N_{all}} = \frac{n}{n + 26} \qquad (14)$$

After corrected with N_{tr},

$$N_{all} = N_{ID\_MSG(0x02n)} + N_{RP\_MSG\_NOACK(msg)} + N_{RP\_FIN()} + 4N_{tr}$$
$$= 8 + (12 + n) + 6 + 4N_{tr} = n + 26 + 4N_{tr}$$

Corrected bus efficiency was $\lambda = \dfrac{n}{n + 26 + 4N_{tr}}$ (15)

Case 1: $\beta = 31.25 Kbps$, $n \in [1,256]$ communication efficiency λ varied with $N_{tr} \in [1,10]$ as shown in Figure 5.33.

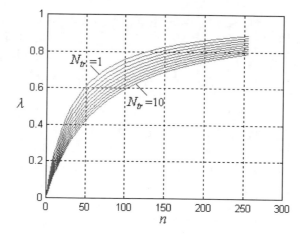

Figure 5.33. $\beta = 31.25 Kbps$, $n \in [1,256]$, communication efficiency λ varied with $N_{tr} \in [1,10]$ under single data exchange.

Case 2: $\beta = 1 Mbps, 2.5 Mbps$, $n \in [1,256]$ communication efficiency λ varied with $N_{tr} \in [10,70]$ as shown in Figure 5.34.

2) Acknowledged message used

$$N_{all} = N_{ID\_MSG(0x02n)} + N_{RP\_MSG\_ACK(msg)} + N_{RP\_ACK()} + N_{RP\_FIN()}$$
$$= 8 + (12 + n) + 6 + 6 = n + 32$$ (16)

Corrected bus efficiency was $\lambda = \dfrac{n}{n + 32 + 4N_{tr}}$ (17)

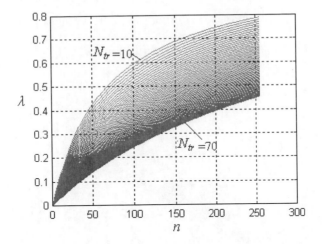

Figure 5.34. $\beta = 1Mbps, 2.5Mbps$,$n\in[1,256]$ communication efficiency λ varied with $N_{tr} \in [10,70]$ under single data exchange and non-acknowledged message used.

Case 1: $\beta = 31.25Kbps$, $n\in[1,256]$ communication efficiency λ varied with $N_{tr} \in [1,10]$ as shown in Figure 5.35.

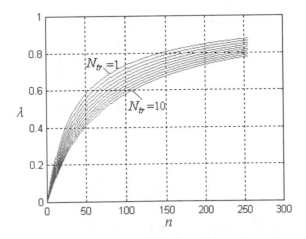

Figure 5.35. $\beta = 31.25Kbps$, $n\in[1,256]$ communication efficiency λ varied with $N_{tr} \in [1,10]$ under single data exchange and acknowledged message used.

Case 2: $\beta = 1Mbps, 2.5Mbps$, $n \in [1,256]$ communication efficiency λ varied with $N_{tr} \in [10,70]$ as shown in Figure 5.36.

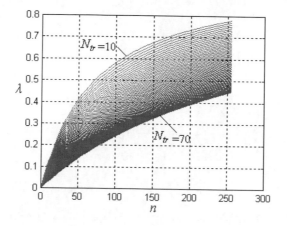

Figure 5.36. $\beta = 1Mbps, 2.5Mbps$, $n \in [1,256]$ communication efficiency λ varied with $N_{tr} \in [10,70]$ under single data exchange and acknowledged message used.

5.3.4.3. Performance Analysis for Data Exchange between Nodes with Maximum Communication Cycles

The assumption was same with before mentioned.

- **Non-acknowledged message used**

$$\lambda = \frac{\sum_{a=1}^{m} n_{ij}}{N_{all}} = \frac{\sum_{a=1}^{m} n_{ij}}{\sum_{a=1}^{m} (n_{ij} + 26 + 4N_{tr})} = \frac{\sum_{a=1}^{m} n_{ij}}{\sum_{a=1}^{m} n_{ij} + 26m + 4mN_{tr}} \tag{18}$$

- **Acknowledged message used**

$$\lambda = \frac{\sum_{a=1}^{m} n_{ij}}{N_{all}} = \frac{\sum_{a=1}^{m} n_{ij}}{\sum_{a=1}^{m} (n_{ij} + 32 + 4N_{tr})} = \frac{\sum_{a=1}^{m} n_{ij}}{\sum_{a=1}^{m} n_{ij} + 32m + 4mN_{tr}} \tag{19}$$

Case 1: $\beta = 31.25 Kbps$,$m=1$, $n \in [1,500]$ communication efficiency λ varied with $N_{tr} \in [1,10]$ as shown in Figure 5.37.

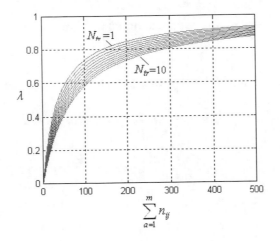

Figure 5.37. $\beta = 31.25 Kbps$,$m = 1$, $n \in [1,500]$ communication efficiency λ varied with $N_{tr} \in [1,10]$ under maximum communication cycles and acknowledged message used.

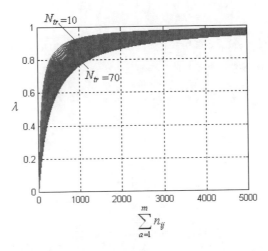

Figure 5.38. $\beta = 1 Mbps, 2.5 Mbps$,$m = 1$, $n \in [1,5000]$ communication efficiency λ varied with $N_{tr} \in [10,70]$ under maximum communication cycles and acknowledged message used.

Case 2: $\beta = 1Mbps, 2.5Mbps$,$m = 1$, $n \in [1,5000]$ communication efficiency λ varied with $N_{tr} \in [10,70]$ as shown in Figure 5.38.

Communication performance under non-acknowledged message used was almost the same with under acknowledged message used.

5.3.5. Comparison of Communication Performance

5.3.5.1. Performance Analysis for Single Data Exchange between Nodes

λ_{msg} represents Communication performance under periodic message transmission; λ_{var} representing Communication performance under variable exchange and LAS forwarding; $\Delta\lambda$ representing the difference of λ_{msg} and λ_{var} .

$$\Delta\lambda = \lambda_{msg} - \lambda_{var} = \frac{n}{n + 26 + 4N_{tr}} - \frac{n}{2n + 28 + 4N_{tr}} \tag{18}$$

Case 1: $\beta = 31.25Kbps$,$n \in [1,128]$, $\Delta\lambda$ varied with $N_{tr} \in [1,10]$ as shown in Figure 5.39

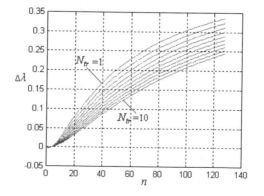

Figure 5.39. $\beta = 31.25Kbps$,$n \in [1,128]$, $\Delta\lambda$ varied with $N_{tr} \in [1,10]$.

It could be seen that $\lambda_{\mathrm{var}} > \lambda_{msg}$ when n < 4 ; $\lambda_{msg} > \lambda_{\mathrm{var}}$ when $n \geq$ 4.

Case 2: $\beta = 1Mbps, 2.5Mbps$,$n \in [1,128]$, $\Delta\lambda$ varied with N_{tr} $\in [10,70]$ as shown in Figure 5.40.

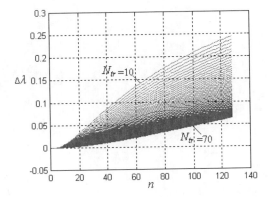

Figure 5.40. $\beta = 1Mbps, 2.5Mbps$,$n \in [1,128]$, $\Delta\lambda$ varied with $N_{tr} \in$ [10,70].

It could be seen that relation of λ_{var} and λ_{msg} varied with n could be described as

$$\begin{cases} \lambda_{\mathrm{var}} > \lambda_{msg}, n < 4 \\ \lambda_{\mathrm{var}} = \lambda_{msg}, n = 4 \\ \lambda_{\mathrm{var}} < \lambda_{msg}, n > 4 \end{cases} \tag{19}$$

5.3.5.2 Performance Analysis for Data Exchange between Nodes with Maximum Communication Cycles

$$\Delta\lambda = \lambda_{msg} - \lambda_{\mathrm{var}} = \frac{\sum_{a=1}^{m} n_{ij}}{2 \times \sum_{a=1}^{m} n_{ij} + 28m + 4mN_{tr}} - \frac{\sum_{a=1}^{m} n_{ij}}{\sum_{a=1}^{m} n_{ij} + 32m + 4mN_{tr}} \tag{20}$$

Performances were described as Figure 5.41 and Figure 5.42.

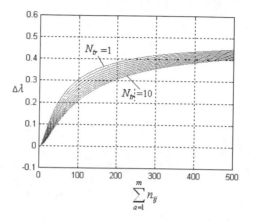

Figure 5.41. $\beta = 31.25Kbps$,$n \in [1,500]$, $\Delta\lambda$ varied with $N_{tr} \in [1,10]$ under maximum communication cycles.

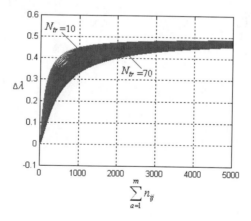

Figure 5.42. $\beta = 1Mbps,2.5Mbps$,$n \in [1,5000]$, $\Delta\lambda$ varied with $N_{tr} \in$ [10,70] under maximum communication cycles.

It could be seen that communication efficiency under periodic message transmission pattern was higher than that under variable exchange and LAS forwarding pattern when $n > 4$ in case of maximum communication cycles. Communication efficiency increased significantly with n increasing.

5.3.6. Conclusion

1. With the 2 patterns, evaluation of n affected communication performance significantly if number of bits in user data was smaller ($n < 500$).effects on efficiency by n decreased with n increasing;

2. With the 2 patterns, it was inverse ratioed to extension between communication efficiency λ and bus speed β *it was* inverse ratioed between robustness of λ in term of N_{tr} and β as well;

3. With the 2 patterns, it was inverse ratioed between communication efficiency λ and turn-around time. Choosing turn-around time should based on network reliability and efficiency, former could be achieved by taking longer turn-around time while later could be achieved by taking shorter one.

4. In case of single data destination node, communication efficiency under periodic message transmission pattern was higher than that under variable exchange and LAS forwarding pattern when $n > 4$. Communication efficiency increased significantly with n increasing.

Communication efficiency under the case of multi data destination nodes with variable exchange pattern were not analyzed and compared, which required further research in the future.

Chapter 6

NETWORKED CONTROL SYSTEM BASED ON CAN ITS APPLICATION IN INDUSTRY

6.1. INTRODUCTION TO CAN

The CAN bus is a broadcast type of bus. This means that all nodes can "hear" all transmissions. There is no way to send a message to just a specific node; all nodes will invariably pick up all traffic. The CAN hardware, however, provides local filtering so that each node may react only on the interesting messages.

The bus uses Non-Return To Zero (NRZ) with bit-stuffing. The modules are connected to the bus in a wired-and fashion: if just one node is driving the bus to a logical 0, then the whole bus is in that state regardless of the number of nodes transmitting a logical 1.

The CAN standard defines four different message types. The messages use a clever scheme of bit-wise arbitration to control access to the bus, and each message is tagged with a priority.

The CAN standard also defines an elaborate scheme for error handling and confinement which is described in more detail in Section 9, "CAN Error Handling."

Bit timing and clock synchronization is discussed in page 8 of this Tutorial. Here's a bit timing calculator you can use to calculate the CAN bus parameters and register settings.

CAN may be implemented using different physical layers (pg 5), some of which are described here, and there are also a fair number of connector types (pg 7) in use. We also provide a number of oscilloscope pictures (pg 6) for those interested in the details of a message.

6.2. CAN MESSAGES

The CAN bus is a broadcast type of bus. This means that all nodes can "hear" all transmissions. There is no way to send a message to just a specific node; all nodes will invariably pick up all traffic. The CAN hardware, however, provides local filtering so that each node may react only on the interesting messages.

6.2.1. The CAN Messages

CAN uses short messages – the maximum utility load is 94 bits. There is no explicit address in the messages; instead, the messages can be said to be contents-addressed, that is, their contents implicitly determines their address.

6.2.2. Message Types

There are four different message types (or "frames") on a CAN bus:

1. the Data Frame,
2. the Remote Frame,
3. the Error Frame, and
4. the Overload Frame.

6.2.2.1. The Data Frame

Summary: "Hello everyone, here's some data labeled X, hope you like it!"

The Data Frame is the most common message type. It comprises the following major parts (a few details are omitted for the sake of brevity):

- the Arbitration Field, which determines the priority of the message when two or more nodes are contending for the bus. The Arbitration Field contains:

  - For CAN 2.0A, an 11-bit Identifier and one bit, the RTR bit, which is dominant for data frames.
  - For CAN 2.0B, a 29-bit Identifier (which also contains two recessive bits: SRR and IDE) and the RTR bit.

- the Data Field, which contains zero to eight bytes of data.
- the CRC Field, which contains a 15-bit checksum calculated on most parts of the message. This checksum is used for error detection.
- an Acknowledgement Slot; any CAN controller that has been able to correctly receive the message sends an Acknowledgement bit at the end of each message. The transmitter checks for the presence of the Acknowledge bit and retransmits the message if no acknowledge was detected.

Note 1: It is worth noting that the presence of an Acknowledgement Bit on the bus does not mean that any of the intended addressees has received the message. The only thing we know is that one or more nodes on the bus has received it correctly.

Note 2: The Identifier in the Arbitration Field is not, despite of its name, necessarily identifying the contents of the message.

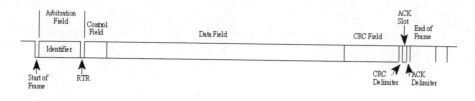

Figure 6.1. A CAN 2.0A ("standard CAN") Data Frame.

Figure 6.2. A CAN 2.0B ("extended CAN") Data Frame.

6.2.2.2. The Remote Frame

The Remote Frame is just like the Data Frame, with two important differences:

- it is explicitly marked as a Remote Frame (the RTR bit in the Arbitration Field is recessive), and
- there is no Data Field.

The intended purpose of the Remote Frame is to solicit the transmission of the corresponding Data Frame. If, say, node A transmits a Remote Frame with the Arbitration Field set to 234, then node B, if properly initialized, might respond with a Data Frame with the Arbitration Field also set to 234.

Remote Frames can be used to implement a type of request-response type of bus traffic management. In practice, however, the Remote Frame is little used. It is also worth noting that the CAN standard does not prescribe the behaviour outlined here. Most CAN controllers can be programmed either to automatically respond to a Remote Frame, or to notify the local CPU instead.

There's one catch with the Remote Frame: the Data Length Code must be set to the length of the expected response message. Otherwise the arbitration will not work.

Sometimes it is claimed that the node responding to the Remote Frame is starting its transmission as soon as the identifier is recognized, thereby "filling up" the empty Remote Frame. This is not the case.

A Remote Frame (2.0A type):

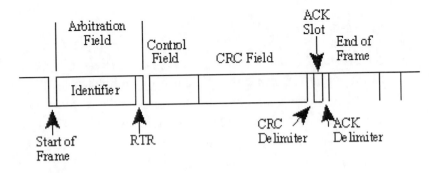

Figure 6.3. Remote Frame (2.0A type).

6.2.2.3. The Error Frame

Simply put, the Error Frame is a special message that violates the framing rules of a CAN message. It is transmitted when a node detects a fault and will cause all other nodes to detect a fault – so they will send Error Frames, too. The transmitter will then automatically try to retransmit the message. There is an elaborate scheme of error counters that ensures that a node can't destroy the bus traffic by repeatedly transmitting Error Frames.

The Error Frame consists of an Error Flag, which is 6 bits of the same value (thus violating the bit-stuffing rule) and an Error Delimiter, which is 8 recessive bits. The Error Delimiter provides some space in which the other nodes on the bus can send their Error Flags when they detect the first Error Flag.

Here's the Error Frame:

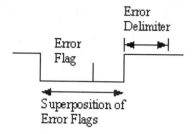

Figure 6.4. Error Frame.

6.2.2.4. The Overload Frame

The Overload Frame is mentioned here just for completeness. It is very similar to the Error Frame with regard to the format and it is transmitted by a node that becomes too busy. The Overload Frame is not used very often, as today's CAN controllers are clever enough not to use it. In fact, the only controller that will generate Overload Frames is the now obsolete 82526.

6.2.2.4.1. Standard vs. Extended CAN

Originally, the CAN standard defined the length of the Identifier in the Arbitration Field to eleven (11) bits. Later on, customer demand forced an extension of the standard. The new format is often called Extended CAN and allows no less than twenty-nine (29) bits in the Identifier. To differentiate between the two frame types, a reserved bit in the Control Field was used.

The standards are formally called

- 2.0A, with 11-bit Identifiers only,
- 2.0B, extended version with the full 29-bit Identifiers (or the 11-bit, you can mix them.) A 2.0B node can be
  - "2.0B active", i.e., it can transmit and receive extended frames, or
  - "2.0B passive", i.e., it will silently discard received extended frames (see below.)
- 1.x refers to the original specification and its revisions.

New CAN controllers today are usually of the 2.0B type. A 1.x or 2.0A type controller will get very upset if it receives messages with 29 arbitration bits. A 2.0B passive type controller will tolerate them, acknowledge them if they are correct and then – discard them; a 2.0B active type controller can both transmit and receive them.

Controllers implementing 2.0B and 2.0A (and 1.x) are compatible – and may be used on the same bus – as long as the controllers implementing 2.0B refrain from sending extended frames!

Sometimes people advocate that standard CAN is "better" than Extended CAN because there is more overhead in the Extended CAN messages. This is not necessarily true. If you use the Arbitration Field for transmitting data, then Extended CAN may actually have a lower overhead than Standard CAN has.

6.2.2.4.2. Basic CAN vs. Full CAN

The terms "Basic CAN" and "Full CAN" originate from the childhood of CAN. Once upon a time there was the Intel 82526 CAN controller which provided a DPRAM-style interface to the programmer. Then came along Philips with the 82C200 which used a FIFO- (queue-) oriented programming model and limited filtering abilities. To distinguish between the two programming models, people for some reason termed the Intel way as "Full CAN" and the Philips way as "Basic CAN". Today, most CAN controllers allow for both programming models, so there is no reason to use the terms "Full CAN" and "Basic CAN" – in fact, these terms can cause confusion and should avoided.

Of course, a "Full CAN" controller can communicate with a "Basic CAN" controller and vice versa. There are no compatibility problems.

6.2.2.4.3. Bus Arbitration and Message Priority

The message arbitration (the process in which two or more CAN controllers agree on who is to use the bus) is of great importance for the really available bandwidth for data transmission.

Any CAN controller may start a transmission when it has detected an idle bus. This may result in two or more controllers starting a message (almost) at the same time. The conflict is resolved in the following way. The transmitting nodes monitor the bus while they are sending. If a node detects a dominant level when it is sending a recessive level itself, it will immediately quit the arbitration process and become a receiver instead. The arbitration is performed over the whole Arbitration Field and when that field has been sent, exactly one transmitter is left on the bus. This node continues the transmission as if nothing had happened. The other potential transmitters will try to retransmit their messages when the bus becomes available next time. No time is lost in the arbitration process.

An important condition for this bit-wise arbitration to succeed is that no two nodes may transmit the same Arbitration Field. There is one exception to this rule: if the message contains no data, then any node may transmit that message.

Since the bus is wired-and and a Dominant bit is logically 0, it follows that the message with the numerically lowest Arbitration Field will win the arbitration.

Q: What happens if a node is alone on the bus and tries to transmit? A: The node will, of course, win the arbitration and happily proceeds with the message transmission. But when the time comes for acknowledging... no node will send a dominant bit during the ACK slot, so the transmitter will sense an ACK error, send an error flag, increase its transmit error counter by 8 and start a retransmission. This will happen 16 times; then the transmitter will go error passive. By a special rule in the error confinement algorithm, the transmit error counter is not further increased if the node is error passive and the error is an ACK error. So the node will continue to transmit forever, at least until someone acknowledges the message.

6.2.2.4.4. Message Addressing and Identification

It is worth noting once again that there is no explicit address in the CAN messages. Each CAN controller will pick up all traffic on the bus, and using a combination of hardware filters and software, determine if the message is "interesting" or not.

In fact, there is no notion of message addresses in CAN. Instead, the content of the messages is identified by an identifier which is present somewhere in the message. CAN messages are said to be "contents-addressed".

A conventional message address would be used like "Here's a message for node X". A contents-addressed message is like "Here's a message containing data labeled X". The difference between these two concepts is small but significant.

The content of the Arbitration Field is, per the Standard, used to determine the message's priority on the bus. All CAN controllers will also use the whole (some will use just a part) of the Arbitration Field as a key in the hardware filtration process.

The Standard does not say that the Arbitration Field must be used as a message identifier. It's nevertheless a very common usage.

A Note on the Identifier Values

We said that 11 (CAN 2.0A) or 29 (CAN 2.0B) bits is available in the Identifier. This is not entirely correct. Due to compatibility with a certain old CAN controller (guess which?), identifiers must not have the 7 most significant bits set to all ones, so only the identifiers 0..2031 are left for the 11-bit identifiers, and the user of 29-bit identifiers can use 532676608 different values.

Note that all other CAN controllers accept the "illegal" identifiers, so in a modern CAN system identifiers 2032, 2047 can be used without restrictions.

6.3. PHYSICAL LAYERS IN CAN

The CAN bus uses Non-Return To Zero (NRZ) with bit-stuffing. There are two different signaling states: dominant (logically 0) and recessive (logically 1). These correspond to certain electrical levels which depend on the physical layer used (there are several.) The modules are connected to the bus in a wired-and fashion: if just one node is driving the bus to the dominant state, then the whole bus is in that state regardless of the number of nodes transmitting a recessive state.

A physical layer defines the electrical levels and signaling scheme on the bus, the cable impedance and similar things.

There are several different physical layers:

- The most common type is the one defined by the CAN standard, part ISO 11898-2, and it's a two-wire balanced signaling scheme. It is also sometimes known as "high-speed CAN."
- Another part of the same ISO standard, ISO 11898-3, defines another two-wire balanced signaling scheme for lower bus speeds. It is fault tolerant, so the signaling can continue even if one bus wire is cut or shorted to ground or Vbat. It is sometimes known as "low-speed CAN."
- SAE J2411 defines a single-wire (plus ground, of course) physical layer. It's used chiefly in cars – e.g., GM-LAN.
- Several proprietary physical layers do exist.
- Modification of RS485 was used in the Old Ages when CAN drivers didn't exist.
- Go to page 6 to view a number of oscilloscope pictures for those interested in the details of a message.

Different physical layers cannot, as a rule, interoperate. Some combinations may work, or seem to work, under good conditions. For example, using both "high-speed" and "low-speed" transceivers on the same bus can work. sometimes.

A great many CAN transceiver chips are manufactured by Philips; alternative vendors include Bosch, Infineon, Siliconix and Unitrode.

A very common type is the 82C250 transceiver which implements the physical layer defined by ISO 11898. The 82C251 is an improved version.

A common transceiver for "low-speed CAN" is TJA1054 from Philips.

The maximum speed of a CAN bus, according to the standard, is 1 M bit/second. Some CAN controllers will nevertheless handle higher speeds than 1M bit/s and may be considered for special applications.

Low-speed CAN (ISO 11898-3, see above) can go up to 125 K bit/s.

Single-wire CAN can go up to around 50 K bit/s in its standard mode and, using a special high-speed mode used e.g. for ECU programming, up to around 100 K bit/s.

6.3.1. Minimum Bus Speed

Be aware that some bus transceivers will not allow you to go below a certain bit rate. For example, using 82C250 or 82C251 you can go down to10 K bit/s without problems, but if you use the TJA1050 instead you can't go below around 50 K bit/s. Check the data sheet.

At a speed of 1 M bit/s, a maximum cable length of about 40 meters (130 ft.) can be used. This is because the arbitration scheme requires that the wave front of the signal can propagate to the most remote node and back again before the bit is sampled. In other words, the cable length is restricted by the speed of light. A proposal to increase the speed of light has been considered but was turned down because of its inter-galactic consequences.

Other maximum cable lengths are (these values are approximate) –

- 100 meters (330 ft) at 500 K bit/s
- 200 meters (650 ft) at 250 K bit/s
- 500 meters (1600 ft) at 125 K bit/s
- 6 kilometers (20000 ft) at 10 K bit/s

If opt-couplers are used to provide galvanic isolation, the maximum bus length is decreased accordingly. Hint: use fast opt-couplers, and look at the delay through the device, not at the specified maximum bit rate.

6.3.2. Bus Termination

An ISO 11898 CAN bus must be terminated. This is done using a resistor of 120 Ohms in each end of the bus. The termination serves two purposes:

- Remove the signal reflections at the end of the bus.
- Ensure the bus gets correct DC levels.

An ISO 11898 CAN bus must always be terminated regardless of its speed. I'll repeat this: an ISO 11898 CAN bus must always be terminated regardless of its speed. For laboratory work just one terminator might be enough. If your CAN bus works even though you haven't put any terminators on it, you are just lucky.

Note that other physical layers, such as "low-speed CAN", single-wire CAN, and others, may or may not require termination. But your vanilla high-speed ISO 11898 CAN bus will always require at least one terminator.

The ISO 11898 prescribes that the cable impedance be nominally 120 Ohms, but an impedance in the interval of [108, 132] Ohms is permitted.

There are not many cables in the market today that fulfill this requirement. There is a good chance that the allowed impedance interval will be broadened in the future.

ISO 11898 is defined for a twisted pair cable, shielded or unshielded. Work is in progress on the single-wire standard SAE J2411.

There is no standard at all for CAN bus connectors! Usually, each Higher Layer Protocol(!) defines one or a few preferred connector types. Common types include

- 9-pin DSUB, proposed by CiA.
- 5-pin Mini-C and/or Micro-C, used by DeviceNet and SDS.
- 6-pin Deutch connector, proposed by CANHUG for mobile hydraulics.
- Go to page 7 to view a few different connector layouts.

6.4. CAN ERROR HANDLING

6.4.1. Errors Handling Mechanisms

Error handling is built into in the CAN protocol and is of great importance for the performance of a CAN system. The error handling aims at detecting errors in messages appearing on the CAN bus, so that the transmitter can retransmit an erroneous message. Every CAN controller along a bus will try to detect errors within a message. If an error is found, the discovering node will transmit an Error Flag, thus destroying the bus traffic. The other nodes will detect the error caused by the Error Flag (if they haven't already detected the original error) and take appropriate action, i.e., discard the current message.

Each node maintains two error counters: the Transmit Error Counter and the Receive Error Counter. There are several rules governing how these counters are incremented and/or decremented. In essence, a transmitter detecting a fault increments its Transmit Error Counter faster than the listening nodes will increment their Receive Error Counter. This is because there is a good chance that it is the transmitter who is at fault! When any Error Counter raises over a certain value, the node will first become "error passive," that is, it will not actively destroy the bus traffic when it detects an error, and then "bus off," which means that the node doesn't participate in the bus traffic at all.

Using the error counters, a CAN node can not only detect faults but also perform error confinement.

6.4.2. Error Detection Mechanisms

The CAN protocol defines no less than five different ways of detecting errors. Two of these works at the bit level, and the other three at the message level.

1. Bit Monitoring.
2. Bit Stuffing.
3. Frame Check.
4. Acknowledgement Check.
5. Cyclic Redundancy Check.

6.4.2.1. Bit Monitoring

Each transmitter on the CAN bus monitors (i.e., reads back) the transmitted signal level. If the bit level actually read differs from the one transmitted, a Bit Error is signaled. (No bit error is raised during the arbitration process).

6.4.2.2. Bit Stuffing

When five consecutive bits of the same level have been transmitted by a node, it will add a sixth bit of the opposite level to the outgoing bit stream. The receivers will remove this extra bit. This is done to avoid excessive DC components on the bus, but it also gives the receivers an extra opportunity to detect errors: if more than five consecutive bits of the same level occurs on the bus, a Stuff Error is signaled.

6.4.2.3. Frame Check

Some parts of the CAN message have a fixed format, i.e., the standard defines exactly what levels must occur and when. (Those parts are the CRC Delimiter, ACK Delimiter, End of Frame, and also the Intermission, but there are some extra special error checking rules for that.) If a CAN controller detects an invalid value in one of these fixed fields, a Form Error is signaled.

6.4.2.4. Acknowledgment Check

All nodes on the bus that correctly receives a message (regardless of their being "interested" of its contents or not) are expected to send a dominant level in the so-called Acknowledgement Slot in the message. The transmitter will transmit a recessive level here. If the transmitter can't detect a dominant level in the ACK slot, an Acknowledgement Error is signaled.

6.4.2.5. Cyclic Redundancy Check

Each message features a 15-bit Cyclic Redundancy Checksum (CRC), and any node that detects a different CRC in the message than what it has calculated itself will signal an *CRC Error*.

6.4.3. Error Confinement Mechanisms

Every CAN controller along a bus will try to detect the errors outlined above within each message. If an error is found, the discovering node will transmit an Error Flag, thus destroying the bus traffic. The other nodes will detect the error caused by the Error Flag (if they haven't already detected the original error) and take appropriate action, i.e., discard the current message.

Each node maintains two error counters: the Transmit Error Counter and the Receive Error Counter. There are several rules governing how these counters are incremented and/or decremented. In essence, a transmitter detecting a fault increments its Transmit Error Counter faster than the listening nodes will increment their Receive Error Counter. This is because there is a good chance that it is the transmitter who is at fault!

A node starts out in Error Active mode. When any one of the two Error Counters raises above 127, the node will enter a state known as Error Passive and when the Transmit Error Counter raises above 255, the node will enter the Bus Off state.

An Error Active node will transmit Active Error Flags when it detects errors.

An Error Passive node will transmit Passive Error Flags when it detects errors.

A node which is Bus Off will not transmit anything on the bus at all.

The rules for increasing and decreasing the error counters are somewhat complex, but the principle is simple: transmit errors give 8 error points, and receive errors give 1 error point. Correctly transmitted and/or received messages causes the counter(s) to decrease.

6.4.3.1. Example (Slightly Simplified)

Let's assume that node A on a bus has a bad day. Whenever A tries to transmit a message, it fails (for whatever reason). Each time this happens, it increases its Transmit Error Counter by 8 and transmits an Active Error Flag. Then it will attempt to retransmit the message and the same thing happens.

When the Transmit Error Counter raises above 127 (i.e., after 16 attempts), node A goes Error Passive. The difference is that it will now transmit Passive Error Flags on the bus. A Passive Error Flag comprises 6 recessive bits, and will not destroy other bus traffic – so the other nodes will not hear A complaining about bus errors. However, A continues to increase its Transmit Error Counter. When it raised to above 255, node A finally gives in and goes Bus Off.

What did the other nodes think about node A? – For every active error flag that A transmitted, the other nodes will increase their Receive Error Counters by 1. By the time that A goes Bus Off, the other nodes will have a count in their Receive Error Counters that is well below the limit for Error Passive, i.e., 127. This count will decrease by one for every correctly received message. However, node A will stay bus off.

Most CAN controllers will provide status bits (and corresponding interrupts) for two states:

- – "Error Warning" – one or both error counters are above 96
- – Bus Off, as described above.
- – Some – but not all! – controller also provide a bit for the Error Passive state. A few controllers also provide direct access to the error counters.

The CAN controller's habit of automatically retransmitting messages when errors have occurred can be annoying at times. There is at least one controller on the market (the SJA1000 from Philips) that allows for full manual control of the error handling.

6.4.3.2. Bus Failure Modes

The ISO 11898 standard enumerates several failure modes of the CAN bus cable:

1. CAN_H interrupted
2. CAN_L interrupted
3. CAN_H shorted to battery voltage
4. CAN_L shorted to ground
5. CAN_H shorted to ground
6. CAN_L shorted to battery voltage
7. CAN_L shorted to CAN_H wire
8. CAN_H and CAN_L interrupted at the same location
9. Loss of connection to termination network

For failures 1-6 and 9, it is "recommended" that the bus survives with a reduced S/N ratio, and in case of failure 8, that the resulting subsystem survives. For failure 7, it is "optional" to survive with a reduced S/N ratio.

In practice, a CAN system using 82C250-type transceivers will not survive failures 1-7, and may or may not survive failures 8-9.

There are "fault-tolerant" drivers, like the TJA1053, that can handle all failures though. Normally you pay for this fault tolerance with a restricted maximum speed; for the TJA1053 it is 125 K bit/s.

6.5. HIGHER LAYERS IN CAN PROTOCOL

The CAN standard defines the hardware ("the physical layer" – there are several) and the communication on a basic level ("the data link layer"). The CAN protocol itself just specifies how to transport small packets of data from point A to point B using a shared communications medium. But in order to manage the communication within a system, a higher layer protocol (HLP) is required.

Higher Layer Protocols include common standards like J1939, CAN-Open, CCP/XCP, and more.

6.6. SIMULATION AND PERFORMANCE ANALYSIS FOR CAN COMMUNICATION

A simulation model for CAN bus communication with 16 nodes was built with Stateflow in MATLAB/SIMULINK. The construction of each node for all the 16 nodes was the same, as shown in Figure 6.5.

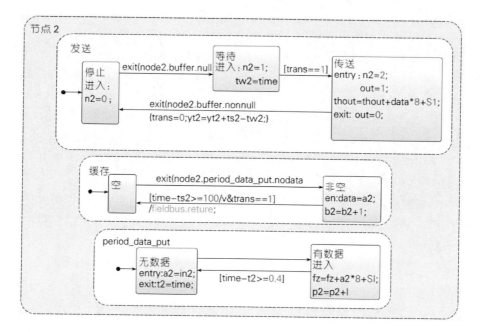

Figure 6.5. Construction of the node.

Transmission, buffering and data acquisition were included in each node module. Only these parts dealing with communication activities were considered and no computing, controlling and data reception activities were included when constructing the node model for the object of the simulation was just for studying the communication performance of CAN bus. Data acquisition module was used for acquiring the input data. The length of data conformed to average distribution. Data was assembled into standard short frame under "data available" status. In real system, data was probably from field or the output from node controller. Buffer module represented the buffer in nodes and the volume of the buffer was assumed to be 1 including two statuses: null and not null.

Bus scheduling module was shown as follows, including bus activities module and arbitration function "compete". Field-bus module included three states: idle, busy, frame isolated.

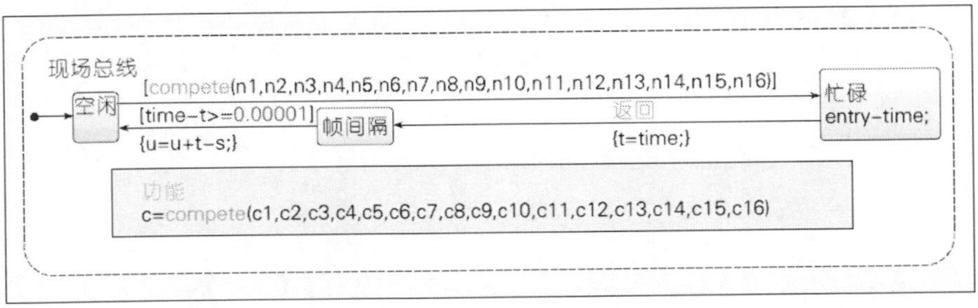

Figure 6.6. Scheduling module.

In this CAN simulation model, the significance of output parameters was as follows:

- u representing the total time of busy state;
- thout representing the total length of all data frames sent by all nodes;
- fz representing the total length of all data frames generated by all nodes;
- b1-b16 representing the amount of frames in 1-16 nodes, which were transmit successfully over the network;
- p1-p16 representing the amount of frames that were asked for transmission by 1-16 nodes.

Therefore, the calculation of throughput was as

$$\frac{thout}{T} = \frac{thout}{2}$$

The average delay was calculated as

$$\frac{\sum_{i=1}^{16} yti}{16}$$

Rate of traffic collision was calculated as

$$\frac{N \times \text{load} - \sum_{i=1}^{16} bi}{N \times \text{load}}$$

Load here means the load of the network traffic. Load completion was calculated as

$$\frac{\sum_{i=1}^{16} bi}{\sum_{i=1}^{16} pi}$$

The performance curves were as follows.

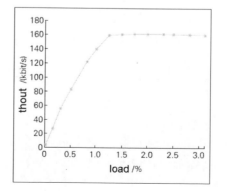

Figure 6.7. Load-throughput performance.

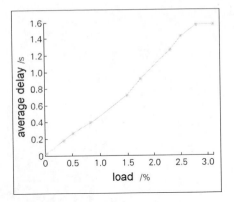

Figure 6.8. Load-average delay performance.

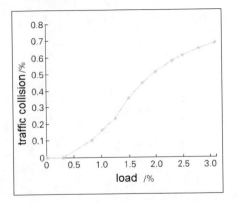

Figure 6.9. Load-traffic collision performance.

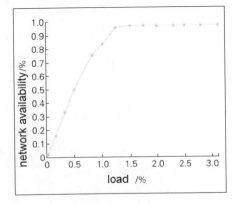

Figure 6.10. Load-network availability performance.

Geng Liang, Wen Li and Guoping Liu

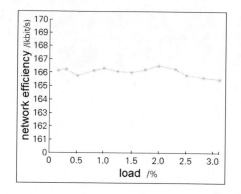

Figure 6.11. Load-network efficiency performance.

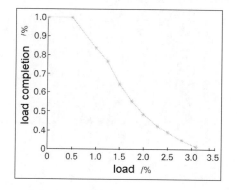

Figure 6.12. Load-load completion performance.

Chapter 7

IEC61499 FOR NETWORKED CONTROL SYSTEM

7.1. INTRODUCTION TO IEC61499

When development of IEC 61499 was begun in 1992, it was originally envisioned to provide common reference architecture for the use of software objects identified as Function Blocks (FBs) [1]. These were used in centralized, scanned controller architectures as exemplified in the IEC 61131-3 [2] standard for programming of Programmable Logic Controllers (PLCs), as well as in the configuration of decentralized, scheduled execution in Distributed Control Systems (DCS) as exemplified in the IEC 61804 series of standards. This led to an architecture that can be mapped to both application domains, as well as implementable as a pure event driven, distributed architecture. Since this project was widely distributed geographically, including researchers from the USA, Canada and Europe, it was necessary to maintain some degree of project control via a Compliance Profile (CP) [5]. Based on the experience obtained in this and other projects, the PAS documents were improved and updated to IEC Standard status in 2005. IEC/TR 61499-3, containing tutorial information based on the obsolete PAS documents, was withdrawn in 2007, since during the transition from PAS to Standard status, a substantial amount of literature and documents about the usage of this standard had become publicly available.

Based on accumulated experience in multiple implementations of IEC 61499, Working Group 15 of IEC Technical Subcommittee 65B (SC65B/WG15) began maintenance work on Parts 1 and 2 of the Standard in 2009. This WG consists of 19 international automation and control experts from eight countries (i.e., Austria, Germany, Italy, Japan, Netherlands, New Zealand, Switzerland, USA) coming from industry, academia and institutes for research and technology transfer. Following the normal sequence for maintenance of International Standards, the work of SC65B/WG15 has resulted in final approval of Second Editions of the IEC 61499 series as International Standards in late 2012.

7.2. KEY POINTS IN IEC61499

IEC 61499-1 defines the *function block type* as the basic unit for encapsulating and reusing Intellectual Property (IP = "know-how"). In object oriented terms, this is a *class* defining the behavior of (possibly) multiple instances. As shown in Figure 7.1, it includes *event* inputs and outputs as well as the more traditional *data* inputs and outputs, to provide for synchronization between data transfer and program execution in distributed systems.

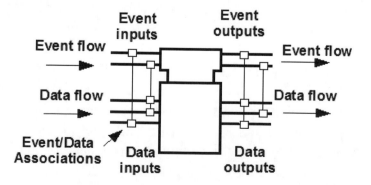

Figure 7.1. A Function Block type.

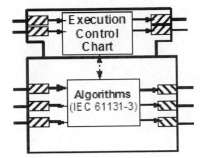

Figure 7.2. A Basic Function Block type.

As its name implies, the *basic FB type* is the "atom" out of which higher level "molecules" are constructed. With IEC 61499-2 compliant software tools, software developers can encapsulate IP in the form of *algorithms* written in one of the IEC 61131-3 programming languages or other languages such as Java or C++. As shown in Figure 7.2, execution of these algorithms is triggered by *Execution Control Charts (ECCs),* which are event driven state machines similar to the well known Harel Statecharts.

Another "atomic" function block type is the *Service Interface Function Block* (SIFB) type. This represents the interface to low level services provided by the operating system or hardware of the embedded device, such as:

- *Graphical User Interface* (GUI) elements such as a slider (illustrated in Figure 7.3), knob or pilot light
- *Communication services* (the CLIENT_2 SIFB illustrated in Figure 7.3 is a communication "client" for a remote "server")
- *Interfaces to hardware* such as a temperature sensor, a motor speed controller, a control valve or a room light intensity controller

IEC 61499-2 compliant software tools and their associated runtime packages can provide a large selection of GUI and communications SIFBs. Providers of *hardware SIFBs* (typically the manufacturers of embedded devices) can use IEC 61499-2 compliant software tools to document how they work in the form of service sequence diagrams.

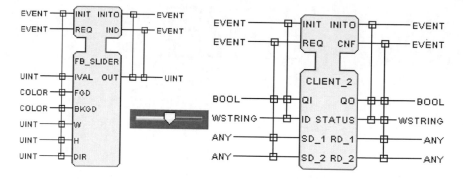

Figure 7.3. Service Interface Function Block types.

Software developers can use IEC 61499-2 compliant software tools to build higher level FB "molecules" called *composite FB types* out of lower level function block "atoms" (component function blocks). This is done by specifying the event and data interfaces of the composite type, then filling it with a diagram showing how its internal component function blocks are connected. In this kind of function block, execution of the algorithms in the component function blocks is controlled by the flow of events from one component to another.

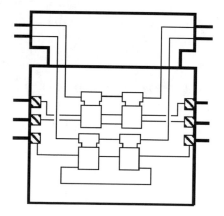

Figure 7.4. A Composite FB type.

In the IEC 61499-1 architectural model, distributable *applications* are built by interconnecting instances of reusable FB types with appropriate event and data connections, in the same manner as designing a circuit board with integrated circuits. Using IEC 61499-2 compliant software tools, these FBs can then be distributed to physical *devices* across a network as shown in Figure 7.5, as long as these devices comply with the applicable compliance profile.

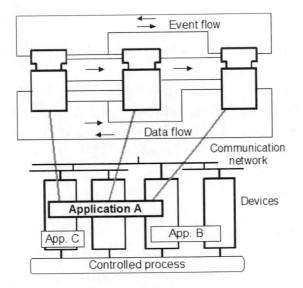

Figure 7.5. Distribution of an Application.

It is also possible to distribute an application across multiple resources within a device. Resources might be multiple processors plugged into a backplane, or multiple tasks within a single processor with a multitasking operating system.

In the IEC 61499 architecture, *resources* are the workhorses that provide the services needed to integrate all the pieces of applications into a working distributed system. IEC 61499-2 compliant software tools can be used to:

- Map the messages that are passed back and forth between devices into the input and output events and data of *communication SIFBs*
- Use event and data inputs and outputs to trigger the performance of the *algorithms* of *basic* and *composite* FBs, and synchronize their operation with other FBs

- Map the data and event inputs and outputs of I/O *SIFBs* to the inputs and outputs of the system, where it can sense what is going on in the physical world and take appropriate physical actions in response.

7.3. IMPROVEMENT IN THE IEC61499 2ND EDITION

The Second Edition of IEC 61499 Parts 1, 2 and 4 will contain changes made in response to approximately 120 editorial and 40 technical comments received from National Committees, with additional editorial changes to conform with IEC requirements. Significant technical changes from the First Edition are listed below.

7.3.1. Execution Control

Interpreting the definitions for executing IEC 61499 FBs, especially how to interpret the definitions for the ECC of basic FBs has been one of the most discussed topics in research and industry in recent years [9, 10]. For this reason, a large part of the refinement work for the second edition has been spent on removing ambiguities in the description of the ECC's behavior in IEC 61499-1. The goal has been to clarify and simplify for device vendors the requirements for implementation of ECC behavior, while at the same time making it more understandable for application developers, so that all can rely on a common understanding of a basic FB's execution behavior.

The first major change in execution control requirements is to resolve *concurrency* issues by requiring that a resource shall ensure that no more than one input event is delivered at any instant in time to the FB. This provision aims at making execution of FB applications more deterministic by excluding possibilities of simultaneous activation of multiple algorithms. If such simultaneous activity is not blocked, it could result in different execution results, even with the same FB application on the same platform.

A second major change resolves data consistency issues by requiring that, in conjunction with the event input delivery, sampling of input data (or its functional equivalent) shall be performed on those input variables associated with the input event using a graphical or textual WITH construct in the declaration of the FB type. Ambiguities in sampling rules could result in different execution results of the same function block application on different devices.

A third major change resolves a confusion that resulted from a change in the semantics of events between the First Edition of IEC Standard 61499-1 and the earlier PAS (Publicly Available Specification) version: in the PAS, an event could be used as a Boolean variable, while in the Standard it was defined as an "instantaneous occurrence." In ECCs the transition conditions of the currently active state are evaluated sequentially on activation by an input event. That means that as long a valid transition condition is found a new state will be entered and its actions (i.e., executing algorithms, sending output events) performed. In the Second Edition of IEC 61499-1, it is clarified that an input event is only valid the first time the transition conditions are evaluated. In any further evaluations (i.e., after the new state has been reached) only conditions without an event in their condition may be evaluated. However, this does not imply that the transition taken at first after activation by the input event needs to have that event in its condition; Also in this case a condition without event in its condition may be taken. For instance, as shown in Figure 7.6, these provisions prevent an infinite iterative or recursive loop between state START and TRIGGERED upon the single occurrence of an EI event with $K > 3$. The importance of this provision for the application developer is explained by the increasing role of ECCs used as a language of application development. During the initial development of the Standard, the ECC was regarded as a simple mechanism for activating different operational modes of the FB (AUTO, MANUAL, etc.). However, practical experience has shown that using ECC as a state machine language, in which various combinations of eventful and eventless transitions may occur, simplifies the representation of application logic and reduces the complexity of algorithms. This results in significant improvements in the readability and maintainability of basic FB types. As in other architectural specification frameworks such as UML [11], this usage of the ECC requires more rigorous semantic definition.

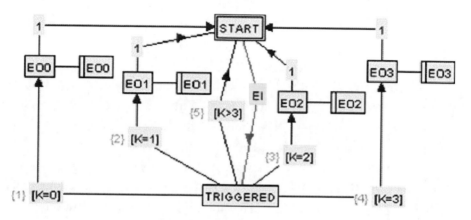

Figure 7.6. Execution Control Chart (ECC) example.

In order to better show the difference between events and data, a new transition condition syntax in the form of event input name was specified by the Second Edition of IEC 61499-1. This is easier to read and reflects the syntax of the Unified Modeling Language (UML), which should make ECCs easier to learn and understand. Additionally, the terminology "clearing a transition" has been changed to "passing a transition" in order to avoid the connotation that a transition could be represented by a user accessible Boolean variable that could be "set" or "cleared." This in fact was an artifact of a long-standing mistranslation of the French term franchisement in the original GRAFCET standard [12].

A final improvement that is given as an example in the Second Edition of IEC 61499-2 is the possibility to represent graphically the priority ordering (i.e., order of evaluation) of multiple transitions from a single EC state, as illustrated in Figure 7.6. This ordering is significant when such transitions are not mutually exclusive, i.e., when multiple transitions have the same associated event or no associated event.

7.3.2. Temporary Variables

The definition of *algorithms* in basic FBs has been extended such that the declaration of algorithms may also include the declaration of temporary variables using a VAR_TEMP declaration as in IEC 61131-3. The behavior of these temporary variables is such that they are only visible within the algorithm in which they are specified. On each algorithm invocation such variables are created and initialized. They may be used and modified during execution of the algorithm but their values do not persist between executions of the algorithm. This greatly improves the readability of basic FBs as variables only needed within an algorithm now need not be declared as internal variables of the FB. A typical application example would be a variable used as loop counter.

7.3.3. Network and Segments

A syntax for segment types has been introduced in the Second Edition of IEC 61499. This enables the specification of the properties of a specific network type or protocol. IEC 61499-2 compliant software tools can now provide libraries of different kinds of segment types for the system configuration, allowing a clear documentation of the overall system structure. In a further step device types can specify which kinds of ports to different segment types they provide, for example as resource types or SIFB types. As part of an IEC 61499 system configuration, links can be specified between such ports and appropriate segments (instances of segment types). This can then be used for ensuring a valid system configuration, and could also provide a basis for future software tool capabilities for automatic network configuration and communication performance evaluation.

7.3.4. Integration with PLCs

In addition to the facilities defined in the First Edition of IEC 61499-1 for the mapping of functionalities defined in IEC 61131-3 into the IEC

61499 architecture, the Second Edition of IEC 61499-1 defines the use of SIFBs that can act as clients of the PLC communication services defined in IEC 61131-5 [13]. These include a READ block for synchronous reading of PLC data, a UREAD block for asynchronous reading, and a WRITE block for synchronous writing of PLC data, as well as a TASK block for remote triggering of PLC tasks as defined in IEC 61131-3.

7.3.5. Simplified Data Access

The First Edition of IEC 61499-1 adopted the access path concept from IEC 61131-3 for use with READ and WRITE management actions to provide access to externally visible interfaces of devices, resources and FBs, and additionally to provide access to internal variables of basic FBs or internal FB elements of composite FBs. However, this concept violates the principles of encapsulation and component orientation of the IEC 61499 FB model. In order to enforce good software design and enhance system performance, reliability, maintainability and safety, the use of access paths has been removed from IEC 61499. With the removal of access paths, the READ and WRITE management commands are now allowed to access only the interface of FBs, devices and resources, and the internals are hidden from them.

7.3.6. Additional Changes and Corrections

In addition to the changes described above, the Second Edition of IEC 61499 contains a number of smaller changes and corrections. These are mainly corrections to add anticipated but forgotten elements, for example a RESET command for management of FB operational states.

Two additional changes provide a unification of language elements across the different FB types. The first change is that service sequences, which allow describing the externally visible dynamic behaviors of a FB, are now allowed for all types of FBs. The second is that definitions for the usage of adapters have been extended from *composite* FB types to basic FB types as well.

Finally, IEC 61499-2 has been updated to contain informative examples of software tool capabilities and updated Document Type Definitions (DTDs) to conform to the changes in IEC 61499-1.

7.4. DEVELOPMENTS IN THE FUTURE

In the process of preparing the Second Editions of IEC 61499 Parts 1, 2 and 4, IEC SC65B/WG15 considered several proposals for extensions to the Standard which could enhance its applicability for the development of distributed automation and control systems. However, these proposals were sufficiently developed in detail or sufficiently tested for immediate standardization. Therefore, the WG plans to develop a New Work Item Proposal (NWIP) to prepare a new Part 5 of the IEC 61499 as a Technical Specification (IEC/TS 61499-5) for provisional application to determine the suitability for standardization of some or all of these extensions following a period of testing in practice.

As mentioned earlier, IEC/TR 61499-3 (Tutorial Information) was withdrawn as obsolete in 2007, since it referred to the pre standard (PAS) version of IEC 61499. Nevertheless, the original content of IEC 61499-3 contains several important points which provide valuable information about the development and application of IEC 61499. Therefore, the SC65B/WG15 is currently discussing the possibility to revise Part 3 of the standard and to include additional tutorial information which can be very useful during the design and implementation of an IEC 61499-compliant implementation of a distributed automation and control system.

7.5. BENEFITS OF IEC61499

The business and financial benefits of widespread adoption of the IEC 61499 Standard are directly impacted by the extent to which to the qualities of open systems targeted by IEC 61499-4 and illustrated in Figure 7.7 are attained.

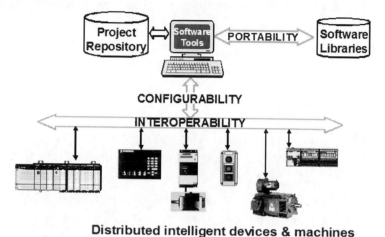

Figure 7.7. Qualities of Open Automation and Control Systems.

These qualities are defined as:

- *portability:* the extent to which software elements (FB types, data types, resource types, device types, and system configurations) can be accepted and correctly interpreted by multiple software tools
- *configurability:* the extent to which a system can be *configured* via selection of *functional units* (FBs, resources, and devices), assigning their locations and parameters and establishing their data and event interconnections
- *inter-operability:* the extent to which functional units in a *system* are able to operate together to perform the required set of automation, control, and data processing functions.

The benefits of adoption of a new architecture such as that defined in the IEC 61499 Standard are also strongly affected by *network externalities,* where the value of the technology to one user depends on how many other users there are:

Technologies subject to strong network effects tend to exhibit long lead times followed by explosive growth. The pattern results from positive feedback: as the installed base of users grows, more and more users find adoption worthwhile.

The adoption pattern of these technologies follows the well-known S-shaped "logistic curve" shown in Figure 7.8, where the vertical axis can be taken to represent the portion of available application "sockets" occupied by the technology (the number of available sockets may actually increase during the lifetime of the technology). Shapiro and Varian characterize this curve as occurring in three phases: Launch, Takeoff, and Saturation.

The optimum timing for the various players in the control and automation marketplace can be identified as follows, corresponding to the indicated ranges on the time scaled horizontal axis:

1. *Launch:* This is the optimum time for providers of software tools and runtime platforms to enter the market, in order to establish the dominant software architecture via broadly accepted compliance profiles.

2. *Takeoff:* This is the optimum time for providers of hardware platforms to enter the market, in order to establish a presence among early adopters of the technology in the system integrator and end user communities. In the case of IEC 61499, such early adopters may be found where the systems to be controlled are inherently distributed and modular, for instance in material handling and sort, building automation, pipelines and the "Smart Grid."

3. *Saturation:* This or late Takeoff is the optimum time for the large majority of automation system users to be using the technology, as economies of scale drive initial system costs down.

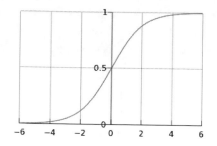

Figure 7.8. Logistic curve.

In order to be ready to adopt the technology at the optimum time, potential adopters should engage in training and maintain close monitoring of the evolution of the technology during the late portion of the preceding phase. In the case of IEC 61499, ample evidence exists to show that the technology is currently in the late Launch phase, so the time for most users and system integrators to begin training, feasibility studies and market monitoring is within the next two years.

7.6. INTEGRATION

In the IEC 61499 architecture, resources are the workhorses that provide the services needed to integrate all the pieces of applications into a working distributed system. IEC 61499-compliant software tools can be used to:

- Map the messages that are passed back and forth between devices into the input and output events and data of communication service interface function blocks (SIFBs).
- Use event and data inputs and outputs to trigger the performance of the algorithms of basic and composite function blocks, and synchronize their operation with other function blocks
- Map the data and event inputs and outputs of I/O SIFBs to the inputs and outputs of the system, where it can sense what is going on in the physical world and take appropriate physical actions in response.

7.7. EXAMPLES

7.7.1. Example 1: Processing a Message

1   A message arrives from another resource (possibly in a remote device) via the communication interface.

2   The resource maps the data in the message into a data output of the communication SIFB, which is wired to the data input of a basic function block; the resource then issues an event from the SIFB, which is propagated to an event input of the basic FB.

3   The arrival of this event causes the resource to execute the basic FB's algorithm, which uses the value of the data input to produce new values for the data outputs, which are wired to an I/O SIFB.

4   The resource then issues an event from the basic FB, which is propagated to an event input of the I/O SIFB.

5   The arrival of this event at the SIFB causes the resource to perform an appropriate action (start or stop a motor, set a room light level, etc.), based on the data input values of the SIFB.

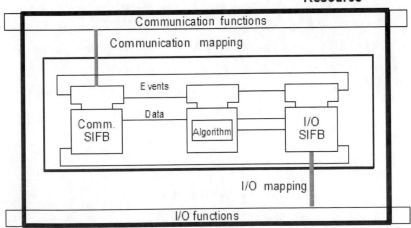

Figure 7.9. Examples 1.

7.7.2. Example 2: Processing an Input Event

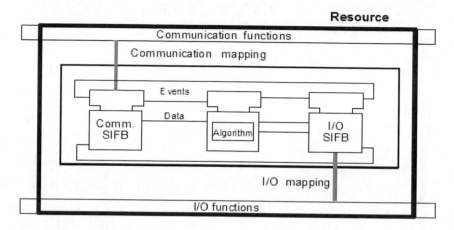

Figure 7.10. Examples 2.

- Something happens at an input interface (a user turns a knob, a limit switch senses the presence of a package on a conveyor, etc.), which causes the resource to map the input data to an output of the I/O SIFB.

- The resource maps the input data into a data output of the I/O SIFB, which in this case is wired to the data input of a communication SIFB. The resource then issues an event from the I/O SIFB, which is propagated to an event input of the communication SIFB.

- The arrival of this event at the communication SIFB causes a message containing the input data to be sent to a resource somewhere else in the system.

7.8. CONFIGURATION

IEC 61499-compliant software tools can be used according to the following procedure to configure distributed control and automation systems from libraries of reusable IEC 61499-compliant components:

1. Configure the devices in the system: their names, types, parameters, and network interconnections.
2. Configure the name, type and parameters of each resource in the devices.
3. Build the required application functionality in each resource by adding and interconnecting function blocks from a library of function block types and setting their parameters as necessary.
4. Add the communication service interface function blocks (SIFBS) necessary for proper transmission of data and synchronization of operations among resources, set their parameters and interconnect them as needed with the application function blocks.

7.9. SOFTWARE TOOLS

Following is a list of IEC 61499-related software tools known to the author. Such tools should meet the requirements defined in IEC 61499-2, and should also have their characteristics defined in a Compliance Profile as specified in IEC 61499-4.

1 FBDK - Function Block Development Kit
2 nxtControl
3 ISaGRAF
4 FBench
4DIAC

7.10. CONCLUSION

The maintenance of IEC 61499 Parts 1, 2, and 4 is completed now, and the Second Edition to be published in late 2012 will be a clear, unambiguous, and industrially useful specification for the use of FBs in distributed and embedded devices and systems. Providers of software tools, runtime platforms and controls hardware should seriously consider entering the market in the next two years. System integrators and end users should begin engagement in training, feasibility studies, and technology monitoring to determine the optimum time for adoption of the IEC 61499 technology. IEC SC65B/WG15 is expected to focus its future work on an improved Second Edition of the Tutorial Information IEC/TR 61499-3 and on the proposal for a new Technical Specification IEC/TS 61499-5 with significant extensions to provide better support for the development of distributed automation and control systems.

REFERENCES

[1]   Thomesse, Jean-Pierre. Field-bus technology in industrial automation, *Proceedings of the IEEE*, v 93, n 6, p. 1073-1101.

[2]   Chen, Gang; Ye, Dong; Che, Rensheng. *Proceedings of the Eighth International Conference on Electronic Measurement and Instruments*, 2007, p. 765-768.

[3]   Weihua, Bao; Hao, Zhang. Analysis and Research on the Real-time Performance of PROFIBUS Field-bus, *World Congress on Software Engineering*, 2009, p. 136-146.

[4]   Carlos Cardeira, a; Zoubir, Mammeri. A schedulability analysis of tasks and network traffic in distributed real-time systems, *Measurement n.*, 15, 1995, p. 71-83.

[5]   Koubias, SA; Papadopoulos, GD. Modern field-bus communication architectures for real-time industrial applications, *Computers in Industry n.*, 26, 1995, p. 243-252.

[6]   Sijing, Zhang; Alan, Burns; Tee-Hiang, Cheng. *Cycle-Time Properties of the Timed Token*.

[7]   Medium Access Control Protocol, *IEEE Transactions on Computers*, Vol. 51, NO. 11, p. 1362-1367.

[8]   Gopal, Agrawal; Biao, Chen; Wei, Zhao; Sadegh, Davari. Guaranteeing Synchronous Message Deadlines with the Timed

Token Medium Access Control Protocol, *IEEE Transactions on Computers*, Vol. 43, NO. 3, p. 327-339.

[9] Eduardo, Tovar. Real-Time Field-bus Communications Using PROFIBUS Networks, *IEEE Transactions on Industrial Electronics*, Vol. 46, NO. 6, p. 1241-1255.

[10] Seung, Ho Hong. Implementation of a Bandwidth Allocation Scheme in a Token-Passing Field-bus Network, *IEEE Transactions on Instrumentation And Measurement*, Vol. 51, NO. 2, p. 246-256.

[11] Seung, Ho Hong. Transmission of a Scheduled Message Using a Foundation Field-bus Protocol. *IEEE Transactions on Instrumentation and Measurement*, Vol. 57, NO. 2, p. 268-275.

[12] Eduardo, Tovar. Factory Communications: On the Configuration of the WorldFIP Bus Arbitrator Table, *Proceedings of ETFA'*, 99, p. 1-18.

[13] Ching-Chih, Han; Kang, G. Shin. Synchronous Bandwidth Allocation for Real-Time Communications with the Timed-Token MAC Protocol. *IEEE Transactions on Computers*, Vol. 50, NO. 5, p. 414-421.

[14] Yuping, Zhang; Chen, Lei. Research of the Scheduling Method for Field-bus. Network Real-time Information, *2011 The 6th International Forum on Strategic Technology*, p. 1125-1135.

[15] Guo, Zhenxue. Features and Applications of WorldFIP field-bus, *Automation and Instrumentation*, (4), 53-55, 2005.

[16] Alameida, L; Tovar, E. Schedulability analysis of real-time traffic in WorldFIP: an integrated approach, *IEEE Trans on Industry Electronics*, 49(5), 1165-1174, 2002.

[17] Wang Zhi, Song Ye-Qiong, Yu Hai-Bin, Sun Youxian. Worst-case response time of aperiodc message in WorldFIP and its improvement in real-time capability. *ISA Transactions*, v 43, n 4, 623-637, 2004.

[18] Chen, Jiming; Wang, Zhi. Performance compare with non-periodic messages schedule of WorldFIP and FF, *Chinese of Scientific Instrument*, 386-390, 26(4), 2005.

[19] Chen, Jiming; Wang, Zhi; Sun, Youxian. A basic study on algorithm of real-time schedule table for field-bus, *Proceedings of the World*

Congress on Intelligent Control and Automation (WCICA), v 3, 1760-1763, 2002.

[20] Wang, Tianran; Zhou, Yue. Analysis and Heuristic Scheduling for Real-time Communication in FF System, *Chinese Journal of Scientific Instrument*, 21(1), 1-6, 2003

[21] Chen, Jiming; Wang, Zhi. Study on schedule problem of non-periodic message traffic in foundation field-bus, *Joural of Zhejiang University*, 37(3), 273-278, 2003.

[22] Geng, Liang. A kind of implementation model based on generalized FBD for distributed intelligent control network, Chinese Control and Decision Conference, *CCDC*, 2008, 411-414, 2008.

[23] Geng, Liang. A kind of function block application model for distributed intelligent control network based on WorldFIP, *Chinese Control and Decision Conference*, 2008, CCDC 2008, 1400-1404, 2008.

[24] Geng, Liang; Guotian, Yang. A kind of communication simulation system for worldFIP field intelligent control network, *Proceedings of 2009 International Asia Conference on Informatics in Control, Automation, and Robotics*, CAR, 2009, 385-389, 2009.

[25] Pang, Y; Yang, SH. Nishitani, Hirokazu. Analysis of control interval for foundation field-bus-based control systems, *ISA Transactions*, v 45, n 3, 447-458, July 2006.

[26] Zhou, Yue; Wu, Qi; Yang, Shaowen. Model and analysis of WorldFIP MAC sub-layer based on DSPN, *Journal of Shenyang Jianzhu University (Natural Science)*, v 23, n 3, 518-521, May 2007.

[27] Eduardo, André Mossin; Rodrigo, Palucci Pantoni; Dennis, Brandão. A field-bus simulator for training purposes. *ISA Transactions*, v 48, n 1, 132-141, January 2009.

[28] Zhai, Weixiang; Bai, Yan; Gao, Feng. Development of intelligent WorldFIP master, *Electric Power Automation Equipment*, v 29, n 2, 121-124+152, 2009.

[29] Shi, John Z; Gu, Fengshou; Goulding, Peter; Ball, Andrew. Integration of multiple platforms for real-time remote model-based

---

condition monitoring, *Computers in Industry*, v 58, n 6, 531-538, 2007.

[30] Benzi, Francesco. Communication architectures for electrical drives, *IEEE Transactions on Industrial Informatics*, v 1, n 1, 47-53, February 2005.

[31] www.worldfip.org.

[32] ALSTOM. *FULLFIP2 User Reference Manual* (ALS 50262 d-en), Paris, France, 2000.

[33] ALSTOM. *MICROFIP User Reference Manual* (ALS 50280 d-en), Paris, France, 2001.

[34] Aibing, Zhang. Development of Interface Card for WorldFIP fieldbus, Msc. Dissertation, *North China Electric Power University*, Beijing, China, 2003.

[35] Geng, Liang. Research and Development of Strategy Configuration Software Package for Distributed Intelligent Sytem Based on IEC61131-3, Ph.D. Dissertation, *North China Electric Power University*, Beijing, China, 2005.

[36] Lv, Qiuxia. The Development of the Field-bus-current Converter Based on the WorldFIP Field-bus. *Control & Automation*, 2005, 21(1), 15-16.

[37] Gao, Yijie, Development of Vibration Measurement Instrument based on WorldFIP, *Modern Electric Power*, 21(4), 16-19.

[38] Zhang, Aibing; et al. The Driver Development of an Interface Card Based on WorldFIP. *Industrial Control Computer*, 2003, 16(2), 32-34.

[39] Zhang, Qizhi. Intelligent Pressure Transmitter based on WorldFIP, *Modern Electric Power*, 2003, 20(2), 60-63.

[40] Geng, Liang. Design and Implementation of Control Strategy Configuration Software for WorldFIP Field-Bus Control System, *Proceedings of CSEE*, 2005, 24(2), 150-156.

[41] Geng, Liang. Development of Scheme Configuration Software for WorldFIP FCS Based on Object Model, *Journal of Scientific Instruments*, 2005, 26(12), 1293-1297.

[42] Geng, Liang. *Research and development of function block application of the fieid-bus intelligent device based on WorldFIP field-bus*, 26(6), 902-904, 2006.

[43] Geng, Liang. A Kind of Implementation Model Based on Generalized FBD for Distributed Intelligent Control Network, *Proceedings of CCDC*, 2008, 347-350, 2008.

[44] Geng, Liang. A Kind of Function Block Application Model for Distributed Intelligent Control Network Based on WorldFIP, *Proceedings of CCDC*, 2008, 1314-1318, 2008.

[45] Geng, Liang. A Kind of Implementation Model Based on Generalized FBD for Distributed Intelligent Control Network, *Proceedings of CCDC*, 2008, 347-350, 2008.

[46] Wang, Kai. Development of Soft PLC Device Based on the FF HSE, *Chinese Journal of Scientific Instrument*, 27(2), 118-122, 2006.

[47] Lai, Yushu. Design Research of a Type of Soft PLC Integrated Monitoring Function, *Measurement and Control Automation*, 23(11), 18-22, 2007.

[48] Huang, Yanlin. Research and Implementation of Soft PLC Technology, *Computer Engineering*, 30(1), 165-167, 2004.

[49] Xie, Yunmin. Monitor System of Sluice Based on Open Soft PLC and CAN Filedbus, *Instrument Technique and Sensor*, (6), 31-32, 51, 2007.

[50] Yuan, Haiying. *Journal of Guangxi University of Technology*, 18(4), 72-75, 2007.

[51] Chen, Hui. Study and realize Soft PLC technology based on ladder language, *Measurement and Control Automation*, 22(9), 266-268, 2006.

[52] Li, Yanhui. Over all Design of Soft PLC Development Platform and discussion on Control Schemes, *Forestry Machinery & Woodworking Equipment*, 36(6), 16-18, 2008.

[53] Huang, Yanyan. Research and Implementation of Soft PLC, *Computer Engineering*, 30(1), 165-167, 2004.

[54] Fadaei, A.; Salahshoor, K. Design and implementation of a new fuzzy PID controller for networked control systems. *ISA Transactions*, 47 (2008) 351-361.

[55] Ma, C.; Chen, S.; Liu, W. Maximum allowable delay bound of networked control systems with multi-step delay. *Simulation Modelling Practice and Theory*, 2007, 15(5), 13-20.

[56] Imera, O. C.; Y¨ukselb, S; Basar, T. Optimal control of LTI systems over unreliable communication links. *Automatica*, 2006, 42(14), 29-39.

[57] Hua, L. S.; Baia, T.; Shib, P.; Wu, Z. Sampled-data control of networked linear control systems. *Automatica*, 2007, 43(9), 3-11.

[58] Hespanha, J; Naghshtabrizi, P; Xu, Y. A survey of recent results in networked control systems. *Proc. IEEE*, 2007, 95(1), 138-162.

[59] Murray, R. M.; Astrom, K. J.; Boyd, S. P; Brockett, R. W.; Stein, G. B. Control in an information rich world, *IEEE Control System Magazine*, 2003, 23(2), 20-33.

[60] Braslavsky, J. H.; Middleton, R. H. Feedback stabilization over signal-to-noise ratio constrained channels. *Proc. American Control. Conference*, 2004, 1492–1496.

[61] Liberzon, D.; Hespanha, J. P. B. Stabilization of nonlinear systems with limited information feedback. *IEEE Transactions on. Automatic Control*, 2005, 50(6), 910-915.

[62] Naghshtabrizi, P.; Hespanha, J. Designing observer-based controller for network control system. *Proc. 44th Conference on Decision and Control*, 2005, 4, 2876-2880.

[63] Elia, N. Remote stabilization over fading channels. *System Control Letter.*, 2005, 54(3), 237-249.

[64] Liberzon, D.; Hespanha, J. P. Stabilization of nonlinear systems with limited information feedback, *IEEE Transactions on Automatic. Control.*, 2005, 50(6), 910–915.

[65] Fadaei, A.; Salahshoor1, K. Design and implementation of a new fuzzy PID controller for networked control systems. *ISA Transactions*, 2008, 47, 351–361.

[66] Li, Q. Evaluation of Delays Induced by Foundation Field-bus H1 Networks. *IEEE Transactions on Instrumentation and Measurement*, 2009, 58(10), 3684-3692.

[67] Pang, Y.; Nishitani, H. Analysis of control interval for foundation field-bus-based control systems, *ISA Transactions.*, 2006, 45(3), 447-458.

[68] Field-bus Foundation. *FF-890-1.3: Foundation specification function block application process, part 1*. Austin, USA. 1999.

[69] Field-bus Foundation. *Foundation specification function block application process Part 3: FF-892- FS1.4*. Austin, USA. 1999.

[70] Field-bus Foundation. *Foundation specification function block application process Part 5: FF-894 - DPS0.95*. Austin, USA. 1999.

[71] Eduardo, Andre Mossin; Rodrigo, Palucci Pantoni; Dennis, Brandao. A field-bus simulator for training purposes, *ISA Transactions*, 2009, 48, 132-141.

[72] Chen, J.; Wang, Z.; Sun, Y. How to improve control system performance using FF function blocks. *IEEE international conference on control application.*, 2002, 2, 1022-1026.

[73] Ferreiro, Garcia R.; Vidal, Paz J.; Pardo, Martinez X. C.; Coego, Botana J. Field-bus: Preliminary design approach to optimal network management. *Proceedings of IEEE international workshop on factory communication systems.*, 1997, 355-362.

[74] Field-bus Foundation. *FF-890-1.3: Foundation specification function block application process, part 1*. Austin, USA. 1999.

[75] Smar Co. *Function blocks instruction manual*, 2003.

[76] Smar Co. DFI302-Field-bus universal bridge, *System302 Manual.*, 2003.

[77] Halevi, Y.; Ray, A. Integrated communication and control systems: Part I - analysis. *Journal of Dynamic Systems, Measurement and Control*, 1998, 110, 367–373.

[78] Nilsson, J. *Real-time control systems with delays*. Ph.D. dissertation, Lund Institute of Technology, 1998.

[79] Oktas, GFx. *Distributed control of systems over communication networks*. Ph.D. dissertation, University of Pennsylvania, 1998.

[80] Tipsuwan, Y.; Chow, M. Y. Network-based controller adaptation based on QoS negotiation and deterioration. *The 27ᵗʰ annual conference of the IEEE industrial electronics society*, 2001, 3, 1794–1799.

[81] Tipsuwan, Y.; Chow, M. Y. Control Methodologies in Networked Control Systems. *Control Engineering Practice*, 2003, 11(10), 1099-1111.

[82] Jin, F. A. Selection of sampling cycle in computer-based control system. *Basic automation*, 1995, (3), 38-40.

[83] www.holobloc.com/fbdk2.

[84] Perry, S Marshall; John, S Rinaldi. *How to Plan, Install and Maintain TCP/IP Ethernet Networks*, USA, ISA, 2004.

[85] http://www.harting.com/.

[86] http://www.siemens.com/.

[87] http://www.phoenixcontact.com.cn/.

[88] Leitão, P. "Agent-based distributed manufacturing control: A state-ofthe-art survey," *Eng. Applic. Artif. Intell.*, vol. 22, pp. 979–991, 2009.

[89] Gang, C.; Zhonghua, Y. and Ping, L. C. "Coordinating agents in shop floor environments from a dynamic systems perspective," *IEEE Trans. Ind. Inf.*, vol. 2, no. 2, pp. 269–280, May 2006.

[90] Herrero-Perez, D. and Martinez-Barbera, H. "Modeling distributed transportation systems composed of flexible automated guided vehicles in flexible manufacturing systems," *IEEE Trans. Ind. Inf.*, vol. 6,no. 2, pp. 166–180, May 2010.

[91] Mehrabi, M. G.; Ulsoy, A. G.; Koren, Y. and Heytler, P. "Trends and perspectives in flexible and reconfigurable manufacturing systems," *J. Intell. Manuf.*, vol. 13, pp. 135–146, 2002.

[92] ElMaraghy, H. "Flexible and reconfigurable manufacturing systems paradigms," *Int. J. Flexible Manuf. Syst.*, vol. 17, pp. 261–276, 2005.

[93] Koren, Y.; Heisel, U.; Jovane, F.; Moriwaki, T.; Pritschow, G.; Ulsoy, G. and Van Brussel, H. "Reconfigurable manufacturing systems," *CIRP Ann. Manuf. Technol.*, vol. 48, pp. 527–540, 1999.

[94] Rooker, M.; Sünder, C.; Strasser, T.; Zoitl, A.; Hummer, O. and Ebenhofer, G. "Zero downtime reconfiguration of distributed automation systems: The CEDAC approach," in *Holonic and Multi-Agent Systems for Manufacturing*, V. Marik, Ed. et al. Berlin, Germany: Springer, 2007, pp. 326–337.

[95] Shengyong, W.; Foh, C. S. and Lawley, M. A. "Using shared-resource capacity for robust control of failure-prone manufacturing systems," *IEEE Trans. Syst., Man Cybern. A, Syst. Humans*, vol. 38, no. 3, pp. 605–627, May 2008.

[96] Christensen, James H.; Strasser, Thomas.; Valentini, Antonio.; Vyatkin, Valeriy.; Zoitl, Alois. *The IEC 61499 Function Block Standard: Overview of the Second Edition*, ISA, 2012.

ABOUT THE AUTHORS

Professor Geng Liang
School of Control and Computer Engineering,
North China Electric Power University,
Beijing, China
Email: liangeng1976@163.com

Mrs Wen Li
Beijing Guodianzhishen Control Technology Co. Ltd,
Beijing, China

Professor Guoping Liu
The University of South Wales, UK

INDEX

A

actuators, xi, 1, 2, 3, 4, 5, 7, 23, 24, 33, 35, 58, 60, 73, 92, 94, 104, 117, 155, 158, 159, 169, 178, 188

addressing, vi, 69, 78, 79, 89, 101, 192, 224, 225, 234, 252

algorithm(s), 6, 23, 34, 35, 38, 47, 152, 155, 157, 172, 177, 183, 184, 185, 193, 194, 197, 198, 220, 221, 222, 223, 252, 269, 270, 271, 272, 273, 275, 280, 281, 286

analog signal, 3, 36

analysis, vi, vii, viii, 7, 18, 20, 25, 28, 32, 34, 36, 38, 39, 44, 52, 100, 109, 110, 136, 142, 154, 155, 158, 162, 169, 184, 211, 212, 221, 223, 226, 228, 231, 234, 235, 238, 240, 241, 262, 285, 286, 287, 291

application laver, vii, 12, 207

arbitration, 17, 47, 245, 247, 248, 249, 250, 251, 252, 253, 255, 258, 263

architecture, 7, 9, 10, 14, 19, 20, 22, 25, 27, 28, 29, 30, 31, 32, 61, 63, 64, 67, 69, 77, 78, 90, 155, 157, 160, 162, 167, 171, 178, 182, 185, 190, 267, 271, 276, 278, 279, 280

asynchronous, 23, 43, 44, 48, 50, 51, 52, 53, 65, 71, 95, 108, 188, 191, 200, 208, 210, 211, 215, 220, 276

B

BAT, 194, 195, 196, 197, 198, 200, 201, 213, 214, 215, 217, 218, 219, 220, 221, 222, 223

bus termination(s), viii, 77, 255

C

cables, 2, 10, 62, 63, 78, 96, 122, 124, 190, 256

CAN, viii, 11, 33, 34, 35, 39, 245, 246, 247, 248, 249, 250, 251, 252, 253, 254, 255, 256, 257, 258, 259, 260, 261, 262, 263, 289

communication performance, 39, 223, 224, 225, 228, 240, 243, 263, 275

composite FB(s), 270, 271, 276, 277

computer(s), 1, 9, 14, 16, 34, 41, 55, 137, 158, 162, 169, 180, 285, 286, 288, 289, 292, 295 configurability, 278

configuration, vii, viii, 31, 58, 59, 67, 69, 73, 81, 82, 85, 96, 100, 101, 126, 136, 140, 141, 154, 157, 158, 160, 163, 164, 166, 168, 173, 180, 181, 184, 188, 190, 193, 194, 200, 234, 267, 275, 282, 286, 288

consistency, 6, 13, 21, 86, 273

control system(s), v, vi, vii, viii, xi, 2, 3, 17, 19, 20, 33, 41, 57, 61, 62, 86, 92, 94, 115, 126, 137, 154, 155, 157, 158, 159, 160, 161, 162, 163, 166, 167, 168, 169, 170, 171, 176, 178, 180, 182, 183, 184, 185, 187, 245, 267, 277, 278, 284, 287, 288, 290, 291,292

controller, 1, 4, 5, 11, 24, 34, 72, 92, 93, 100, 118, 129, 154, 155, 160, 170, 178, 183, 185, 212, 225, 226, 247, 250, 251, 252, 253, 257, 258, 259, 260, 263, 267, 269, 290, 292

CSMA/CD, 6, 37, 178

cyclic, vi, 58, 60, 69, 72, 73, 74, 75, 76, 81, 82, 83, 88, 93, 100, 105, 151, 155, 159, 169, 185, 191, 195, 201, 258, 259

D

data frame(s), 35, 55, 67, 192, 246, 247, 248, 263

data link layer, 12, 30, 31, 58, 132, 190, 191, 206, 212, 225, 261

device description, 81, 117, 119, 134, 137, 138, 139, 140

distributed control system (DCS), 1, 2, 17, 154, 156, 267

E

electromagnetic compatibility (EMC), 22, 23

engineer workstation (EWS), 154, 158, 160, 163, 164, 165, 176, 180, 181

error detection, viii, 12, 247, 257

error handling, viii, 245, 257, 261

Ethernet, 1, 16, 17, 31, 32, 34, 37, 54, 56, 60, 62, 95, 99, 100, 102, 121, 124, 125, 154, 155, 157, 158, 160, 162, 163, 166, 168, 170, 171, 172, 176, 178, 180, 182, 183, 184, 185, 292

evaluation, 39, 228, 243, 274, 275, 291

event, viii, 133, 146, 171, 172, 191, 200, 267, 268, 269, 270, 271, 272, 273, 274, 278, 280, 281, 282

execution control, viii, 173, 174, 175, 269, 272, 274

execution control chart (ECC), 269, 272, 273, 274

F

factory instrumentation protocol (FIP), vii, 11, 12, 13, 19, 116, 187, 188, 189, 190, 191, 192, 193, 194, 196, 197, 198, 201, 203, 207, 209, 211

fault tolerance, 5, 6, 15, 261

fibre distributed data inter-face (FDDI), v, 42, 43, 47, 48, 50, 51, 53, 54, 55, 56

field-bus, 1, 2, 3, 4, 5, 6, 7, 8, 10, 11, 12, 13, 14, 15, 17, 18, 19, 20, 21, 22, 23, 24, 25, 26, 27, 28, 29, 31, 32, 33, 34, 35, 39, 57, 64, 66, 67, 85, 88, 92, 103, 115, 116, 117, 118, 120, 121, 122, 123, 125, 126, 127, 129, 132, 133, 134, 136, 138, 140, 151, 152, 154, 155, 157, 158, 159, 160, 162, 163, 164, 165, 166, 168, 169, 184, 185, 187, 188, 189, 190, 191, 200, 223, 224, 263, 285, 286, 287, 288, 289, 291

field-bus message specification (FMS), 13, 22, 33, 62, 64, 69, 92, 120, 132, 133, 134

FOUNDATION, 3, 31, 32, 33, 34, 115, 116, 117, 118, 119, 120, 121, 123, 125, 126, 129, 134, 138

frame check, 56, 59, 90, 96, 193, 258

function block, 83, 117, 118, 119, 127, 129, 132, 134, 135, 136, 137, 140, 141, 154, 155, 158, 159, 163, 164, 166, 167, 168, 169, 173, 178, 184, 185, 267, 268, 269, 270, 273, 280, 281, 283, 287, 289, 291, 293

G

general station description (GSD), 81, 82, 84, 91, 101

H

H1, 11, 12, 21, 31, 32, 64, 66, 71, 76, 88, 120, 121, 122, 123, 125, 126, 156, 162, 291

H2, 11, 12, 21, 120, 121

HCF/LCM, 195, 214, 219

human machine interface, 1, 154, 158

I

I/O, 36, 38, 60, 61, 73, 92, 160, 166, 168, 178, 272, 280, 281, 282

identification, 59, 202, 252

IEC61499, viii, 171, 172, 173, 175, 176, 185, 267, 268, 272, 277

industrial network, xi, 1, 3, 28, 35, 37

information, 4, 6, 7, 16, 19, 20, 21, 25, 34, 35, 58, 59, 60, 62, 71, 72, 73, 81, 82, 83, 86, 89, 90, 91, 116, 117, 130, 136, 138, 140, 188, 189, 207, 209, 213, 223, 267, 277, 284, 286, 290

integration, viii, 8, 17, 41, 60, 62, 64, 81, 223, 275, 280, 287

intelligence, 5, 17, 27, 223

international organization for standardization (ISO), 14, 22, 29, 32, 33, 64, 120, 254, 255, 256, 261

inter-operability, 117, 278

L

local area network (LAN), LAN, 1, 17, 35, 52, 54, 254

logical link control (LLC), 15, 22, 56

M

MAP, 8, 10, 11, 16, 19, 22, 30, 32, 37

master, 12, 13, 20, 58, 64, 68, 69, 70, 71, 72, 73, 74, 75, 76, 82, 87, 90, 92, 94, 95, 96, 100, 103, 104, 105, 108, 110, 111, 117, 126, 139, 166, 287

medium access control (MAC), vi, 6, 15, 16, 17, 22, 30, 33, 35, 37, 39, 42, 45, 48, 56, 58, 67, 95, 101, 103, 105, 106, 285, 286, 287

message deadlines, 42, 46, 48, 109

message priority, 251

N

network traffic, 6, 36, 38, 178, 264, 285

O

open system interconnection (OSI), 14, 15, 28, 30, 31, 54, 57, 64, 87, 93, 95, 103, 120, 188, 189

operator workstation (OWS), 154, 158, 163, 165, 176, 180, 181

organization, vi, 9, 14, 25, 28, 99, 103, 115, 116

OSI/ISO model, 14, 15

P

performance, vi, vii, viii, xi, 35, 36, 37, 39,
   42, 97, 116, 117, 122, 132, 142, 151,
   154, 155, 157, 158, 183, 184, 212, 223,
   224, 226, 228, 231, 234, 235, 238, 240,
   241, 257, 262, 264, 265, 266, 271, 276,
   280, 285, 286, 291
periodic and non-periodic traffic, 39
peripherals, vi, 56, 60, 86, 92, 100
physical layer, 12, 13, 14, 21, 26, 30, 188,
   189, 190, 213, 246, 253, 254, 256, 261
portability, 278
priority, 34, 37, 38, 39, 44, 47, 51, 52, 53,
   74, 75, 102, 105, 107, 108, 109, 110,
   111, 112, 113, 132, 142, 143, 144, 145,
   147, 148, 149, 150, 151, 182, 195, 197,
   201, 202, 204, 216, 221, 223, 245, 247,
   253, 274
producer/distributor/consumer (PDC)
   model, vii, 212
PROFIBUS, vi, 3, 11, 12, 13, 22, 31, 32, 33,
   34, 35, 39, 57, 58, 59, 60, 61, 62, 63, 64,
   65, 66, 69, 70, 73, 74, 75, 76, 78, 81, 82,
   83, 84, 86, 87, 89, 91, 92, 93, 94, 96, 97,
   98, 99, 100, 103, 104, 105, 106, 107,
   108, 109, 110, 111, 112, 113, 116, 285,
   286
PROFIBUS – FMS, 62
PROFIBUS - PA, 62
PROFIBUS DP, 33, 60, 61, 63, 64, 69, 74,
   76, 87, 89, 92, 94, 96, 97
PROFIBUS DP or PA, 60
PROFIBUS PA, 57, 62, 63, 64, 66, 75, 76,
   78, 92, 97, 98, 116
PROFINET, vi, 60, 97, 99, 100, 101, 102,
   103
PROFISAFE, 85, 86, 87, 88, 89, 90, 91
programmable logic controllers (PLC), 1, 8,
   36, 72, 86, 154, 156, 160, 162, 166, 167,

   168, 171, 176, 178, 180, 181, 185, 188,
   276, 289
promptness, 207, 210, 211
proportional/integral/derivative (PID), 2,
   118, 127, 129, 135, 137, 140, 156, 160,
   163, 164, 165, 166, 171, 172, 173, 174,
   176, 182, 183, 290
protocol(s), v, vi, viii, xi, 3, 4, 6, 7, 8, 11,
   12, 13, 14, 15, 16, 17, 18, 26, 27, 28, 30,
   31, 32, 33, 34, 35, 37, 39, 42, 43, 44, 45,
   46, 48, 50, 54, 56, 57, 58, 59, 60, 63, 64,
   69, 87, 90, 91, 92, 93, 94, 95, 96, 99,
   101, 103, 107, 108, 109, 110, 116, 119,
   125, 134, 166, 183, 187, 188, 189, 190,
   191, 192, 195, 207, 211, 217, 224, 256,
   257, 261, 262, 275, 285, 286

R

real-time, vi, 1, 6, 14, 16, 18, 22, 23, 24, 25,
   31, 32, 33, 35, 36, 37, 38, 41, 42, 47, 60,
   99, 100, 101, 102, 104, 107, 108, 109,
   110, 112, 124, 152, 154, 155, 183, 187,
   188, 191, 211, 213, 220, 223, 285, 286,
   287, 291
refreshment, 207, 208, 209, 210, 211
reliability, 22, 23, 25, 35, 41, 73, 116, 223,
   243, 276
resource(s), 15, 25, 38, 39, 41, 42, 44, 46,
   47, 60, 85, 90, 91, 134, 135, 271, 272,
   275, 276, 278, 280, 281, 282, 283, 293

S

scheduling, v, vi, vii, 14, 15, 16, 35, 38, 40,
   47, 142, 151, 152, 153, 155, 169, 185,
   194, 195, 197, 198, 213, 217, 218, 221,
   223, 225, 263, 286, 287
semantic, 274

sensors, xi, 1, 2, 4, 5, 7, 10, 11, 23, 24, 33, 35, 58, 60, 92, 94, 104, 117, 127, 129, 188

simulation, viii, 262, 263, 287, 290

software tools, viii, 121, 269, 270, 271, 275, 278, 279, 280, 282, 283, 284

standardization, vi, 7, 11, 13, 14, 18, 22, 29, 98, 187, 277

standards, 3, 7, 8, 9, 10, 20, 30, 33, 34, 42, 54, 57, 74, 81, 82, 87, 103, 188, 191, 250, 262, 267, 268

synchronous, 42, 43, 44, 45, 46, 48, 50, 51, 52, 53, 54, 66, 107, 108, 109, 110, 188, 200, 208, 209, 215, 220, 276, 285, 286

synchronous and asynchronous service, 51

timed-token protocol(s) (TTPs), 43, 50, 51, 52

transducers, 5, 60, 73

transmission delay, 156, 158, 164, 170, 171, 176, 178, 179, 182, 183, 185

transmitter(s), 5, 62, 63, 75, 81, 83, 86, 142, 143, 155, 158, 159, 160, 162, 163, 247, 249, 252, 257, 258, 259, 288

U

UDFB-DA, 154, 173, 174, 176, 177

unified modeling language (UML), 274

user application, 117, 132, 134

T

target token rotation time (TTRT), 39, 43, 44, 45, 46, 49, 50, 51, 53, 105, 142, 143, 151

temporary variables, viii, 275

W

WorldFIP, 187, 188, 189, 190, 191, 192, 193, 194, 195, 196, 200, 204, 206, 207, 211